Julia Leyda
American Mobilities

**American Culture Studies** | Volume 14

*In memory of my grandmother, Hazel (Azzia) Richard De Ville (1906-1992), and my mother, Seraphia De Ville Leyda (1936-1989).*

**Julia Leyda** is Visiting Professor in the Graduate School for North American Studies and a Fellow in the DFG Research Unit "Popular Seriality: Aesthetics and Practice" at the John F. Kennedy Institute, Freie Universität Berlin. Her research interests include cuteness, the financialization of domestic space, and contemporary cli-fi.

Julia Leyda

# American Mobilities

## Geographies of Class, Race, and Gender in US Culture

[transcript]

**Bibliographic information published by the Deutsche Nationalbibliothek**
The Deutsche Nationalbibliothek lists this publication in the Deutsche Natio-nalbibliografie; detailed bibliographic data are available in the Internet at http://dnb.d-nb.de

© 2016 transcript Verlag, Bielefeld

Cover layout: Kordula Röckenhaus, Bielefeld
Cover illustration: Photo collage by C.E. Shore: "Horse-Drawn Wagon Loaded with Sacks of Potatoes" (circa 1940). US National Archives and Records Ad-ministration. "Dust Bowl, Dallas, South Dakota" (1936). US Department of Agriculture. "Visitors Leave their Cars Parked along a Road to Photograph Buffalo in the Field" (1938). US National Archives and Records Administra-tion "B&O Passenger Train, Chicago" (1943). Jack Delano, US Library of Congress. "Chrysler Building, Midtown Manhattan, New York City" (1932). Samuel Gottscho, Gottscho-Schleisner Collection, US Library of Congress.
Printed in Germany
Print-ISBN 978-3-8376-3455-6
PDF-ISBN 978-3-8394-3455-0

# Contents

# Acknowledgments

The author wishes to thank Christopher Shore for, simply, everything. Warmest gratitude also goes to those colleagues, friends, and family whose support made this project possible: Jayme Burke, Roger and Shelley Cavaness, John Eckman, Le'a Kent, Merrill Marchal, Jolie Préau, Julie Prebel, John Sheehan, Wendy Somerson, and Anneliese Truame. Certainly having the best dissertation committee in the universe helped mightily—all my thanks to Susan Jeffords, Steven Shaviro, Matthew Sparke, and Priscilla Wald for their consistent encouragement and enthusiasm.

## Permissions
Chapter 1 first appeared in *Arizona Quarterly* 56.2 (2000); revised version printed by permission of the Regents of the University of Arizona.

Chapter 4 is reprinted with permission from *Cinema Journal*.

Chapters 5 and 6 are reprinted with permission from the *Japanese Journal of American Studies*, where they were published as articles in 2008 and 2002, respectively.

# Foreword

This book is the product of a very personal experience of American mobility: a transnational academic career that has traversed three continents over the course of the past twenty years. Embarking on my doctoral study in 1995, I could hardly have imagined the trajectory that would carry me from Seattle to Germany to Japan and then, in 2015, back to Germany again. The timeliness of the "transnational turn" in American Studies also strikes me as exceedingly well-timed for my own career, coming as it did just as I was beginning to make my place within the transnational networks of Americanists in Europe and Asia while maintaining ties to the United States.

Had I remained in the U.S., it is entirely likely that I never would have published my dissertation in book form, but rather moved on to another research project in order to acquire tenure in the U.S. academic system. Indeed, in the national academic context where I found myself—Japan—the publication of a monograph was not in fact even a requirement for tenure; peer-reviewed journal articles and international conference presentations were esteemed more highly than a (frequently self-published) monograph and thus I adapted to my situation and built my CV accordingly. However, upon relocating to Germany, I discovered that the conventions dictate that, for a professorship, an academic must have her dissertation between two book covers sanctioned by a publishing house. This requirement at first caused me some small degree of chagrin, given the intervening years since my doctoral defense, in which I had ranged far and wide into some new territory both literally—in my countries of residence—and metaphorically, in my research and teaching.

It felt, somehow, dishonest to publish in 2015 a dissertation that had been written in the previous century (!). But then I hit upon the notion of publishing, in place of four of the original dissertation chapters, the four peer-reviewed journal articles that grew up out of them, along with the remaining two unpublished chapters, constituting a kind of greatest hits of my early career that ranges from text written as a doctoral student to the reworked and often hardly recognizable revisions produced under the rigors of an early career academic, and under the guidance of anonymous reviewers and generous colleagues. What follows here is then a published record of my doctoral research, completed at the University of Washington between 1995 and 1998, and then substantially revised over the subsequent years. I have retained the original Dedication, Acknowledgments, and Introduction, only amending when necessary to clarify the provenance of particular chapters. The full text of the original dissertation is available online in the usual repositories for the unnaturally curious, but this more convenient and (I hope) more compelling version will be the final text of a (for me) fascinating first book-length undertaking.

# Introduction: American Mobilities

> Is it conceivable that the exercise of hegemony might leave space untouched? Could space be nothing more than the passive locus of social relations, the milieu in which their combination takes on body, or the aggregate of the procedures employed in their removal? The answer must be no.
> HENRI LEFEBVRE/*THE PRODUCTION OF SPACE*

> According to the ideology of separate spheres, domesticity can be viewed as an anchor, a feminine counterforce to the male activity of territorial conquest. I argue, to the contrary, that domesticity is more mobile and less stabilizing; it travels in contradictory circuits both to expand and contract the boundaries of home and nation and to produce shifting conceptions of the foreign.
> AMY KAPLAN/*"MANIFEST DOMESTICITY"*

Mobility has been a key feature in American culture from the settlement of the original colonies to the nation's expansion toward new territories. Even after the closing of the frontier in 1890, Eastern populations continued to spread westward in search of property and prosperity. The allure of available land and natural resources drew Americans to all corners of the country hoping to establish a better life for themselves and their families. Through the turn of the century, the urbanization that accompanied industrialization continued to draw rural populations until, by the prosperous 1920s, more Americans lived in the city than in the country. During the 1920s, cities in the western states swelled, particularly in California, as middle-class white Americans scrambled to escape what had become known as the (racialized) nightmares of urban life: immigration, overcrowding, pollution, disease, and crime. But the 1920s were also a time of economic warning signals: agricultural industries were already depressed and while stock prices were inflated, real wages were stagnant. The progress of America was slowing down.

After the crash of 1929, the Depression forced a phenomenon I call "negative mobility" into the national imagination. In the 1930s, geographic mobility could no longer be equated with nation-building progress; rather, the migration, displacement, and homelessness of millions of unemployed Americans during the Depression constituted a real threat to the nation itself. Instead of signifying upward social mobility, geographic movements during the Depression resulted from involuntary relocation in search of work, food, and shelter.[1] Up to this point in American history, westward movement had always implied progress, development, and opportunity, and thus been linked ideologically with upward class mobility. However, during the 1930s and in the two subsequent decades, the United States underwent a reconfiguration of space that touched every facet of daily life and cultural production. The Great Depression was the first time in American history when massive migrations resulted not from the push of expansion, urbanization, or immigration, but out of economic crisis—negative mobility preoccupied the nation. The Depression forced thousands of Americans to leave their homes because of downward class mobility, not in search of land ownership but because they could no longer afford rent or mortgage payments. Territorial expansion—moving west, homesteading, and build-

---

1   Some statistics may give a sense of scale: in 1933, almost half of all home mortgages were in default, resulting in a thousand foreclosures every day (Hobsbawm 100-103). That year 40 million men, women, and children nationwide lived without a dependable source of income and 10 percent of the white population lived on relief, compared to 18 percent of African Americans (Takaki 367).

ing railroads—was replaced in the national imagination with this new kind of negative mobility motivated by economic survival and represented in ways that illustrate the reinterpretations of domesticity generated by the Depression.

Representations of homelessness in the form of Hoovervilles, Okies, and hoboes began to appear in the public culture as Americans grappled with the increasingly difficult daily struggles for basic human requirements. A 1934 reportage piece in *American Mercury*, Meridel Le Sueur's "Women Are Hungry," portrays the particular and often unnoticed suffering of women from all stations of life—teacher, farm girl, and old and young mothers.[2] The last section, entitled "Moon Bums," describes two teenage "girl bums" the writer interviewed as they waited to hop a freight south for the winter: "Fran and Ethel stood with their bundles. They looked like twigs as the light from the engine swathed over them. They looked like nothing" (157). The women tell her about one of their recent domestic situations: "Last winter they had lived in dry goods boxes outside of Chicago with two fellows who were carpenters and made the shacks, and the girls did the cooking and the fellows did the foraging" (155-56). Fran and Ethel recount a grotesque imitation of domesticity, as unmarried homeless men and women live in marginally private, improvised outdoor houses acting out their traditional gender roles, the women explain, because "a man isn't picked up in the city like a girl is. A girl is always considered a moral culprit when she begs in the city, and she is sterilized or sent away to a farm or a home which she hates" (156). Their ironic re-enactment of traditional domestic roles was short-lived, obviously, because they were again hopping a train for another winter home, but Le Sueur's reportage stresses many of the elements of negative mobility that this book will explore at length in its chapters: the ways the domestic private sphere is crowded into the public during the 30s through the phenomenon of negative social and geographic mobility, and the lingering effects of these sociospatial disruptions on the next two decades.

---

2    The piece is also remarkable in its attention to the formerly middle-class teacher with a Ph.D. in a light spring suit, whose sense of personal shame for her poverty prevents her from seeking relief until her despair and advanced stages of starvation provoke her suicide.

World War II brought a different kind of mobility to the home front: enormous economic expansion and geographic movement toward the centers of the war industry. According to the Census Bureau report in 1945, at least 15.3 million people had moved to a different county since the bombing of Pearl Harbor in 1941 (Chafe 10). Unlike the Depression, when masses of people were evicted or forced to leave home due to poverty, the war brought the promise of high-paying jobs and millions of Americans were willing to relocate.[3] People were earning and spending more: between 1939 and 1944, salaries and wages more than doubled, nightclub income rose 35 percent, and racetrack betting in New York in 1944 climbed to a daily average of $2.2 million (Chafe 9-10). The war pulled white women and African Americans into jobs that had formerly belonged exclusively to white men, who were now fighting the foreign war. Patriotism and higher wages motivated many women to leave their jobs for the defense plants—over half the working women in Mobile, Alabama, for example, changed to war work, which paid an average of 40 percent higher wages (Chafe 13). Although women in manufacturing in 1945 still only earned 65 percent of their male co-workers, that was much more than their previous jobs in stenography, laundry, and waitressing paid (Chafe 15).

The booming economy gave new hope to the African American unemployed and working poor, who had suffered worst during the Depression. Migrants from the South poured into American cities to work in the war industries: over half a million African Americans left the South in search of defense jobs, and in Los Angeles the black population increased from 75,000 in 1940 to 135,000 in 1945 (Takaki 398). World War II brought opportunities for geographic and socio-economic mobility to the nation on the heels of its worst economic crisis, and over 400,000 African American women left domestic employment for war industry jobs (Chafe 18). The new earning power and geographic mobility did not resolve the social restrictions that limited African Americans' participation in American life, but as historian William Chafe argues, "war had provided a forge within

---

3   The 1940s brought terror and ruin to the 100,000 Japanese Americans who lost their homes and jobs when forced to relocate to internment camps. An expansion of this study would take up the negative mobility narratives of internment as an important corollary to the limited but significant gains made by women and African Americans during the war.

which anger and outrage, long suppressed, were seeking new expression" (21). Race riots in Detroit and Harlem increased black protest nationwide and forced government officials to acknowledge that segregation was a problem, although the Office of War Information claimed that nothing could be done about it until after the war (Chafe 22). As the NAACP's Walter White pointed out, "World War II has immeasurably magnified the Negro's awareness of the disparity between the American profession and practice of democracy" (qtd. in Chafe 29).

Women, too, were reluctant to give up their wartime jobs to return to their homes or previous lower-paying positions: 75 percent wanted to continue working rather than succumb to the negative mobility that a return to the domestic sphere would constitute for them (Chafe 28). But the end of the war brought a campaign to return women to the private sphere, arguing that the 11 million returning veterans needed their jobs. The fear of economic collapse due to the reduction or elimination of defense industry jobs put many in mind of the recent horrors of the Depression: "As *Fortune* magazine commented, 'the American soldier is depression conscious [...] worried sick about post-war joblessness'" (qtd. in Chafe 29). The fear of another Depression in the minds of postwar Americans, combined with the hope for peace and prosperity in the aftermath of the war, created a strange national climate of consumerism, conservatism, and conformity—the 1950s. In a way that wasn't possible in the tumultuous 30s and 40s, America focused on the home as the quintessential figure for the nation: the safety of the American family home represented the security of the nation in the postwar era, even as the national defense industries geared up for the Cold War arms race.

The strong focus on the home had material effects on the postwar economy, as well as representations of the nation. Prosperity in the 1950s resulted in a massive housing boom—13 million new homes were built—and the emergence of the new professional managerial class (Chafe 117). In the years between 1947 and 1957, the number of salaried middle-class workers rose 61 percent (Chafe 115). Families were growing faster than ever, as the rate of population growth during the Baby Boom (1946-64) more than doubled the growth of the 1930s, equaling the growth rate of India (Chafe 123). Not only were middle-class families growing in size and income, they were also becoming the preferred symbol of the nation, in both international and domestic contexts; the renewed interest in the domestic private sphere during the 50s paralleled the escalating tensions of the Cold War. In her study of family life in the 1950s, Elaine Tyler May argues that "locating the family within the larger political culture, not outside it [...] illuminates both the cold war ideology and the domestic revival as two sides of the same coin: postwar Americans' intense need to feel liberated from the past and secure in the future" (10). People's memories of the previous two decades fostered this powerful longing for security, and I argue that the Great Depression as well as World War II exerted strong influences on the postwar sense of home. Rather than reading the 50s as a convenient midpoint of the century, the beginning of the "postwar" period, I suggest that we look at the ways in which the 50s are historically and culturally continuous with, and in part constituted by, the 30s and 40s.

The subject of this book is to trace the way representations of mobility produced and circulated during the Depression, World War II, and the Cold War connect the private sphere—the family, the home—and the public sphere—work, war, government. The negative mobility of the Depression eliminated the possibility for a private sphere for many Americans, who literally lost their homes and livelihoods. Geographic migrations during the 1930s were motivated by desperation: eviction, starvation, and unemployment. Effectively marking the end of negative mobility on such a scale, World War II moved still more Americans out of their homes, this time towards upward economic mobility, as millions moved to work defense jobs and women were hired in war work. 1940s Americans were still worried about poverty, but they benefited from the continued economic expansion even into the 1950s as income and consumer spending continued to increase. The Depression forced Americans in subsequent decades to rethink the assumption that geographic mobility was the key to the class mobility and private security they desired.

*American Mobilities* focuses on a pivotal point in the century when Americans realized that mobility—of capital and of labor—could have its disadvantages—instability, vulnerability—which would in later decades again become apparent. Mobility is a crucial element in all of these changes in social space: people, jobs, and capital moved from East to West, from rural to urban to suburban, and between private and public spheres during the 1930s, 40s, and 50s. A historical perspective that includes pre-war, wartime, and postwar periods together helps us to better understand the origins of contemporary representations of mobility: uneven transnational flows of capital and labor, racialized appeals to anti-immigration and anti-affirmative action laws, and the breakdown of the nation-state in the wake of the dissolution of the Soviet Union. In the new millennium, questions of mobility prove to be an important thread that runs through the twentieth century from the desperation of the Depression through the prosperous years of economic and international expansion and back into global financial crisis. Historian Eric Hobsbawm observes economic and ideological continuities between the Depression and postmodern eras:

Those of us who lived through the years of the Great Slump still find it almost impossible to understand how the orthodoxies of the pure free market, then so obviously discredited, once again came to preside over a global period of depression in the late 1980s and 1990s, which, once again, they were equally unable to understand or to deal with. (103)

This comparison also drives an essay by Fredric Jameson that suggests that late 20th-century finance capital can be productively read in terms of the 1930s:

What is wanted is an account of abstraction in which the new deterritorialized postmodern contents are to an older modernist autonomization as global financial speculation is to an older kind of banking and credit, or as the stock market frenzies of the eighties are to the Great Depression. (261)

These parallels point to the need for books like the present one, that encourage us to consider the role of the Depression, as well as World War II and the Cold War in the twentieth-century United States.

How did the reconfigurations of space that took place in the United States during these three decades affect people's lives and identities as they are represented in cultural texts? How do American cultural texts from the first half of the twentieth century represent forms of social and geographic mobility? What does the recurring motif of geographic movement signify in terms of the shifts between public and private spheres in the context of the national crises of the 30s, 40s, and 50s—Depression, World War, and Cold War? These questions inform my study of the representations of social and geographic mobility in this period. As I attempt to answer these questions, the methodologies of literary study are my most important paradigm: close reading of language, attention to narrative structures, and above all an interest in representation. These approaches alone could not take me where I want to go, however, since my questions reach into other fields of knowledge: history, geography, and cultural studies. Delving into history becomes indispensable when some of the texts most crucial to my inquiry have been largely neglected by historians and literary critics; if there is little or no general cultural knowledge of African American independent cinema of the 1930s, for example, the task of synthesizing information from primary sources and orienting it for the larger purposes of my study becomes necessary. Similarly, the rich field of critical geography, especially the work of Derek Gregory and David Harvey, provides me with ongoing theoretical conversations about space and movement from which to draw terms and concepts when my own explorations of (representations of) space and mobility exceed the reach of conventional literary inquiry. Borrowing judiciously from many disciplines enriches the scope of this study and enables a more thorough investigation of the representations of mobility in twentieth-century American literature and culture.

This book explores the ways in which representations of social mobility and their co-construction with discourses of class, gender, and race function in textual and cinematic spaces of the 1930s, 40s, and 50s. The project investigates the role these issues played in the reconfiguration of American space from rural to urban, from East to West, from domestic to international. Texts from this period represent space in ways that problematize American assumptions that socio-economic mobility is available to all: time and again, characters in these novels and films learn that having a car and a road doesn't necessarily mean you can get somewhere. Because American national identity has always concerned itself with movement—into the wilderness, across the continent, into middle and upper classes, into outer space—the trope of mobility is particularly important during times of national crisis, when the public imagination needs more than ever a believable myth of American history. The images of mobility that permeate the fiction and film during the years between the Depression and the Cold War are intimately implicated in these historical events.

I would like to define some of the key terms that I will use in this book, particularly mobility, space, place, and the domestic. As I use the term, mobility denotes both the ability to move and movement itself. Some characters have the ability to move geographically but still lack the most important mobility: upward social and economic movement. For this study, mobility encompasses the socio-economic and the geographic because the texts frequently represent both, often connecting or equating them. Often, too, geographic mobility across American space represents international expansion, in the form military or commercial intervention. The emphasis on moving on, moving out, and moving up not only links the texts in this study; it also characterizes American national identity throughout history. As Morris Dickstein argues, representations of movement prevailed in virtually every facet of American culture in the 1930s: Busby Berkeley's choreography, Dorothea Lange's and Margaret Bourke-White's photographs of migrant workers, and the streamlined styles of modernist design. Extending Dickstein's premise to the subsequent decades, this book argues that during the 1930s, 40s, and 50s, from the national crisis of the Depression to the patriotic boom of World War II and the Cold War, Americans were fascinated with mobility and that fascination manifested itself in representation.

Movement presumes space, which brings us to a term fraught with grandiose and diverse meanings in recent literary and theoretical work. Henri Lefebvre defines social space as "neither a 'subject' nor an 'object' but rather a social reality—that is to say, a set of relations and forms" (116). In this sense, these chapters contribute to a history of American space as it is represented in literature and film and as it is reconfigured in social practices and fractures along the lines of race, gender, and class. This project draws on the methods of both literary study of representation and the geographic study of space, attempting to breach the distance between the two methodologies to read space as a relational, socially created phenomenon. Relational space, in this study, is represented in fiction and film at all scales—houses, streets, cities, states, territories, and nations—and their representations in American cultural texts are implicated in the changing and contested values that shape Americans' lives.

Given the popularity of the term "space" in literary scholarship, I would like to elaborate more specifically what I mean when I employ it. As scholars in transnational American Studies continually challenge themselves not to reinscribe the dominance of the U.S., but rather contribute to the critique of that dominance with the goal of empowering non-U.S. and non-Western voices, those of us who presume to write about space need to be cautious not to abstract the concept to the degree that it operates outside of material history. In his essay, "Isaiah Bowman and the Geography of the American

Century," Neil Smith describes what he calls the "spatial turn" in the 20th century, which, he notes frequently, is also known as the American Century. The spatial turn signals "a dislocation of economic expansion from absolute geographical expansion" marked by uneven development which contributes to "economic expansion organized in and through 'relational' rather than absolute space" (Smith 20; 46).

This division of space into absolute and relational is a critical move that many geographers make: separating abstract, absolute, or metaphorical space from material, social, or actual space in order to emphasize the latter's alternative to a fixed, container model that cannot change. Absolute space refers to space with definite boundaries, for example, private property or nation states, which can contain events and objects—this notion of space operates in the proclamation of the closed frontier, for example, which says that there is no new or unclaimed territory within the borders of the U.S. (Smith 16). On the other hand, the relational space Smith refers to marks the "spatial turn" to the global and eventually transnational 20th century in which the U.S. operated (and dominated) in "spheres of influence" and "trade zones" rather than imperial colonies like those of nineteenth-century England. After the closing of the frontier and the spatial turn of the American Century, the movement of American capital no longer equals the movement of American settlers; relational space depends on uneven development, not virgin territory. The increased mobility of American capital coincided with, and indeed fostered, the immobility of "others" whose stasis is attributed to idiosyncrasies of culture or biology, rather than economics.

I argue that the spatial turn in the early decades of the twentieth century—"modernity"—gives us a geographical context in which to look at the changes taking place both in cultural and in economic arenas. In the 30s, 40s, and 50s, American expansion in the relational space of foreign diplomacy coincided with the Great Depression in which national economies collapsed, and the exportation of Hollywood films worldwide accompanied the trade routes of United Fruit and TWA. I want to stay aware of the risk involved in these kinds of generalizations, which lies in the ease with which terms like "space" and "mobility" can become unmoored from material places and social constructions of identity—thus making it difficult to pin down the power relations involved. I aim to keep my own work grounded in this sense: to focus on mobility as a way of understanding the uneven distributions of power that underlie both economic and cultural production.

The American Century is the century of uneven development, as Neil Smith argues, and this book seeks to find ways to talk about space and mobility without losing sight of the material relations that take "place" in public and private spheres.

A specific location in space, then, is the common-sense understanding of a "place." Place, as I employ the term, connotes a location that is both geographically grounded and invested with cultural meaning: for example, "rural" may not be a single point on a particular map, but it is grounded in its opposition to "urban." The concept of "place" emphasizes the links between space and identity, although in a more literal way than the metaphorical "politics of location," the method of inquiry into identity that has so fruitfully informed the work of feminist scholars from Adrienne Rich to Caren Kaplan.[4] In this book, the term "place" refers to a concept that depends on both geography and the social constructions of identity that accompany that geographical location. In the introductory essay to *Knowing Your Place: Rural Identity and Cultural Hierarchy*, editors Barbara Ching and Gerald W. Creed explain their book's focus on rural identity as a first step in "questioning the cultural ascendancy of urbanity" that has prevailed, as Raymond Williams has shown, since before Roman times, and that privileging of the urban has only gained ground since the first stages of industrialization (Ching and Creed 30). In this sense, my use of the term place is more rooted in geography than many recent studies allow; frequently place or location is used metaphorically to refer to terms of identity such as gender, nationality, and/or race. Like Ching and Creed, I employ the term as a kind of "middle ground in which 'place' can be metaphoric yet still refer to a particular physical environment and its associated socio-cultural qualities" (7).

One place that is crucial to the argument of this project is the site of the domestic. "Domestic" has two distinct and usually quite separate meanings, both of which depend on their opposite concepts for specificity: the private home as opposed to the public sphere and the nation as opposed to the foreign. In her essay "Manifest Domesticity," from a special issue of *American Literature* entitled "No More Separate Spheres," Amy Kaplan troubles

---

4    Kaplan argues for a politics of location "that investigates the productive tension between temporal and spatial theories of subjectivity [that] can help us delineate the conditions of transnational feminist practices in postmodernity" (138).

the boundaries between these two definitions, paying particular attention to their gendered dimensions:

When we contrast the domestic sphere with the market or political realm, men and women inhabit a divided social terrain, but when we oppose the domestic to the foreign, men and women become national allies against the alien, and the determining division is not gender but racial demarcations of otherness. (582)

Kaplan's essay makes an important step toward linking the discourses of gender, imperialism, and nation in current critical conversations about antebellum America; building on her thesis, I suggest that both definitions of domestic are necessary for an understanding of U.S. culture during the first half of the twentieth century. Kaplan's revision of the "domestic" private sphere—as inherently implicated in domestic and international politics and markets—provides a way to read purportedly "private" issues such as race and gender in terms of the major social and political, "public" upheavals in the 1930s, 40s, and 50s. Indeed, many of the representations of conflict this book considers arise from the inadequate separation of these spheres, when racialized or gendered others, for example, move into the public sphere. This movement takes the form of social as well as geographic mobility, as the socially constructed meanings associated with one place are carried into the other.

Geographical mobility in the 30s is frequently associated with social movement; however, for the rural poor in Faulkner's *As I Lay Dying* and the working class in Le Sueur's *The Girl*, racialized notions of class influenced by the eugenics movement mark poor whites as "white trash" unable to succeed and unworthy of success in spite of their attempts to move from rural to urban spaces. In Chapter One, I read these two novels through the term "white trash" as it is used to racialize poor whites by middle-class town- and city-dwellers who interpret poverty as a matter of taste or choice rather than the result of social and economic forces. Raymond Williams's *The Country and the City* is crucial to this chapter and subsequent chapters, since it articulates the far-reaching ways that national rural/urban dichotomies can be situated in terms of class. Just as, according to Williams, rural life constituted the obsolete other for the industrializing urban English, poor whites in the U.S. have historically been the object of specifically American forms of othering in class as well as racialized distinctions. Attention to whiteness in recent academic work has yielded many important studies from critics in a variety of fields, including Duane Carr, David Roediger, and Alexander Saxton. But my first chapter has also been influenced by the recent anthology edited by Annalee Newitz and Matt Wray, entitled *White Trash: Race and Class in America*. It was their ahistorical and undertheorized approach to contemporary class and race issues that inspired me to attempt a literary historical genealogy of the term, grounded in the texts and geographies of the Depression. Representations of rural life, I argue, should be read in terms of a larger trajectory: judging poor white rural Mississippians as "trash" allows them to be ridiculed and their poverty to be individualized rather than understood as part of the structurally uneven national movement toward industrialization, urbanization, and consumerism. Similarly, the Girl in Le Sueur's novel is classified by a relief worker as unsuitable to reproduce based on her poverty, pregnancy and single status, all of which bring into play the eugenics-inspired discourses of social work that targeted poor women for institutional intervention. Both texts depict the ideological, aspirational precarity of the middle class that compels them to distinguish themselves from poor whites on the basis of biology rather than address the economic and social bases for their poverty.

Both texts also depict extreme conflations of public and private spheres: everything that belongs inside comes out as Addie Bundren's funerary procession becomes a grotesque public spectacle while her body decomposes in its coffin. The funeral should be a family matter, her coffin should be in the ground, and her putrefying insides should be underground. The novel ends with the introduction of Anse's new wife, figured as a commodity obtained in town as were his new teeth and the children's bananas. In *The Girl*, the bodies of the poor are commodified as instruments of labor and subject to invasion by the state as improperly fertile. The Girl's politicization takes place in a community of homeless women protesting the inadequacy of state prenatal care, and the birth of her daughter is witnessed as a political event by the gathering protesters. The concerns of the home—marriage, childbirth, and death—become problematically public in Faulkner's and Le Sueur's Depression-era texts, as "domestic" concerns serve to define public notions of identity—class, race, and gender. This chapter received favorable editorial reviews from *Arizona Quarterly*, where it was published as an article with some revisions in 2000; I have included here the version from the journal, which improved under the guidance of the anonymous reviewers. The chapter's section on Faulkner's *As I Lay Dying* was later incorporated, with further revisions, into a chapter on that novel and *Absalom, Absalom!* entitled "Shifting Sands: The Myth of Class Mobility" for Richard C. Moreland's *A Companion to William Faulkner* (Blackwell, 2007).

As the private moves into the public sphere, American national space is increasingly represented in terms of the public spaces of cities during the 30s and 40s, and a trajectory from East Coast to West Coast charts a reconfiguration of national urban space. Chapter 2 reads the novels *Imitation of Life* by Fannie Hurst and *If He Hollers Let Him Go* by Chester Himes, examining the roles of the two coastal locations as national sites of commerce, inflected by place and by raced and gendered notions of workplace and the private sphere. Although the change in emphasis from East to West during the 1930s and 1940s has been documented it has not been fully theorized by cultural critics, so I turn to the changing representations of domestic and commercial space as a way of reading the reconfiguration of national space in these two texts. Hurst's novel describes Bea Pullman's movement from domestic to commercial, from East Coast westward and then abroad, in her enormously successful corporation; simultaneously, Hurst represents Bea's life as a successful businesswoman, increasingly disembodied and removed from the domestic sphere. Neither wife nor homemaker, Bea chastises herself as a failure because she doesn't conform to her mother's traditional notions of femininity. Himes's novel, on the other hand, portrays Bob Jones's experiences of racism in the Los Angeles shipyards during World War II, emphasizing the parallels between racial and sexual violence and between national racist institutions and international military expansion. Bob's difficulties in the public sphere of industrial work and city streets illustrates the sometimes painful consequences of mobility when African American workers across the country migrated to California and into occupations previously reserved for whites. As representations of white women and African Americans moved out of the home and into the formerly white male workplace, the social spaces of the nation— and the way they are represented in literary texts—underwent massive and often violent changes.

Westward movement during this period shifts the national imagination of urban space from New York to Los Angeles, a new city in the mythic West where California's colonial past erupts in fictional texts, architectural styles, and decorating trends. In Los Angeles, geographical mobility in the form of automobiles comes to symbolize a particularly modern, American, and "Western" freedom. The dialectic of foreign and domestic takes some sharp turns throughout the history of space in the Los Angeles area, as shifting power relations around race and ethnicity affect who has the power to claim citizenship and social mobility. Chapter 3 draws on the multicultural history of Southern California to read reassertions of whiteness in the newly emerging genre of California novels: from James M. Cain and Raymond Chandler to Budd Schulberg and Nathanael West, the geographic and socio-economic mobility that characterizes representations of California doesn't always pan out the way it promises to. I turn to John Findlay's study of post-1940 western cities, *Magic Lands*, which provides a theoretical framework for reading Los Angeles in this period. Findlay's notion of the "magic city" as a phenomenon of the American West helps me to explain the images of Los Angeles as a new kind of city, a conscious departure from the cities of the East Coast and Midwest, that now represents the home of the modern nation. The movement of large numbers of Americans from East to West during the 30s and 40s helps to establish a new sense of the nation, figured as a new urban form: the Western city.

Among the most important new residents of Los Angeles were the Jewish immigrants who founded the Hollywood movie industry, and Neal Gabler's comprehensive study of the Hollywood Jews, *An Empire of Their Own*, provides a unique cultural history of the American cinema by exploring how the immigrants' mobility narratives helped shape the way the rest of America imagined itself through the cinema. The film industry in the 30s and 40s enjoyed intimate access to the American public's most private processes of identification, and the on-screen representations of social and geographic mobility from this time period participate in public notions of nation and citizenship. This chapter situates the historical and literary representations of the Hollywood Jews' social mobility in the larger context of the changing American notion of the city as a western phenomenon. Concluding with a look at the quintessential symbol of Los Angeles—the automobile—Chapter 3 examines the use of the car as a symbol of social mobility and, frequently, immobility, as the hard-luck denizens of the Los Angeles underworld in the novels of James M. Cain and Raymond Chandler try and often fail to achieve socio-economic success. I preserve the original chapter here; a shorter version of was published in 2004 as part of the

Netherlands Association of American Studies conference proceedings volume edited by Jaap Verheul. That chapter is entitled "Los Angeles in the 1930s: Magic City, White Utopia, or Multicultural Museum?" and deals primarily with the novels of Nathanael West and James M. Cain.

The trajectory from rural to urban spaces and from East to West Coast culminates in the parallel constructions of American expansion into the West with U.S. imperialist movement in Europe and Asia during the 1940s. In the original dissertation's Chapter 4, a reading of two low-budget films produced during the years of preparation for and participation in World War II, *Harlem Rides the Range* (1939) and *I Walked with a Zombie* (1943), I placed these popular texts in the context of past and present nation-building and empire-building narratives. The chapter was substantially revised prior to publication in *Cinema Journal* in 2002, during which process I cut the entire discussion of the zombie film to focus exclusively on the black-cast western; it is this revised version I include here. Like Bob Jones's struggle for rights and recognition in the public sphere in Chapter 2, the African American cowboy films of the late 30s and early 40s depict a heroic and patriotic African American male citizen who participates in the important process of national consolidation of space in the American West. The appearance of black actors in the traditionally white role of cowboy hero complicates the racial hierarchies, not only within the film genre, but also in the context of the national imagination of American masculinity. *Harlem Rides the Range* also depicts American geographic mobility, in the westward movement at the frontier as well as the reterritorialization of the west (and the western) as a site of African American heroism, further demonstrating the primacy of the mobility trope in relation to the dual meanings of the domestic as both the private sphere of home and as it implies the national public sphere of American cultural politics.

*Maud Martha* is the only work of fiction by Gwendolyn Brooks (1917–2000), the first African American poet to win a Pulitzer Prize. It is a short novel or novella made up of a series of vignettes centering around the title character, a young African American woman, covering the period from her childhood to early adulthood in Chicago. To better understand the representations of class and space as co-constructions in *Maud Martha*, in Chapter 5 I employ a key concept from geographical theory: the "imaginative geography." What geographers emphasize is the material, embodied nature of imaginative geographies: they are not just images. Rather they are products of, and influences on, physical lived experience as raced, gendered, classed, and otherwise marked and unmarked bodies in society. This chapter considers two crucial vignettes from the novel as it argues that, in the spatial event of reading, the text's imaginative geographies play a role in the development of literary meaning, in that a reader's impression is informed by the text's representations of the characters' thoughts, dreams, and actions as portrayed in the text. But they can also be a product of reading literature, in that the act of reading fosters an imaginary experience of other places, other lives, and other bodies. This kind of textual mobility constitutes another facet of this book's central argument: that American literature and culture of the early 20th century demands a consideration of this crucial trope. This chapter was initially left out of the dissertation but was presented as a conference paper at the MLA in Chicago in 2007 and published as an article in the *Japanese Journal of American Studies* in 2008.

The concluding chapter originally traced the representations of space and mobility in the films of John Ford from the Depression through the Cold War, including *Wee Willie Winkie* (1937), *The Grapes of Wrath* (1940), and, most importantly, *The Searchers* (1956). For its 2002 publication in the *Japanese Journal of American Studies*, I deleted the discussion of the other films in order to expand and deepen my geographical reading of *The Searchers*. Ford's signature use of Western landscapes and the stark contrast he makes between claustrophobic domestic settings and outdoor "wild" spaces position audiences to envision the U.S. as an expansionist world power. In their representation of American space, Ford's films problematize the complex interrelations between public and private spheres, played out in the geographical locations that came to represent, in his distinctive cinematic shorthand, the nation. Ford's deployment of the mobility trope in his horses, wagons, and buckboards contrasts with his representations of the interior world of the home, for example, in the constricting, oppressive feeling that arises from his use of ceilings and doorways. His films create a geographical and social way to narrate the power relations that reside in the landscapes and the indoor spaces of his films, as well as the "domestic" and foreign policy issues confronting the nation during the 1950s in particular. In this analysis of *The Searchers*, I argue that the domestic sphere is ultimately structured by the public sphere, as the Cold War western constructs a picture of a static, unmoving home that depends on the presence of a mobile man of action, capable of violence in his duty to protect the home. The surly but benevolent John Wayne character is the figure for American militarism in the Cold War, when the Duke's brash frontier violence is depicted as obsolete but still unfortunately necessary.

Understanding the ways in which the domestic discourses of the 30s are still present in quite different forms in the 40s and 50s can offer us a broader perspective on 1990s representations of mobility and the domestic, the decade when these chapters were written. Lauren Berlant argues that the Reagan era's focus on family values has resulted in "collapsing the political and the personal into a world of public intimacy" (*Queen* 1). Public attention to private issues, including President Bill Clinton's relationship with Monica Lewinsky and the public's access to the narrative of their sex acts, only underscores Berlant's argument that personal actions and values are substituted for political discourse in contemporary American culture. But while the fact that Clinton's private affairs threatened his political career in a way unthinkable during FDR's presidency illustrates the vast differences between postmodern and modern media and standards of public discourse, I argue that exploring the continuities as well as the differences can lead to a fuller understanding of the century as a whole.

Recalling President Clinton's frequent self-comparisons and references to an earlier president famous for his intimacy with the nation, Franklin D. Roosevelt, during his campaign and both terms in office, I suggest that Clinton's brand of public intimacy is modeled on FDR's: through his use of the new public medium of radio, Roosevelt "gave many people a feeling that he was their personal friend and protector, that they could tell him things in confidence" (McElvaine 6). Just as Roosevelt projected this impression of intimacy via his radio programs in which he addressed the American in the second person as though in conversation, Clinton appeared on late night talk shows and MTV town meetings, trying to prove that he was personally interested in reaching into Americans' homes. Little did Clinton know how intimately Americans would know him—years after that campaign, the Lewinsky affair prompted him to plead for privacy to sort out his family problems. But I suggest that the public intimacy with the Presidency began with FDR, an origin in the Depression which forges a link between the 30s and the 90s, oriented around the threshold between public and private spheres.

Mapping the representations of private and public spheres as they intersect with gender, class, race, nation, and sexuality in 1980s and 90s road movies, for example, can inform readings of such important films as *Stranger than Paradise* (1984), *Powwow Highway* (1989), *Thelma and Louise* (1991), *Lost Highway* (1996), and *Breakdown* (1996). These films—like the films in Chapters 4 and 6—represent American mobility and its relationship to national identity in ways that can tell us much about contemporary domestic and foreign policies. Tuning in to the discourses of the movement, including the American genre of the road film, underscores the connections between the brink of the millennium and the decades of and after the Great Depression, when the Bundrens, the Girl, Bob Jones, Mildred Pierce, Philip Marlowe, Bob Blake, Maud Martha, Ethan Edwards, and dozens of other characters followed their aspirations of the American Dream of socio-economic and geographic mobility in wagons, on horseback, on foot, by train, or along the highways of the nation.

## WORKS CITED

Berlant, Lauren. *The Queen of America Goes to Washington City: Essays on Sex and Citizenship*. Durham: Duke UP, 1997. Print.

---. "The Theory of Infantile Citizenship." *Public Culture* (1993): 395-410. Print.

Carr, Duane. *A Question of Class: The Redneck Stereotype in Southern Fiction*. Bowling Green: Bowling Green U Popular P, 1996. Print.

Chafe, William H. *The Unfinished Journey: America Since World War II*. 3rd ed. New York: Oxford UP, 1995. Print.

Ching, Barbara and Gerald W. Creed. "Introduction: Recognizing Rusticity: Identity and the Power of Place." *Knowing Your Place: Rural Identity and Cultural Hierarchy*. New York: Routledge, 1997. 1-38. Print.

Gregory, Derek. *Geographical Imaginations*. Oxford: Blackwell, 1994. Print.

Harvey, David. *The Condition of Postmodernity: An Enquiry into the Origins of Cultural Change*. Oxford: Blackwell, 1990. Print.

Hobsbawm, Eric. *The Age of Extremes: A History of the World, 1914-1991*. 1994. New York: Vintage, 1996. Print.

Jameson, Fredric. "Culture and Finance Capital." *Critical Inquiry* 24 (1997): 246-65. Print.

Kaplan, Amy. "Manifest Domesticity." *American Literature* 70 (1998): 581-606. Print.

Kaplan, Caren. "The Politics of Location as Transnational Feminist Critical Practice." *Scattered Hegemonies: Postmodernity and Transnational Feminist Practices*. Eds. Inderpal Grewal and Caren Kaplan. Minneapolis: U of Minnesota P, 1994. 137-52. Print.

Le Sueur, Meridel. "Women Are Hungry." 1934. *Ripening: Selected Work, 1927-1980*. Old Westbury: Feminist P, 1982. 144-57. Print.

Lefebvre, Henri. *The Production of Space*. 1991. Trans. Donald Nicholson-Smith. Oxford: Blackwell, 1997. Print.

Leyda, Julia. "Black-Audience Westerns and the Politics of Cultural Identification in the 1930s." *Cinema Journal* 42.1 (2002): 46-70. Print.

---. "Home on the Range: Space, Nation, and Mobility in John Ford's *The Searchers*." *Japanese Journal of American Studies* 13 (2002): 83-106. Print.

---. "Los Angeles in the 1930s: Magic City, White Utopia, or Multicultural Museum?" *Dreams of Paradise, Visions of Apocalypse: Utopia and Dystopia in American Culture*. Ed. Jaap Verheul. Amsterdam: VU UP, 2004. 130-36. Print. Eur. Contributions to Amer. Studies 51.

---. "Reading White Trash: Class, Race, and Mobility in Faulkner and Le Sueur." *Arizona Quarterly* 56.2 (2000): 37-64. Print.

---. "Shifting Sands: The Myth of Class Mobility." *A Companion to William Faulkner*. Ed. Richard C. Moreland. Malden, MA: Blackwell, 2007. 165-79. Print.

---. "Space, Class, City: Literary Geographies of Gwendolyn Brooks's *Maud Martha*." *Japanese Journal of American Studies* 19 (2008): 123-37. Print.

Newitz, Annalee, and Matt Wray, eds. *White Trash: Race and Class in America*. New York: Routledge, 1997. Print.

Rich, Adrienne. "Notes Toward a Politics of Location." *Blood, Bread, and Poetry: Selected Prose, 1979-1985*. New York: Norton, 1986. Print.

Roediger, David. *Towards the Abolition of Whiteness: Essays on Race, Politics, and Working Class History*. New York: Verso, 1994. Print.

Saxton, Alexander. *The Rise and Fall of the White Republic: Class Politics and Mass Culture in Nineteenth-Century America*. New York: Verso, 1990. Print.

Smith, Neil. "The Lost Geography of the American Century." *American Empire: Roosevelt's Geographer and the Prelude to Globalization*. Berkeley: U of California P, 2003. Print.

Takaki, Ronald. *A Different Mirror: A History of Multicultural America*. Boston: Back Bay-Little, Brown, 1993. Print.

Williams, Raymond. *The Country and the City*. New York: Oxford UP, 1973. Print.

# 1 Reading White Trash

Class, Race, and Mobility in Faulkner and Le Sueur

The *Oxford English Dictionary* defines the word "trash" as "a worthless or disreputable person; now, usually, such persons collectively . . . white trash, the poor white population in the Southern States of America," including British usages of "trash" that denote poverty and worthlessness. The American examples, however, include the addition of "white," creating the racialized term "white trash," as in an 1831 usage: "'You be right dere,' observed Sambo, 'else what fur he go more 'mong niggers den de white trash?'" Another usage appears in a white man's 1833 journal entry: "The slaves themselves entertain the very highest contempt for white servants, whom they designate as 'poor white trash.'" Although this example attempts to trace the term "white trash" to slaves, I suggest that whatever the origin of the expression, it was most likely the invention of middle-class whites, who attributed it to slaves and encouraged animosity among slaves and poor whites in order to prevent cross-racial alliances that would challenge white hegemony. Indeed, the *OED* etymology cites a white man's journal entry, in which the term is ascribed *to* African Americans *by* whites, who most benefit from it.

According to Eugene Genovese's history of slavery, *Roll, Jordan, Roll*, middle-class whites "explained away the existence of such racial contacts and avoided reflecting on the possibility that genuine sympathy might exist across racial lines" (23). Fear of slave rebellion with the aid of poor whites who resented the planter class fostered the hostile attitudes toward white trash: for example, many Southern states instituted "stern police measures against whites who illicitly fraternized with blacks" and attempted to keep white and black laborers separate (Genovese 23). Although poor whites and blacks sometimes helped one another, more often animosity prevailed, bolstering the power of the upper and middle class whites. Despite a few examples of cross-racial sympathy in Genovese's oral histories, on the whole "interracial solidarity could not develop into a serious threat to the regime" because of the dominance of racist discourse over class consciousness and the strength of poor whites' desire for upward class mobility (Genovese 24).

Throughout the nineteenth and early twentieth centuries, the racial and classed term white trash has peppered American oral and written culture, yet few scholars have seriously questioned how this term functions in American language and literature.[1] The paucity of research on the term is in itself telling: white trash is an epithet whose history is still largely unexamined. In 1990s everyday usage, the term white trash caricatures a group of people—poor whites—implicitly justifying through ridicule their disenfranchisement and alienation from society. A historically informed, critical examination of how the term white trash functions in the 1930s demonstrates how middle-class whites constructed white trash identity to explain the socio-economic immobility of other, less prosperous whites. The discourse of "trash" circulated in connection with claims about genetics and eugenics, adaptability to changing capitalist markets, and gender identity. The term signifies specific racialized class identities contingent on time and place, but always serving to distinguish the trash from upwardly mobile whites, who, no matter how poor, still have the potential for upward mobility that the trash lack. Emphasizing individual biological traits—concerns proper to the private sphere—middle-class whites could evade the fact that poor whites' poverty results from structural problems in the economy—the public sphere of capital and labor, production and consumption. By examining the way the term works in the 1930s, a time of economic crisis when the issue of class took center stage in public discourse and when urbanization and consumer capitalism reached into the private homes of even the

---

1    Sylvia Jenkins Cook, Nicole Rafter, and Duane Carr have published studies of American "poor whites," but Annalee Newitz and Matt Wray's 1997 *White Trash: Race and Class in America* is the most recent scholarly work to take up the issue. While their anthology signals an increased critical interest in "white trash," the overall content is undertheorized and ahistorical.

poorest states in the South, we can better comprehend how the term operates in contemporary texts and contexts.

Meridel Le Sueur's *The Girl* (1939)[2] and William Faulkner's *As I Lay Dying* (1930) suggest the historically specific ways in which poor whites are read as white trash in 1930s American texts. Reading these two novels together is a response to a current dearth of critical scholarship in two main areas: first, the issue of race in the study of Le Sueur, and second, the need to read Faulkner in terms of class. That is, recent work on Le Sueur has focused on reviving interest in her work and situating it in the context of feminism and the left literary tradition; conversely, while library shelves brim with recent scholarship on Faulkner, especially excellent studies on race, gender, and nation,[3] very few critically examine how class is represented in his fiction. Myra Jehlen's 1976 book, *Class and Character in Faulkner's South*, points to a promising direction in Faulkner scholarship: it considers his novels not primarily in terms of their modernist formal characteristics, but for their treatment of social issues, specifically the ways in which his work represents the poor whites of Yoknapatawpha and engages with the social history of class in Mississippi. Since the 1970s, dozens more Faulkner studies have emerged, but no major study of class since hers. On the other hand, Meridel Le Sueur's work, while nowhere nearly as popular as Faulkner with readers or critics, has received more and well-deserved attention in recent years, especially in Paula Rabinowitz's *Labor and Desire: Women's Revolutionary Fiction in Depression America* (1991) and Constance Coiner's *Better Red: The Writing and Resistance of Tillie Olsen and Meridel Le Sueur* (1995). Both these studies perform the crucial and belated

---

2    Although it wasn't published in its entirety in the 1930s, I still consider *The Girl* a 30s novel, as do Le Sueur scholars Coiner, Foley, and Rabinowitz. One obvious reason is the fact that Le Sueur published three chapters in *Anvil* and *New Masses* during the 30s. Additionally, *The Girl* is a 30s text in proletarian content, formal experimentation, and Le Sueur's Marxist feminism, also evident in her nonfiction published during this period. In fact, even if the "feminist" elements were revised or expanded (with 70s feminist hindsight) for the 1978 publication, given the 1930s preoccupation with class politics, this proletarian novel occupies a 1930s radical literary space along with Tillie Olsen's *Yonnondio: From the Thirties*, also not published during that decade.

3    See Clarke, Ladd, Roberts, Saldívar.

tasks of taking up neglected women writers of the left and documenting the conditions under which they produced their work and under which their work was (poorly) received or suppressed altogether; both read Le Sueur's work in the context of proletarian and women's writing. This chapter continues and extends Rabinowitz's and Coiner's projects by taking up the issue of racialized class identity in Le Sueur's proletarian feminist novel. Faulkner and Le Sueur, although very different in many integral ways, round out a picture of white trash during the Depression.

The trope of movement, both geographical and socioeconomic, plays a crucial role in these representations: the privileging of industrial over agrarian and the modern city over the antiquated countryside marks trash subjects as deficient in geographical capital. These subjects occupy a low position on an axis of class and geographical privilege in what Pierre Bourdieu calls "socially ranked geographical space" (124). For the characters in these two novels, attempting to move from private to public sphere, from country to city, and from working to middle class involves difficult and often unsuccessful movements across those geographical and socio-economic boundaries. The first section of this chapter demonstrates how white trash characters are treated as classed and racialized others by urban whites. The second section examines the ways in which white trash characters read their own bodies as natural resources and as commodities. The third section historicizes the term in the context of studies of class and whiteness, particularly the work of Evan Watkins and George Rawick. The final section maps the position of poor whites, in racializing and commodifying tropes as well as tropes of movement and stagnation, as trash along the road to modernization in the urbanizing nation, and often as obstacles to modernization. The hope that geographic movement will lead to class mobility permeates the two novels, and the failure of that hope for mobility marks the characters as white trash in the racialized and classed sense of the term.

## "LIKE THEY DO": THE BUNDRENS AS CLASSED AND RACIALIZED OTHERS

The construction of the Bundrens as white trash in *As I Lay Dying* serves a crucial purpose in the racialized class ideology that undergirds the narrative: Anse Bundren is figured by Faulkner's text as lazy, dishonest, self-righteous, duplicitous trash, and many observers in the novel attribute various of these characteristics to his children as well. Anse as white trash allows the other white farmers to see themselves as hard-working, honest white men somehow constitutionally or biologically different from the white trash. The white men who live in Anse's county may be only marginally better off than he, but they are more socially adept and ambitious; for them, Anse functions as a classed white other, in a different category from their own, even though they, like Anse, live in the country and function as part of the antiquated agricultural mode of production in the Depression-era New South.

The function of geography in the white trash identity is also central: town whites must "other" the rural whites to preserve their own class and racial identity as white capitalists. As Raymond Williams demonstrates in *The Country and the City*, the country is represented as the site of backwardness, inefficiency, and ignorance at precisely the point in history when national participation in consumer capitalism picks up steam; for these rural whites in the New South, that point is only now arriving. With the changes in production and consumption come changes along other social axes, including relations of geography and race. The Bundrens suffer condescension and discrimination from town- and city-dwellers because of their roots in the rural poor. Certainly, as Williams argues, the overdetermined categories of country and city have been invoked historically to signify not simply geographical difference but also differences in morals, modes of production, and stages of capitalism. These white trash characters from the rural United States are perceived by the other characters as "country" and therefore obsolete, primitive, and stupid.[4] Marking the Bundrens as trash obviates the need to explain their lack of mobility in the "land of opportunity" the middle classes need to believe exists. When country-dwellers travel to town, they face the prejudices of the townsfolk at every turn, particularly in their uneasy role as consumers with very little purchasing power. Simultaneously threatened and reassured by the presence of poor country white trash, the townspeople distance themselves from the trash by emphasizing their difference via their rural customs and by racializing the white trash as somehow biologically or genetically inferior to themselves.

---

4   Cook has illustrated how these attributes have been ascribed to poor whites since the 1700s.

The importance of geographical capital in *As I Lay Dying* comes up frequently. For example, the youngest son Vardaman's obsession with a toy train in a shop window illustrates how geography is implicated in capitalism even in the rural counties of Mississippi. He wonders about commodity consumption and its relation to the town/country binary as he worries that a town boy might have bought the train: "When it runs on the track shines again. 'Why ain't I a town boy, pa?' I said. God made me. I did not said to God to made me in the country. If He can make the train, why cant He make them all in the town" (66). Later in the journey, as Dewey Dell entertains him with stories of the train, he worries again about a town boy buying the train: "Dewey Dell says it wont be sold because it belongs to Santa Claus and he taken it back with him until next Christmas. Then it will be behind the glass again, shining with waiting. [...] She says he wont sell it to no town boys" (100-102). Even as a very young child, Vardaman has internalized the devalued geographical capital associated with rural whites, and his anxiety troubles and intensifies his position as a consumer, "shining with waiting" for the toy he desires.[5]

The family's perceived geographical and cultural capital plays out differently for Vardaman's father, Anse. Anse Bundren's racialized class position is articulated in the novel through others' perceptions of him. To the townsfolk and better-off neighbors, Anse's personality flaws and his poverty are cause and effect. With little or no regard for the physical toll of poverty and hard work, Anse's character is consistently perceived by other whites as lazy, greedy, and deceitful, characteristics historically attributed to white trash to justify their lack of social mobility. Tull, a white man who lives on a farm near the Bundrens but who is significantly more socially skilled and financially stable, alludes to Anse's financial situation as rooted in greed, suggesting that Anse would withhold information if he stood to profit from it: "I'd believe him about something he couldn't expect to make anything off of me by not telling" (23). The easy morals of white trash Anse are here thrown into relief by Tull's implication that he and Anse differ in this moral realm; as Anse would behave dishonestly for financial gain out of greed, so Tull would not. The implication is that Anse is greedy because he is poor, poor because he is lazy, and lazy because he lacks ambi-

---

5    Susan Willis and John T. Matthews provide provocative readings of Vardaman's consumerism.

tion. Tull's circular logic in his assessment of Anse relies on the class-specific semantic difference between ambition and greed: ambitious people desire success and achieve it through hard work, while greedy people desire material wealth and achieve it through dishonest means. Unaware of this class bias, Tull sees himself as ambitious and Anse as greedy.

Even if Tull's stated opinion of Anse were true, he doesn't mention any possible motives Anse would have outside of greed, his family's poverty, for example, or his own inability to work. Although many townsfolk believe a natural, racialized difference separates them from the Bundrens, none acknowledge the physical results of the class differences manifested in Anse's body. Duane Carr aptly points out that, amidst the neighbors' and townsfolk's casual condemnation of Anse's laziness, only Darl mentions his father's work-related disabilities due to a previous bout with heatstroke and bad shoes as a child laborer. Anse's refusal to work up a sweat stems from the fact that "as a young man he had been a hard worker who fell deathly ill 'from working in the hot sun,' a reality that gives credence to his otherwise superstitious belief that if he works up a sweat he will die" (Carr 83). And although numerous characters remark upon Anse's custom of working his children as he rests in the shade, only Darl observes that his father's feet are "badly splayed, his toes cramped and bent and warped, with no toenail at all on his little toes, from working so hard in the wet in homemade shoes when he was a boy" (11). The narrative gives the reader examples of how Anse's body is scarred by his life of work, but few notice the physical explanations for Anse's "laziness," seeing him simply as shiftless white trash.

As for his neediness, Anse is seen as part of a specific group of people. After Anse trades his son's horse for a mule team without permission, Armistid vents his frustration over Anse's neediness. He describes Anse returning from the trade looking "kind of funny: kind of more hangdog than common, and kind of proud too. Like he had done something he thought was cute but wasn't so sho now how other folks would take it" (189). Armistid sees Anse as a disingenuous and manipulative individual, but also definitive of his class—rural white trash. Like Anse, Armistid is a farmer in rural Yoknapatawpha county, but he and his wife Lula have a barn, a mule team, and apparently more middle-class sensibilities than the Bundrens, who can't afford false teeth and who must barter and mortgage for most of their necessities. Distinguishing himself from Anse, Armistid contemplates his annoying qualities: "durn if there aint something about a durn fellow *like* Anse that seems to make a man have to help him, even when he knows he'll be wanting to kick himself the next minute" (192; my emphasis). Armistid is talking about a "fellow like Anse"—not just Anse himself, but a group or class of fellows like him, of his type, who need help from Armistid, "a man" who will angrily regret it "the next minute." Here Anse is rhetorically lumped together with needy, seemingly humble people who share his attributes such as laziness, deceit, and reliance on others, who appear to need help from "a man" but, Armistid believes, are really angling for their own gain. Anse and other white trash take advantage of the generosity of others, especially white middle-class men, just as the racialized discourse about class still resonates today in representations of "welfare mothers." Foregrounding a similar representation of idle poor that recurs throughout English literature and histories, Williams notes that it is "not only the recurrent and ludicrous part-song of the rich; but the sharper, more savage anxiety of the middle men, the insecure," who have a greater stake in denouncing the poor and demarcating the lines of distinction between the trash and the middle classes (44). In *As I Lay Dying*, those who have the greatest stake in marking Anse as a white trash other are those who occupy positions closest to his, socio-economically and geographically: farmers and townsfolk who want to be perceived as "modern" and middle class and who see in the Bundrens' backwardness evidence of their own progress, whether literally progress to town or toward the class status that town represents.

Changes in the New South were slow in coming in the 1930s and not always met with glee. Anse's resistance to change, perceived as stubbornness or simply inertia, provokes Samson, a farmer, to comment on Anse's unswerving attempt to get Addie's body to Jefferson:

I notice how it takes a lazy man, a man that hates moving, to get set on moving once he does get started off, the same as he was set on staying still, like it aint the moving he hates so much as the starting and the stopping. And he would be kind of proud of whatever come up to make the moving or the setting still look hard. (114)

While Anse is usually lazy, when he does "get set on moving" he defies all logic in pursuit of his goal, which is seen as somehow consistent with his laziness. A slave to inertia, Anse at rest remains at rest while Anse in motion remains in motion. Like the backward country folk he represents, Anse resists change even in the face of enormous human and financial costs. As Duane Carr points out, Faulkner wrote *As I Lay Dying* around the time Southerners realized that the "progress promised by advocates of a New South had not come to pass, that instead the South had acquired industrialization without prosperity, becoming [...] simply a poverty-stricken replica of the North" (81). In the context of the New South's economic upheavals, Anse and his class of poor rural whites are perceived by striving and middle-class whites as "trash" whose obsolescence is hastened by rapid economic changes to which they are struggling to adapt; the Bundrens are the debris that must be cleaned up for moral reasons and to enable social and economic progress.

In their attempts to distance themselves from the Bundrens, other more successful town whites read them as biologically inferior white trash, particularly in terms of their consumption, thus linking race and class identities. The teenage girl character, Dewey Dell Bundren, is consistently perceived as racialized white trash when she attempts to purchase an abortifacient in two different drug stores: both male storekeepers see her as "a country girl" who would "as soon put a knife in you as not if you two-timed her" and neither of them sells her what she seeks (242). The first druggist, Moseley, measures her potential as a consumer based on her demographic group, judging from her appearance (she wears a gingham dress, straw hat, and no shoes) that she "would maybe buy a cheap comb or a bottle of nigger toilet water" (199). In Moseley's description of Dewey Dell's entrance, he conveys the subtle way in which he categorizes her: "she kind of bumbled at the screen door a minute, like they do, and came in" (198). His "like they do" immediately groups Dewey Dell with rural white trash, perhaps more specifically white trash women, who behave in similar ways when they venture into the drugstore. Not only do "they" hesitate at the door, "they" also often buy "cheap" goods—Moseley estimates Dewey Dell has "a quarter or a dollar at the most"—such as a comb or some toilet water (199). The druggist's demarcation of Dewey Dell's likely purchase, toilet water, as somehow signifying "nigger" conveys the ease with which discourse about class, i.e., a poor white girl, slips into a complementary discourse on race signifying white trash. Dewey Dell's predicted "choice" signals that her tastes will run close to the tastes of African Americans, in the druggist's estimation.

Moseley's perception of Dewey Dell is shaped by the process of class-inflected "distinction," in the sense that Pierre Bourdieu uses the term. As Bourdieu has shown, emphasis on taste and consumer preferences (i.e., she'll choose "a cheap comb") rather than economic limitations (i.e., she can only afford cheap goods) allows those in slightly higher class positions to explain away the class differences that distinguish them from the poor as merely differences in taste. Bourdieu's study interprets contemporary French class structures, but his point clearly applies to different national and temporal contexts: "A class is defined," he writes, "as much by its being-perceived as by its being, by its consumption—which need not be conspicuous to be symbolic—as much as by its position in the relations of production (even if it is true that the latter governs the former)" (483). Dewey Dell's class is defined by the townspeople's perception of it and by her (imagined) consumption as much as by her place in the relations of production, i.e., daughter of a poor farmer. The additional tactic of racializing her further distances Dewey Dell from Moseley in his perceptions of her. The association of white trash like Dewey Dell with African Americans—assumed to be poor by definition, but with the added stigma of supposed biological inferiority—allows the middle-class townsfolk to distance themselves from the trash in socio-economic terms and simultaneously to view them as inherently different.

## "THEY DON'T NEED US TO REPRODUCE OUR KIND": RACIALIZED POOR WHITES IN *THE GIRL*

In modern biological taxonomy, "class" denotes a group of genetically related organisms; it is a term of nomenclature that distinguishes one set of living things from another based on physical and hereditary traits. In the field of social science, on the other hand, "class" signifies membership in a socio-economic group, which, as Bourdieu points out, often also shares cultural and regional similarities such as "taste." In the literature of the American eugenics movement at the turn of the century, however, "class" emerges as a term signifying both biological and socio-economic status, clumsily conflating the two meanings. A Eugenics Record Office report from 1913 explains the "manifest function" of the science of eugenics in terms that conflate genetics and socio-economic class: its purpose is to "devise some plan for cutting off the supply of defective and degenerate social misfits, and for promoting the increased fecundity of the more sterling families" (Laughlin 8). The dangers posed by this attitude within social service and public health institutions is evident in the words of Joseph DeJarnette of the Western State Hospital of Virginia: "In the case of a farmer in breeding his hogs [...] he selects a thoroughbred, [...] but when it comes to our own race any sort of seed seems to be good enough, and the rights of the syphilitic, epileptic, imbecile, drunkard and unfit generally to reproduce must be allowed" (qtd. in Hasian 27). These eugenics proponents are quite clear about their aim to curtail not only hereditary disease but the reproductive rights of whole segments of the population: indeed, poverty is a hereditary disease. That women were most often the site of institutional intervention is unfortunately no surprise:

poor women were characterized as the carriers of 'germplasm' and those afflicted with this disease became the targets of massive publicity campaigns to cleanse America of the dysgenic [...] These narratives attracted an enthusiastic audience among welfare workers, criminologists, and members of the reading public, who saw in them proof of the claims of the hardline eugenicists. (Hasian 81)

Meridel Le Sueur's novel *The Girl* confronts the biological and sociological meanings of class in hazardous encounters with newly professionalized social workers who strongly resemble the welfare workers Hasian mentions.[6] These encounters between poor women and middle-class professional women exemplify the direct influence of the eugenics movement on social institutions and on public perceptions of class in the 1930s.

The nameless main character in *The Girl* experiences the social welfare system in its early stages in Depression-era Minneapolis when she applies for relief. The Girl's relationship with the middle-class female social worker is textually constructed to emphasize the class differences that prevent the two women from being allies and, indeed, cause the Girl to be forcibly detained by the woman who pretends to be her friend during their interview. The social worker racializes the Girl as white trash, although she never uses the term—her actions and attitudes toward the Girl demonstrate this perspective. The institutional view of the Girl as white trash becomes

---

6    For a fascinating study of the professionalization of social work, see Kunzel.

clear as she learns first-hand that forced sterilization and shock treatments are the primary forms of "relief" for sexually active single poor women like herself and her friend Clara. The Girl's case file reads: "The girl is maladjusted, emotionally unstable, and a difficult problem to approach. [...] She should be tested for sterilization after her baby is born. In our opinion sterilization would be advisable" (114). As an unemployed single pregnant poor woman, the Girl represents the people the eugenics discourses mark as dysgenic. Because the social worker sees the Girl only in terms of her purportedly dysgenic properties, she cannot make the feminist connection that Le Sueur's other female characters make across the lines of age, experience, politics, and sexuality. Whereas the Girl is seen as trash and treated as such by the social worker, she is also seen by the reader as "not trash" but as a character struggling to come to terms with her class and gender identity in the politically charged atmosphere of the Depression. This woman-reading-woman within the narrative demonstrates Le Sueur's commitment to the necessity of feminist connections along with class consciousness and workers' struggle even as it complicates the role of middle-class professional women in bureaucracies that oppress poor women.

Le Sueur's attempt to short-circuit or critique a middle-class woman's "reading" of the Girl as white trash has specific implications for 1930s middle-class readers who might wish to erase their class differences and identify only with the poor women's gendered oppression: the novel shows that you can't ally on the basis of gender without also taking into account class.[7] Amelia, an activist for the Workers' Party, provides a class-conscious reading of the social worker's racializing recommendations, which clearly mark the institution as subscribing to eugenicist policies informed by the E.R.O. studies of white trash: "it's because they don't need any more children from workers. They don't need us to reproduce our kind" (124). After admitting to the caseworker that she has had sex outside marriage and is now pregnant, the Girl is involuntarily committed to a relief

---

7   As Paula Rabinowitz argued in her recent talk, representations of the working class depend on descriptions of bodies, which, whether they are ravaged and dehumanized by a life of hard work or idealized as work-hardened and hypermasculine in left literature of the 30s, are always gendered and usually male. Representing the female working-class body is one of Le Sueur's triumphs: the Girl is both emaciated from poverty and explosively alive in her sexuality.

maternity home where she meets dozens of women in her situation, guarded by police matrons and electric window alarms, awaiting sterilization after delivery. The novel suggests that policies controlling the reproduction of poor whites in the 1930s are motivated not simply by a class-based assumption that they are too poor to support children; the white women in the welfare home are racialized and biologized in much the same way recent European immigrants were marked as unfit. Hasian writes, "[l]ong before the Immigration Restrictions Acts of 1924, foreign men and women who came to America found themselves being depicted as parasitic carriers of tainted germplasm that threatened the purity of native Americans" (49). The public discourses about eugenics in the 1930s heavily inform Le Sueur's novel, in a time when scientists targeted poor women, among other groups, for "eugenic" interventions (i.e., sterilization); Le Sueur's critique of these interventions registers in terms of both the gender and class identity of the victims—women treated like trash.

The novel's representations of poor men and women group them together as a class without eliding the significant differences in their oppression based on their gendered experiences. Whereas the women in the novel are physically exploited and abused as sexual and reproductive bodies, the men are physically exploited as labor, while both women and men are figured as dehumanized commodities. The women's gendered oppression is manifested in the Girl's sexual experiences with her boyfriend, on the job, and in her friend Clara's decline from prostitution into illness, shock-treatment-induced vegetative state, and finally death. But the narrative structure of this crucial chapter insistently associates the physical destruction of men with that of women: the mutilated male body of a murdered Wobbly is described along with the forced sterilization and shock treatments to which poor women are subject. Moreover, the men's roles are also gendered: the Girl's boyfriend Butch's masculinity surfaces in the text via constant references to sports such as baseball, his desire to act as breadwinner, and his conflicted feelings about the Girl's pregnancy, signifying his struggles with a strongly embodied, socially coded, classed masculinity.

Butch is torn between the ideology of the heterosexual nuclear family and the economic realities of extreme poverty: on the one hand, social constructions of masculinity call for him to be a working father, with a domestic wife and a well-fed baby. On the other hand, he faces the impossibility of fulfilling that construction during the Depression without a job or a home. Butch's character has bravado but is gradually beaten down by the Depression, starting when his brother Bill is killed and concluding with his own death. His arrogant tirades sound increasingly plaintive as his circumstances grow more desperate: "I know what it takes for winning. I'm a natural winner" (15). Butch is a complex character, brutal and unsympathetic but with moments of tenderness that win the Girl's affections. For example, he beats the Girl when he learns she slept with the gangster Ganz for money, even though Butch himself had pressured her into it. His jealous rage stems from his sense of betrayal, that Ganz has threatened Butch's bourgeois ownership over the Girl, but his own pressure on her to prostitute herself for money conflicts with his feeling of ownership as well as with his imagined patriarchal role as breadwinner. His financial situation never allows Butch to fully play the role he so badly wants: middle-class husband and worker. The conflict between the idealized family that Butch wants to head and the reality of unemployment and destitution defines his character. Since he can't resolve the conflict by achieving legitimate class mobility, he is killed trying to get rich illegally.

The Girl loses Butch in a violent battle for control over capital, namely a bank robbery—for Butch it represents not just money for survival during the Depression, but specifically start-up capital, since he wants to use his share to open a service station. The impossibility of upward mobility crushes the Girl's hopes in an especially thorough way in her narration of her experience in the bank robbery and on the lam from the law. She drives Butch, who is bleeding to death from a gunshot wound, away from the scene of the crime and stops for gas. They have fantasized about operating a service station along a modern highway, but in their conversation with the worker-owner of the station, that dream evaporates even from their fantasies. The man tells them that although he and his wife saved up for years they will lose everything when the oil company repossesses the business.

When Butch and the Girl hear the service station owner's story they realize that even hard work doesn't guarantee a decent living, even the illusion of ownership doesn't pay off for the working class as it does for the tycoons. During Butch's death scene he shouts in his delirium:

What have they done to us, what have they done to this now? Where are the oats, the wheat, I was sure they were planted. Look [...] the wealth of the country, the iron-ore-wheat-with-my-body-I-thee-wed, with my worldly goods I thee endow [...] What are they doing to you now honey? They own the town. They own the earth and the sweet marrow of your body. (95)

In his confusion of married love and the commodities exchange, the body and the gross national product, Butch laments the fact that he and the Girl can only aspire to the ideal middle-class heterosexual marriage, just as they can only dream of owning their small gas station. Butch's language echoes Marx's in the first volume of *Capital*, which illustrates his theory of the commodity with an extended example of iron and corn:

A commodity, such as iron, corn, or a diamond, is therefore, so far as it is a material thing, a use-value, something useful. [...] Use-values become a reality only by use or consumption; they also constitute the substance of all wealth, whatever may be the social form of that wealth. (303)

Butch's conflation of his body and "worldly goods" with the commodities iron and wheat not only references Marx; the chain of signifiers also implies that the worker's body, represented in the speech as Butch's own body ("with-my-body-I-thee-wed") and the Girl's body ("sweet marrow of your body"), itself is a commodity. The connection between the worker's body, the Marxian commodity, and Butch's own wealth ("my worldly goods") suggests that it is a use-value insofar as the use-value is, in Marx's words, "the substance of all wealth." Indeed, the novel provides ample proof that the bodies of the workers are valuable only "by use or consumption." In the economic crisis of the Depression, fewer workers are needed and thus become expendable trash, for sterilization and layoffs. The consumption of the worker's body slows as its use-value decreases, making its labor still less valuable.

The form of that consumption becomes allegorical in Butch's lament: "They own the sweet marrow of your body" suggests ownership of the human being both as a worker and as an organism of flesh, blood, and bones. The image of "sweet marrow" takes the association farther, suggesting cannibalism: someone or something owns the body and can crack open the bones and suck out the marrow, finding it sweet. Elsewhere in the novel, Amelia brings up cannibalism in a Swiftian moment, railing against the often fatal lack of prenatal care for poor women: "it's too bad they can't kill our babies and eat them like suckling pigs! What tender meat that would be! Stuffed babies with mushrooms. Why not?" (120). The motifs of devouring the bodies of the poor and the commodification of the worker's body operate as metaphors for the Depression-era capitalism that devastated so many lives in the 1930s; at the same time, these views of the poor body as a commodity obviate the workers' roles as consumers and producers. For women, the commodification takes the form of sexual and reproductive objectification as well as alienated labor. Clara, a prostitute, dies after the shock treatments she received on the relief workers' orders, prompting the Girl to echo Butch's language in his final speech:

Clara never got any wealth. She died a pauper. She never stole timber or wheat or made poor flour. She never stole anyone's land or took it for high interest on the mortgage. She never got rich on the labor of others. She never fattened off a war. She never made ammunition or guns. She never hurt no one. Who killed Clara? *Who will kill us?* (130)

The Girl's questions are more pointed than Butch's, however, and she names specific injustices departing from his more poetic lament. Clara is innocent because she was poor, she "never got any wealth." Moreover, she never resorted to the criminal and legal methods that wealthy people use to acquire and maintain their wealth: stealing commodities or land, producing substandard foods or weapons of destruction, profiting from the cheap labor or misfortunes of others. The Girl then links herself to Clara with the pronoun "us," concluding that Clara died because of her poverty, and that since they are both poor women they share the same fate.

With the deaths of Butch and Clara, the Girl's desire for middle-class prosperity gives way to the frustration of poverty, enabling her to comprehend the corruption of the wealthy and the oppression of the poor in the capitalist system. As a sex worker, Clara exemplifies the woman as commodified labor in the extreme, selling her body because "it's the only thing you got that's valuable" (49). Although she is a prostitute, Clara lives in her own imaginary bourgeois dream-world. Even as she tries to teach the Girl how to pick up men on the street she explains her hope to marry a rich man: "someday you will have Irish tablecloths and peasant pottery and a pew in church and dress up and go every Sunday because you haven't had to hustle on Saturday nights" (8). In the future she will occupy a very different relation to poverty: it will be represented only as an antiquated, decorative flourish, reduced to an aesthetic as "peasant pottery" and linens made by faraway poor people for her desiring middle-class consumption. Wishing to see herself as a consumer rather than as commodified labor, Clara exemplifies Bourdieu's claim that class distinctions are articulated through participation in consumerism and the display of taste. Like Butch, Clara dies young, starving and broken, her dreams reduced to sad clichés.

Male bodies are also vulnerable, and their mortality is marked as different from the women's but also linked in their class relations. In one powerful chapter that demonstrates the multiple ways the bodies of the poor are literally marked by their class position, the Girl reads the letter in which her case worker recommends sterilization, Clara returns from shock treatments in a vegetative state, and Amelia tells the Girl about the lynching of Wesley Everett, a white male Wobbly, in Centralia, Washington. Amelia laments the widespread support of the lynching by the townspeople:

When they hung Wesley Everett they hung him by a long rope so *they* could all have souvenirs and you go there, in the best houses, you'll find a piece of that rope, and they are glad to show it to you. That's the kind they are, she said." (120; original emphasis)

Faced with the material bodies of the poor being mutilated and murdered, the Girl's class consciousness emerges and moves her to question the oppression she has heretofore endured stoically. Likewise, the lynching should not lead to a simple equation of anti-leftist violence with racist lynching; however, it does resemble racist lynching in its enactment of distancing, dehumanizing, and, like the category white trash, attempting to racialize the white male victims by associating them with the more frequent victims of lynching, African American men. In a complicated sequence of associations and allusions, the lynching of Everett's white male body suggests that although he constituted a socio-economic threat as a Wobbly, his body was destroyed in a specific way commonly used to destroy racially threatening bodies. Thus the very method of Everett's murder links him with African American victims of racial violence, who are marked in pseudo-scientific literature as biologically inferior, even as his political affiliation with the working class links him with the targets of eugenics discourse, the dysgenic white trash carrying genetic material that perpetuates the "biological" trait of poverty.

While the male bodies in *The Girl* are destroyed through their attempts to work or obtain money, the female bodies are manipulated and strictly controlled, especially in terms of sex and reproduction. The men's body count is actually much higher than the women's: Bill is shot scabbing; the Girl's father dies alone, bitter, and poor; Butch and Hoinck are shot in the bank robbery; Amelia's husband is dead; Sacco and Vanzetti are executed; and Wesley Everett is publicly lynched—all attest that women are not the only victims of class oppression. Rather, the male and female bodies are used in different ways: for production and/or for (controlling) reproduction. Coiner reads the deaths of so many men by the end of *The Girl* as a heavy-handed narrative tactic aimed at bringing the women together in the female-only collective that ends the novel on a utopian socialist-feminist note. I concur with her astute critique of Le Sueur's final chapters, in which the "elimination of all male characters by a *deus ex machina* [...] implies that cooperation among women and freedom from sexual domination are possible only in a world where men no longer exist" (118). While I agree with Coiner's reading, we may also read the male deaths as more than an awkward plot device. The systematic killing-off of all the male characters is also a commentary on the ways in which male workers' bodies are commodified and used up, if not killed outright.

## TOWARD A HISTORICIZED "WHITE TRASH"

Historicizing the term white trash as it functioned earlier in the century demonstrates how important and consistent the trash identity is to modern as well as postmodern developments in twentieth-century American capitalism. In my use of the expression white trash to refer to 1930s poor whites, I provide a theoretical backstory for Evan Watkins's term "throwaways"— poor people regarded as expendable, replaceable workers who threaten middle-class narratives of socio-economic success. Watkins defines "throwaways" as "isolated groups of the population who haven't moved with the times, and who now litter the social landscape and require the moral attention of cleanup crews" (3). While throwaways exist in the postmodern era where technology has replaced Social Darwinism as the narrative that justifies social determinism, throughout the 1930s Social Darwinism provided the systems of what Watkins calls natural coding, including eugenics and race theories, in which class mobility was linked to natural se-lection. "White trash" alludes to Watkins's term "throwaways" in that both explicitly position the working-class subject in relation to the capitalist economy in modernity and postmodernity, even as these relations are ef-faced by the emphasis on obsolescence prevalent in the dominant discourse, whether natural in the 1930s, or technological in the 1980s.[8]

Alluding to Watkins's postmodern "throwaways" with the term white trash forges a connection and continuity between the two, while at the same time allowing for their different historical moments. Throughout the twen-tieth-century, American capitalism has positioned specific groups within the working classes as obsolete obstacles to progress. In the 30s, consumer-ism and commodification had not yet reached the frenzied pitch they have in postmodernity. Accordingly, following these different relations of pro-duction and consumption, the term "trash," which suggests something that is used up, broken, and ultimately replaceable, like a chipped coffee cup, is preferable to the term "throwaways," which connotes something designed to be disposable, like a Styrofoam cup. "White trash" is thus the more ap-propriate term for analysis of early twentieth-century class relations. The glories of industrialization have not yet reached the backwoods of the Bundrens or the unemployed Girl in these novels, let alone the flexible ac-cumulation and just-in-time inventory practices that mark the socio-economic conditions of Watkins's throwaways. Furthermore, for the 1930s white trash subject, the Depression hampered economic expansion and rural development thereby restricting access to increasingly "modern," and later "postmodern," modes of production and consumption.

The rural white trash characters in the novels are seen in racialized as well as classed terms by town- and city-dwelling white characters: the ge-ography- and class-specific characteristics attributed to the Girl and the Bundrens also posit them as allegedly biologically inferior subjects, lazy, immoral, child-like, and promiscuous. In the U.S., as the *OED* etymology

---

8    As Watkins points out, "obsolescence involves conditions of both cultural and economic production in the present, not what has survived, uselessly, from the past, as obsolescence stories would have it" (7). This view of the poor has al-lowed Americans to explain away the harsh living conditions that mark the his-tory of poor whites in the U.S., enabling the unspoken distinction among whites, while obscuring the material conditions that shape that history.

of "trash" demonstrates, the class prejudices of English society met the fundamental racism that specially characterizes American culture. I interpret this dual identification of the white rural poor as classed and racialized by invoking George Rawick's argument that white racism intensified as modes of production changed from agrarian to industrial. Forced by these changing modes of production, whites adapted to new restrictions such as timetables, the public/private split, urbanization, and delayed gratification, but felt compelled to distance themselves from their previous ways of life, which were recategorized as lazy, primitive, and promiscuous and projected onto African Americans. In his study of whiteness, David Roediger summarizes Rawick's thesis:

Englishmen and profit-minded settlers in America "met the West African as a reformed sinner meets a comrade of his previous debaucheries." The racist, like the reformed sinner, creates "a pornography of his former life. [...] In order to ensure that he will not slip back into the old ways or act out half-suppressed fantasies, he must see a tremendous difference between his reformed self and those whom he formerly resembled." Blackness and whiteness are thus created together. (64)

Rawick's point about the co-construction of "blackness" and "whiteness," linking shifts in racism to shifts in capitalism, predicts the overlaps between the classed other and the racialized other in *The Girl* and *As I Lay Dying*: the white trash characters in both novels are seen as both classed and racialized. The discursive slippage between racialized and classed identities results from this very co-construction, and the inseparability of race and class at this point in American history supports this argument. Specifically, in Depression-era Minnesota and in the New South Mississippi, the crisis of capitalism leads to a renewed emphasis on racial difference that acts as a diversion from class. The context of changing stages of capitalism grounds the racialized class distinction: white trash are the racialized and biologized "former self" to the whites in the working and middle classes who are striving to be upwardly mobile and must reject the "others" in order to protect their faith in their own success. In addition to projecting "bad" capitalist identities onto white trash others, upwardly mobile whites associate the bad poor with other "bad" subjects excluded from the opportunities of "free enterprise," i.e., people of color. In this way, the rest of the white culture can legitimize their own access to mobility as a function of racialized difference, not class difference; white trash are biologized, racialized, and naturalized in their socio-economic position so that the white middle and upper classes can minimize or ignore any resemblance between themselves and the white trash characters.

In the context of the Depression, embattled middle-class whites find racial ideology easier to fall back on than facing the flaws inherent in capitalism; similarly, the pseudo-scientific discourse of eugenics allows insecure middle-class whites to racialize white poverty instead of addressing the economic conditions that created it. Both these "natural" discourses, racist essentialism and eugenics, attempt to explain biologically why poor whites were not as upwardly mobile as the American work ethic claimed: if hard work and frugality are the equation for success, so the reasoning goes, they must not be hard workers or sensible with their money. With the creation of a distinction among whites, the trash can be separated out from the rest of white society, not because of capitalism or economics, but rather because they are read as biologically inferior and genetically locked into a legacy of poverty.

## MOBILITY IN THE 1930S: TRASH ON THE HIGHWAY

The movement of individual characters from country to city in *The Girl* and *As I Lay Dying* accompanies the geographic shift on a national scale from agriculture to industry and from rural to urban spaces: the 1920 census identifies the majority of Americans as urban dwellers. As the balance of the U.S. population shifted from a rural to an urban majority, new relations of space and movement developed in tandem with the changing modes of production that encouraged urbanization. While some Americans were buying new cars and making money in growing industrial markets, many others were not as successful and thus not as mobile. The mode of transport also suggests a great deal about the characters and their place in the changing nation: the Bundrens in a wagon and the Girl hitchhiking and walking suggest that "traffic is not only a technique; it is a form of consciousness and a form of social relations" (Williams 296). Working-class characters are affected by developments in the modes of transport which, when they are left behind by the new kinds of traffic, signal a "growth and alteration of consciousness: a history repeated in many lives and many places which is fundamentally an alteration of perception and relationship" (Williams 297).

The highway and the ability to use it carry symbolic value in *As I Lay Dying* and *The Girl*. For Faulkner's Anse Bundren, the roads represent a tax expenditure that may speed the destruction of his family's subsistence-level farm economy; for the Girl, the highway holds the memory of her dead lover Butch and his futile ambition to own a service station. The grueling incremental progress of the Bundren family's wagon and the Girl's brief tragic flight from and return as a hitch-hiker to the city exemplify the profoundly limited opportunities held out by geographical mobility for working people in depressed parts of the country. Private rituals and behaviors are forced into the public sphere as these characters struggle to adjust to their negative mobility: dead bodies, Anse's new wife, Dewey Dell's secret quest for an abortion, and the birth of the Girl's baby all take place in public places . The white trash characters of these novels struggle to find their place in the public spheres of the modern urban world, which is larger and faster than they can handle. As Williams points out, "The division and opposition of city and country, industry and agriculture, in their modern forms, are the critical culmination of the division and specialization of labour which, though it did not begin with capitalism, was developed under it to an extraordinary and transforming degree" (304). To the rural poor in Faulkner's novel, increased geographical mobility means exposure to consumer goods they can't afford and the growing likelihood of urban migration in search of higher cash wages. For the Girl, it means moving from country to city looking for work, but the descriptions of city life throughout the novel contrast vividly with the popular image of the gleaming modern city of industry and consumer heaven. Faulkner's death knell of the premodern rural South and Le Sueur's woman-centered Midwestern proletarian novel depict and problematize their characters' positions on the highway of modernity.

The meandering wagon trip and tragicomic attempts to fix Cash's broken leg suggest more than Anse's ineptitude, however. They also symbolize the dialectic of mobility and immobility that pervades the novel. When the wagon breaks up in the flooded river, Cash tries to hold onto Addie's coffin and winds up nearly drowned with a broken leg. After an agonizing day of traveling with Cash's leg in splints, Anse decides to pour cement on the leg to keep it from moving. Cash's condition worsens, clearly a result of the poorly conceived cast: his leg and foot turn first red "like they had been boiled" and then black "like a nigger's" (213; 224). Again a Bundren is likened to a "nigger," this time by young Vardaman remarking on the gangrenous leg, layering another symbol of immobility onto Cash's already ridiculous situation by linking him, specifically his injured leg, with African Americans, who were also shut out of the economic promise of mobility in the New South. In the first place, Cash loses his mobility when his leg breaks and he must lie on the coffin in the wagon, wincing at every jolt. Moreover, the journey itself signifies mobility only superficially, since the circumnavigation of floods and other calamities that befall the Bundrens more emphatically marks their inability to reach their destination, rather than real movement. And finally, his blackened foot further suggests that it has been slammed in the door of the Southern recovery, in a way similar to poor Southern blacks. The highway is not just to Jefferson via Mottson, but to modernity via consumerism, and the Bundren family wagon is a worn-out, barely roadworthy vehicle, representing as it does (complete with corpse) the outmoded and bottomed-out agrarian economy of the New South. As a remedy, the cast on Cash's leg is not only ineffective; it inflicts further damage. Similarly, the roads built to foster greater mobility of goods and people for the state of Mississippi in *As I Lay Dying* bring the Bundrens misfortune, pain, and loss.

Driving in circles, mending broken wheels, crossing flooded rivers, the traveling Bundren family is the living (and dead!) proof that just because there is a road doesn't mean everyone can get somewhere. In the 1920s the Mississippi highway system was in its infancy, and Anse speculates whether such a modernization is even worth the tax money, bringing as it does the increased mobility of labor and consumer desires for commodities: "Durn that road. [...] A-laying there, right up to my door, where every bad luck that comes and goes is bound to find it. [...] it seems hard that a man in his need could be so flouted by a road" (35; 38). He further laments the temporary losses of Darl to the draft during World War I and then of Cash to wage labor in carpentry and the seduction of mail-order tools. These losses are in addition, of course, to the loss of the money in taxes to build the road in the first place, as the Bundren sons increasingly work as wage laborers rather than exclusively on Anse's farm: "[g]ot to pay for the way [literally the road] for them boys to have to go away to earn it [money]" (37). In his usual hyperbole, Anse attempts to blame Addie's death on the road, since "[s]he was well and hale as ere a woman ever were, except for that road" (37). His resentment of the highway illustrates, on the one hand, the healthy suspicion and resistance to change typical of many poor whites during the economic restructuring in the 20s and 30s South. On the other hand, however, Anse is right: the road *is* killing his family's way of life, signaling the urbanization and modernization of even the agrarian South. Like Watkins's throwaways, white trash characters like Anse Bundren are positioned as virtually immobile trash along the highway, the waste of change.

The Girl's parents moved around often as she was growing up, looking for work and a comfortable home: they "moved from one house and city to another in the Midwest, always trying to get into something bigger and better" (9). At one point, her father moves the family to a Wisconsin bee and plum farm, although they have no agricultural training or experience. The working-class desire to move up in social and economic hierarchies comes through in her father's explanation for the move: "think of it, honey and plums, that will be different from the coal mines where I was raised" (27). Predictably, the farm fails: drought, disease, and crop failure belie her father's idyllic visions of pastoral bliss. The honey and plums her father dreamed of didn't feed eight children, and the Girl recalls being sent out to work for room and board (and abuse) at a neighboring farm when she was eleven. The dream of escaping the city to a happy country life surfaces again at the speakeasy, when Belle and Hoinck suggest moving to Canada to establish a homestead: "Belle threw her arms around us laughing, throwing back her wild head. We'll go in my car" (13). But the Girl recognizes the desperation and futility in their plan and knows "that car wouldn't cross the Mississippi" (13). The dream of mobility doesn't come true for her family when they move to the farm, while the crowd at the speakeasy can only fantasize about moving to a better life: inferior vehicles, unattainable fantasies, and inadequate geographical capital prevent the poor characters in *The Girl* from securing any real upward mobility. Whether the move is from city to country or vice versa, the trash characters can't achieve what they seek: class mobility.

From the opening chapter the Girl is marked as a newcomer to the big city, a country kid still wet behind the ears, even though she spent much of her childhood in industrial towns. Clara and Belle take on the roles of educator and protector, since as a "virgin from the country scared of her own shadow," she needs them to teach her how to survive waitressing in the speakeasy and maneuvering the city streets (2). Her allegedly rural origins are far from idyllic, however, since she leaves her parents' small-town home because they haven't enough food or money to support her there. As Williams points out and the novel illustrates, the country often serves as a mythical repository for the "good old days" and a "golden age gone by" that never existed and that often masks the realities of rural experience. The Girl's father falls prey to that myth and the family pays dearly for it on the plum farm; the Girl even romanticizes the country in her fertility metaphors for female sexuality. But if we historicize the pastoral mode as always already nostalgic for a fictive past, questions arise. What struggles are elided by this pastoral myth and who benefits from their elision? How does the elision of the modern industrialized country affect the people who live there, or who move from there to the city? In *The Girl* and *As I Lay Dying* these questions lead to a revealing reading of the geographies of city and country, in which neither is as prosperous as popular wisdom would allow. As a result, for the poor there is no actual paradise on earth, city or country, although popular representations of these two places motivate the poor to migrate toward the greener grass on the other side of the fence.

Although the Girl has made her way in the big city, she is no more successful than her father was on the plum and honey farm or in the coal mines of his youth. And though she grew up moving from place to place, the Girl's only road experience in the novel is driving the getaway car from the failed robbery. She ends up hitchhiking back to town alone after Butch dies, leaving the car, out of gas, on the shoulder of the highway, a symbol of her own immobility. Now car-less and hitchhiking, she goes to a thrift store and looks at the second-hand shoes: "I tried one on and it was like stepping into another's grief" (96). The Girl folds a bit of newspaper to stuff the holes in her own shoes, preferring her own grief for her only reliable mode of transportation, her feet. Like Cash's broken leg, the Girl's feet symbolize her physical mobility but also her metaphorical immobility. In the Minnesota winter she walks instead of drives, in shoes that are falling apart like Anse's bad shoes in his childhood of hard work. And like the Bundrens' wagon trip, as the Girl walks in her bad shoes she moves about but doesn't get anywhere: "The streets used to be only something you walked through to get someplace else, but now they are home to me" (107). In the high-speed, technologically advanced modern age, the Bundrens and the Girl are one step above immobile—they can move from one place to another, but only laterally and literally. The class status they are born into and the Depression economy in which they must survive ensure that they will be stuck, if not where they started out, then somewhere comparable or worse. The characters in the two novels even have their immobility written on their bodies: the broken leg and the freezing and deformed feet symbolize their ill-equipped and ill-fated efforts at movement. The highways, roads, and streets in *As I Lay Dying* and *The Girl* represent the national push to modernize towns and cities and to urbanize rural areas, but the characters in the novels have nowhere to go and little way to get there.

## WORKS CITED

Bourdieu, Pierre. *Distinction: A Social Critique of the Judgment of Taste.* Trans. Richard Nice. Cambridge: Harvard UP, 1984. Print.

Carr, Duane. *A Question of Class: The Redneck Stereotype in Southern Fiction.* Bowling Green: Bowling Green U Popular P, 1996. Print.

Clarke, Deborah. *Robbing the Mother: Women in Faulkner.* Jackson: U of Mississippi P, 1994. Print.

Coiner, Constance. *Better Red: The Writing and Resistance of Tillie Olsen and Meridel Le Sueur.* New York: Oxford UP, 1995. Print.

Cook, Sylvia Jenkins. *From Tobacco Road to Route 66: The Southern Poor White in Fiction.* Chapel Hill: U of North Carolina P, 1976. Print.

Faulkner, William. *As I Lay Dying.* 1930. New York: Vintage, 1985. Print.

Foley, Barbara. *Radical Representations: Politics and Form in U.S. Proletarian Fiction, 1929-1941.* Durham: Duke UP, 1993. Print.

Genovese, Eugene D. *Roll, Jordan, Roll: The World the Slaves Made.* New York: Random House-Pantheon, 1973. Print.

Hasian, Marouf Arif, Jr. *The Rhetoric of Eugenics in Anglo-American Thought.* Athens: U of Georgia P, 1996. Print.

Jehlen, Myra. *Caste and Class in Faulkner's South.* New York: Columbia UP, 1976. Print.

Kunzel, Regina. *Fallen Women, Problem Girls: Unmarried Mothers and the Professionalization of Social Work, 1890-1945.* New Haven: Yale UP, 1993. Print.

Ladd, Barbara. *Nationalism and the Color Line in George W. Cable, Mark Twain, and William Faulkner*. Baton Rouge: Louisiana State UP, 1996. Print.

Laughlin, Harry Hamilton. *Report of the Committee to Study and to Report on the Best Practical Means of Cutting Off the Defective Germ-Plasm in the American Population*. Cold Spring Harbor: Eugenics Record Office, 1914. Print.

Le Sueur, Meridel. *The Girl*. 1939. Albuquerque: West End P, 1990. Print.

---. "Women Are Hungry." 1934. *Ripening: Selected Work, 1927-1980*. Old Westbury: Feminist P, 1982. 144-157. Print.

Ling, Peter J. *America and the Automobile: Technology, Reform, and Social Change*. New York: Manchester UP-St. Martin's, 1990. Print.

Marx, Karl. *The Marx-Engels Reader*. 2nd ed. Ed. Robert C. Tucker. New York: Norton, 1973. Print.

Matthews, John T. "*As I Lay Dying* in the Machine Age." *boundary 2* 19.1 (1992): 69-94. Print.

Newitz, Annalee, and Matt Wray, eds. *White Trash: Race and Class in America*. New York: Routledge, 1997. Print.

Olsen, Tillie. *Yonnondio: From the Thirties*. New York: Delacorte, 1974. Print.

Rafter, Nicole. *White Trash: The Eugenic Family Studies, 1877-1919*. Boston: Northeastern UP, 1988. Print.

Rabinowitz, Paula. "Girls are to Boys as the Bourgeoisie are to the Proletariat: What Do Gender and Class Have to Do with One Another?" Center for Labor Studies. University of Washington, Seattle. 22 May 1998. Lecture.

---. *Labor and Desire: Women's Revolutionary Fiction in Depression America*. Chapel Hill: U of North Carolina P, 1991.

Roberts, Diane. *Faulkner and Southern Womanhood*. Athens: U of Georgia P, 1994. Print.

Roediger, David. *Towards the Abolition of Whiteness: Essays on Race, Politics, and Working Class History*. New York: Verso, 1994. Print.

Saldívar, Ramón. "Looking for a Master Plan: Faulkner, Paredes, and the Colonial and Postcolonial Subject." *Cambridge Companion to William Faulkner*. Ed. Philip Weinstein. New York: Cambridge UP, 1995. 96-120. Print.

Saxton, Alexander. *The Rise and Fall of the White Republic: Class Politics and Mass Culture in Nineteenth-Century America*. New York: Verso, 1990. Print.

Watkins, Evan. *Throwaways: Work Culture and Consumer Education*. Stanford: Stanford UP, 1993. Print.

Williams, Raymond. *The Country and the City*. New York: Oxford UP, 1973. Print.

Willis, Susan. "Learning from the Banana." *A Primer for Daily Life*. New York: Routledge, 1991. 41-61. Print.

# 2 Incorporation and Embodiment

## Gender, Race, and Space in Hurst and Himes

> In the three years in L.A. I'd worked up to
> a good job in a shipyard, bought a new
> Buick car, and cornered off the finest col-
> oured chick west of Chicago.
> CHESTER HIMES/*IF HE HOLLERS LET HIM*
> *GO*

In the above quote from *If He Hollers Let Him Go*, protagonist Bob Jones sums up the three main issues this chapter takes as its focus, namely, path-breaking career advancement; geographic mobility as an American fascination; and the intersections of gender and sexuality with geographic and spatial concerns. In Chester Himes's 1945 novel, as in Fannie Hurst's *Imitation of Life*, published twelve years earlier, these issues are crucial to the main characters in their pursuit of upward class mobility. The time frame of the publication of the novels—1933 to 1945—is exceeded by their settings in that Hurst's narrative begins in the 1910s, moving through World War I and into the 1930s. Thus, the combined historical reach of the two texts extends from 1911 to the height of U.S. involvement in World War II. During this time—from World War I to the Depression to World War II—class was of particular importance for white women and for African Americans, who were moving into new areas of employment motivated first by economic necessity and later by national labor shortages. Whereas *Imitation of Life* portrays a nation in which white women are expected to cultivate domesticity—with the assistance of African American women servants—and leave paid work and big business to men, *If He Hollers Let Him Go* addresses the friction arising from the entry of white women and African Americans into the wartime work force in jobs formerly reserved for white men.

As American business and military ventures expanded in the first half of the century, rapid changes in racial and gender norms manifested themselves in the public spaces of the major American cities on the East and West Coasts. In Hurst's novel, Bea Pullman defies gender restrictions against women in business in the East Coast centers of commerce while she negotiates the conflict between her business career and the traditionally feminine domestic sphere, a role Bea displaces onto her African American maid and confidante, Delilah. But in *If He Hollers Let Him Go*, set in Los Angeles during World War II, race comes out of the home and into the public sphere, where Bob Jones struggles with racism on the streets and on the job. Himes's novel depicts the crisis of spatial and racial boundaries as Bob's wartime job brings him into daily intimate contact with white men and women, showing not only his experiences of racism, but the ways in which Bob copes with racism through the strange permutations of sexism and class prejudice available to him as an ambitious African American man. It is in the public sphere, in the workplace, that Bob and Bea fight to overcome the disadvantages that mark their individual identities as they participate in American expansion worldwide: Bea's company goes global while Bob works on ships for the Navy during World War II. These two novels are the best choices for this inquiry because they both take an outright interest in the traditionally "domestic" issues of race and gender that many texts of the time period kept below the surface of the narrative.[1] They also mark out the terrain in which public and private space is being recon-

---

1  As if there wasn't enough othering going on in both novels, the specter of the lesbian is invoked in order to reinforce the heterosexual main characters: Bea's female employees develop crushes on her and Bob's girlfriend Alice takes him to her lesbian friend Stella's house for a party, where he meets Stella and her lover, who appears jealous of Alice's relationship with Stella. One could argue that because so many other categories of identity—race, gender, class—are so overdetermined, the heterosexuality of the protagonists must be asserted as a kind of last resort. However, such an analysis would regrettably take far more elaboration, so I leave it out for lack of space.

figured, during a period in which American notions about work underwent enormous shifts: from the restrictive 1910s and 20s to the 1940s war in which women and African Americans were recruited to work "white men's" jobs once off-limits but now their patriotic duty.

Hurst's novel, like the two films based on it, has been read primarily in terms of the race relations between Bea and Delilah: Lauren Berlant's essay "National Brands/National Body" is perhaps the best known study, in which she reads the book and both films[2] following the changing focus of each text and how each represents the American national body politic through raced female bodies. Berlant's essay traces Bea's disembodiment as a woman and her incorporation as a business, and the simultaneous positioning of Delilah as Bea's "prosthetic body" or "social hieroglyphic." Berlant's focus is on the "dialectic between abstraction in the national public sphere and the surplus corporeality of racialized and gendered subjects" who are supposed to belong in the private sphere (114). But her use of the term "space" remains largely metaphorical rather than grounded in real places and locations, which limits her reading to a binaristic model of Delilah's circumscribed domestic sphere opposed to Bea's public corporation.[3] Where Berlant notes Bea's movement into the "capitalist public sphere" and "national existence" as a corporation (117), I will emphasize the geographic articulations of that mobility. Rather than reading Bea's company

---

2    Of the three versions of the story, the most recent has been the most popular: Douglas Sirk's 1959 film version. I attribute its popularity to a number of factors, including its highly critical portrayal of American society, its proximity to the Civil Rights movement in the U.S., its availability, and Sirk's celebrated auteur status among film critics. Hurst's novel has been out of print since a 1990 reprint and the earlier film version, John Stahl's 1934 release, has just this year been released on video—until now, it has been infrequently broadcast on cable.

3    Berlant argues that "Delilah's fractured public identity—as herself, as an autonomous iconic image, as a servant of 'B. Pullman'—foregrounds the irregular operations of national capitalism on the bodies of racially and sexually gendered subjects" ("National" 121). In the scheme of this chapter, however, Delilah's "public identity" operates only in the context of the domestic, private sphere. Given this precedent of a raced "public" identity, the character of Bob Jones in Himes's novel resonates more powerfully as an African American active in the public sphere, not as a servant or a trademark but as an industrial worker.

trademark, Delilah's face, as Berlant does so well, this chapter examines the ways in which the company's movement, predicated as it is on the traditional raced and gendered roles occupied by Delilah, echoes national expansion both "domestic" and foreign. That is, playing upon the multiple meanings of "domestic," I read the novel in terms of its representations of women's roles at home, in the national public sphere of business, and in the national movements from rural to urban, from East to West, and from "domestic" to worldwide corporate markets.[4] This chapter explores the interplay between gendered and racial embodiment and the public sphere of big business by focusing on *Imitation of Life*'s explicitly geographic dimensions: Bea's upward class mobility, her company's geographic expansion, and the sites of her racial, gendered, and sexual identities. Bea's East Coast origins and her embrace of a middle-class WASP identity combine disastrously with traditional notions of domesticity and femininity. Although she achieves her ambitions in business, Bea never gets what she keeps saying she really wants: a home and a domestic role as wife and mother. Hurst positions Bea as trapped between the two spheres that make up the world as she sees it, and like a soul in limbo, she never finds her "right place."

Chester Himes is most often read for his popular detective novels, such as *Rage in Harlem* and *Cotton Comes to Harlem*.[5] When critics mention *If He Hollers Let Him Go*, it is always in the context of race and class: Bob Jones is a working African American facing the daily battles of racist oppression, and the novel is frequently labeled a social protest novel.[6] Along similar lines, author Himes is also well-known for the job discrimination he experienced as a writer fired by Jack Warner of Warner Brothers studio because Jack didn't want any "niggers" on his lot. This chapter reads Himes's first Los Angeles novel as a crucial 1940s text, illustrating the movement of American labor, capital, and imagination to the West Coast during World War II. In the quote that opens this chapter, Bob locates himself and his girlfriend in Los Angeles, emphasizing again that they are "west of Chicago": in my map of the nation between the two dates of publication, 1933 and 1945, these two novels contribute to the trajectory of westward mobili-

---

4   Amy Kaplan's essay "Manifest Domesticity" enacts a similar deconstruction of the "domestic" in the field of nineteenth-century American Studies.

5   See Crooks, Walters, and Diawara.

6   See Boris and Skinner.

ty from East to West Coast, and from the U.S. to Europe and Asia in the form of corporate and military expansion. Bob's character occupies the threshold of public and private spheres throughout the novel, as he witnesses whites acting out their racialized sexual anxieties in the public domain of the workplace and the shared spaces of the city. The resistance he meets as he tries assert his male citizenship privileges is often registered on his body as physical pain or violence, demonstrating what happens when race leaves the home and moves into the public sphere.

Reading the two characters, Bob Jones and Bea Pullman, together allows for a better understanding of the widely divergent experiences of mobility, filtered through race and gender, represented in the two works. For both characters, mobility is the most important issue: moving into the middle classes, expanding their economic and geographical reach, pioneering spaces previously closed to them in work and private life. The two characters experience their lives primarily in terms of their own pursuit of economic success, but for each the obstacles that arise to block their access depend on their gendered and racialized identities and on their geographical locations. Bea benefits from her whiteness but struggles against her female body, whereas Bob expects to benefit from his male gender privilege, but suffers constantly from the pain of his racialized body. I read Bea's business, her incorporation, as her attempt to escape her white female body, relying instead on her African American servant Delilah to perform the feminine domestic role. While Bea's flight from embodiment is grounded in the metaphor of the corporation, Bob's reluctance to accept the limitations of his racialized black body results in literal as well as metaphorical acts of violence against his racial embodiment.

## ALL ABOARD FOR ARCTIC INCORPORATED: HOME STYLE ENTREPRENEURSHIP

According to Alan Trachtenberg's study of American corporate expansion, "[h]ardly any realm of American life remained untouched" by the changes in business organization that, by 1929, meant that "the two hundred largest corporations held 48 percent of all corporate assets (excluding banks and insurance companies) and 58 percent of net capital assets such as land, buildings, and machinery" (4-5). Bea Pullman's business career in this

1933 novel allows me to trace the global mobility of American capital in terms of her personal pursuit of upward economic mobility, with the added insights of a female perspective: although she "had scarcely been aware of the woman-suffrage movement as it came to fruition," successful Bea is feted in the media as a pioneer career woman (Hurst 219). *Imitation of Life* is a useful text because Hurst's third person narrator allows us to read Bea's spectacular international business successes through the lens of Bea's traditional notions of domesticity and femininity. Placing Bea's woman-owned business in the context of American corporate expansion therefore also requires that we consider the functions of gender, class, and race in her socioeconomic and geographic mobility narratives. As Anne McClintock has argued, "the mass-marketing of empire as a global system was intimately wedded to the Western reinvention of domesticity, so that imperialism cannot be understood without a theory of domestic space and its relation to the market" (17). Bea's company is founded on tropes of empire, conquest, and mobility, while it sells comfort food to displaced city-dwellers through the mammy character of Delilah and Bea's mass-produced imitation of domesticity. Not only does Bea's ambition stand for her desire to succeed—it also derives from her nostalgia for domestic stability that she was conditioned as a white middle-class woman to expect. My reading of *Imitation of Life* is predicated on the claim that gender, class, and race are "articulated categories" in the study of empire; that is, they cannot be studied fruitfully in isolation from one another (McClintock 5). Rather, the novel supports a reading of economic and geographic expansion that must also consider the narrative's reliance on racial, classed, and gendered identities, particularly among women and particularly in the intersections between the corporate and the domestic spheres. It is in this double sense of the word that I elaborate here on Bea's "incorporation": her business and her repressed white female body.

Bea's franchise moves from the East Coast westward at a time when the national ideal of urban space also headed west. As John Findlay has pointed out, the American West functions as a utopian national space not only in its rural dimensions, such as the "virgin land" beyond the frontier, but also in its new, modern cityscapes: in the 1930s and 40s, Los Angeles in particular represented the "virgin cities" of the Western U.S. in the national imagination (2). Bea's business empire goes mobile, following the national movement of people and capital towards the West Coast, and then international.

As the "incorporation of America," as Trachtenberg describes it, moved westward and crossed national boundaries, mobility comes to signify not only economic success but also geographic expansion; while the American nation had more or less reached its borders, American companies continued to expand their reach into wider national markets and into markets abroad. As she narrates the successes of her company, Hurst also paints Bea's personal life as less than satisfying—she is widowed young, celibate most of her life, and enjoys almost no time with her daughter; at the same time as her corporation flies high, Bea desperately avoids having to deal with her female body.

*Imitation of Life* opens with the funeral of Bea's mother, when she is only seventeen years old, and narrates her life story as she marries at eighteen, has a daughter, loses her husband and cares for her invalid father and infant daughter on her own. When she takes in an African American woman, Delilah, and her daughter, Peola, Bea begins to form a non-traditional imitation of a nuclear family: Bea is the breadwinner and decision-maker while Delilah cares for the home and dependents. After building a very successful business around Delilah's face and waffle recipe, Bea is a famous entrepreneur in spite of, and later because of, her gender.[7] The novel is punctuated by historical events: Bea is married on Election Day in 1916, her first businesses succeed largely due to their appeal among young soldiers during and immediately after the First World War. As her business succeeds, Bea opens waffle shops further and further west: starting out in Atlantic City, then branching out to Philadelphia and New York, she soon operates in New Haven, Baltimore, Buffalo, Cleveland, Detroit, Chicago, Kansas City, and Tulsa. Following the progress of Bea's business allows us to trace the continuing expansion of American interests westward and globally, as well as the role of World War I as an economic boost that saved the nation from a threatening economic slump. After the war, Bea's company expands to Europe and Asia, mirroring the global economic expansion of American businesses at that time.

The tension between Bea's desires for both upward socio-economic mobility and a traditional domestic life is played out in the novel through her relations with other women and her career trajectory from widowed

---

7   Berlant's essay explores the implications of the trademark that uses Delilah's face rather than Bea's at greater length.

homemaker to international corporate executive. Ironically, in many ways her personal affinities with traditional femininity enable her business's expansion via the economic and geographic mobility she enjoys both personally and as a corporation—as a major player in the business world, she must create a persona for herself with virtually no role models, striving to combine the staid, repressed middle-class femininity of her mother with the aggressive entrepreneurial spirit of (male) American business success stories. The novel finally shows Bea's obsession with traditional domesticity to be a self-deluding folly, as her family splinters and she loses the man she wanted to marry. As she negotiates the treacherous terrain of these seemingly opposed social roles and personalities—wealthy businesswoman and homebody—Bea manages her own identity, relying heavily on her traditional notions about class, gender, ethnicity, and race.

Bea's success proves to be an enormous leap in one generation from her mother's perspective on working women, although she does retain many of her mother's romanticized notions of middle-class domesticity. Mrs. Chipley had always told Bea that some young women could "work for 'pin money'" if they liked, but it made them "mannish, like those Woman's Rights advocates" (19). Working "through necessity" was of course out of the question, since a woman should be married and have a husband who supports her. Bea accepts her mother's position on working women and marries the man her father chooses for her, the lodger Mr. Pullman, who has lived with them for many years and works as a condiment salesman on the boardwalk. Before her (ironically named) husband dies in a train wreck, Bea contemplates her good fortune to have a husband and a home instead of "having to brave that strange cold world out there into which girls were actually voluntarily venturing nowadays for such positions as stenographer, teacher, saleslady, or [...] cashier" (70). After her husband's death Bea is forced to find a way to make a living, but positions in sales are highly competitive and teachers and stenographers have coursework and training Bea lacks. Instead she starts selling the mail-ordered maple syrup Mr. Pullman had sold to hotels and restaurants as a lunchtime side job. No longer a lucky married woman, she now has to consider venturing out into the "strange cold world" of work, and in order to succeed, must masquerade as a man on paper, using her late husband's business cards that represent her as B. Pullman and avoiding direct contact with the clients.

When she first hatches the plan to impersonate her late husband to make a living, Bea has mentally reviewed the options for a working woman: "Salesladying and teaching and stenography seemed to be about the beginning and the end" (76). She literally becomes a male impersonator, as Lauren Berlant points out, because she has suffered "the indignity of being all wrong for all the public positions she seeks" (118-19). Like many entrepreneurs, Bea realizes she must create her own opportunities out of the remnants of her domestic life: expanding her late husband's maple syrup business and renting out an upstairs room for extra money. In addition to passing for a man on paper, Bea's new public persona makes her body more masculine: "she had become taller during this period. [...] hardened and slenderized," perhaps by so much walking and lifting, but also by her new manly occupation (97). Hurst describes the new Bea as gaining an "undeniable look of stature and added length of face. [...] a leaner face, an obsessed face [...] a quality of straight-lipped concentration" from her work experience in the "ice-fields of business" (97-98). But when she approaches successful men in the business community about a small loan to open a waffle shop, Bea's body betrays her and she is repeatedly told to find employment working for a man or to get married and have babies, as a realtor tells her: "Go get yourself a husband or a lover. Or at least a job behind somebody else's desk" (137). Women working for wages or supported by men's wages don't threaten these male businessmen, since they still have relatively little power themselves and remain under the control of husbands, male employers, or both. But a woman in a business of her own frightens them, since she would not have to answer to a male authority.

For white women in the 1930s and 40s, a successful career in big business was virtually unheard of; Bea Pullman achieves her success by literally impersonating her husband on paper and hiding behind the common assumptions that business is a male realm. For Bea, her married surname of Pullman suggests her husband, his death in the train, but also her ticket out of poverty and to wealth that she never would have attained had he lived. She pulls the Pullman out of the ashes, passes for a man, and makes it her vehicle to wealth, her upward mobility both geographic and economic. For readers in 1933, Pullman also recalls the many accomplishments of George Pullman, entrepreneur and namesake of the famous sleeping cars, including the design of the company town and an exhibit at the Columbian Exposition of 1893, the White City. According to historian James Gilbert, Pullman coaches "reproduced the separated spaces of the middle-class home with its separate dining, sleeping, and living quarters" complete with porters, cooks, and special linens (147). His company town, modestly named Pullman, Illinois, was a similarly artificial, engineered environment geared toward uplifting his employees and maintain a loyal and healthy workforce by furnishing them with a bland, healthy, middle-class alternative to the tenements of Chicago. Pullman's employees also undertook one of the bitterest strikes in the history of the American labor movement in 1894, which halted rail traffic nationwide until President Cleveland ordered the strikers back to work, leaving the images of burning railroad cars and anti-labor violence in the national memory. The confluence of domesticity, rail mobility, and exploited labor in the name Pullman can be discerned in the themes of the novel, as well as in Bea's own personal associations with the name.

For Bea, the name Pullman further suggests a rosy childhood memory of a railroad car marked in her mind's eye with impressions of race and class, implying the cross-country geographic and economic mobility that will propel Bea into the upper echelons of big business. She names her waffle shops "B. Pullman" and her inspiration for their design scheme comes from her early memory of a train trip. Like the sleeping cars designed by George Pullman in the nineteenth century, the dining car of her childhood had "snowy napery, shining silverware, and white-coated, white-eye-balled rows of dark-skinned waiters, flashing by the corner of Mississippi and Arctic Avenues," and she wants her customers to feel transported back to a similar experience of glamorous travel and middle-class comfort complete with white linens and African American servants (126). Whiteness contrasts with blackness throughout this passage, in which Bea designs the image of her soon-to-be successful business; in particular, Bea's fixation on the "stiffly white napery," also described as "white napery so heavy and glossy," betrays her obsession with whiteness as she fantasizes about her future (126). At the very moment when she conceives of her entrepreneurial business career, the emblems of her widowhood, African American biological racial difference, class privilege, labor struggle, domesticity, and geographic and economic mobility become impossibly intermingled in Bea's fusion of nostalgia and self-promotion; her business and her pleasure, her finances and her femininity, are wrapped up in a tangle of purity and progress, of white linen napkins and speeding trains.

The emphasis on whiteness continues while she looks out the window, as "an evening the color of watered milk flowed over and seemed to immerse Arctic Avenue in bluish pallor" (127). The awkwardness of the metaphor aside, it creates an image of milk overflowing, which, as a description of the moonlight, adds to the jumble of images that suggest the home, maternity, and sustenance. However, the iciness of the street name, Arctic Avenue, and the "bluish pallor" also suggest frigidity and ill health, even death; earlier, too, Bea referred to the "cold world of work" and the "ice-fields of business." The moon, feminine symbol of poetic inspiration, tempts Bea outside for an evening walk along the "white sands," musing first on her lost chances for love as a nineteen-year-old widow and then abruptly deciding that "the napery must be the snow white of Delilah's inimitable laundry-work" (129). Not only does this passage plainly link whiteness—the moon, milk, pallor, Arctic Avenue, white sand, snow, and clean linen—with femininity, domesticity, and middle-class comfort, Bea also makes a connection, by bringing up the "white-coated, white-eye-balled, dark-skinned waiters," between white napery and racial purity. In *Imitation of Life*, Bea shares the Victorian obsession with "smiling servants in crisp white aprons" and "clean, white bodies and clean, white clothing," that McClintock argues in her analysis of the marketing of soap in the age of British imperialism, was a Victorian construct that "stemmed not only from the rampant profiteering of the imperial economy but also from the realms of ritual and fetish" (211). The laundry washes out the dirt of labor, often represented visually in soap ads as blackface, "bringing moral and economic salvation to Britain's 'great unwashed' but also [...] magically embodying the spiritual ingredient of the imperial mission itself" (McClintock 211). In the above passages, Bea clearly associates the work of black servants with crisp white linen and that most imperialist of conveyances, the railroad. Although she is an American in the early twentieth century, the novel constantly emphasizes Bea's traditional values and nostalgia for domesticity as well as frequent references to England, echoing the British Victorian middle classes in her fetishization of the white napery and black servants she associates with it.

## BEA'S COLONIAL AESTHETIC: RACE, EMPIRE, AND THE SEPARATE SPHERES

The implications of Bea's white napkin fetish come full circle when we read it alongside her obsession with American Colonial style and Hurst's fondness for imperialist metaphor: the public and private echo the colony and the metropole, as "Imperialism suffused the Victorian cult of domesticity and the historic separation of the private and the public, which took shape around colonialism and the idea of race" (McClintock 36). Rather than discrete spheres of home and periphery, Bea's world is an improvised amalgam of the domestic, the colonial, and racial and class difference. Throughout the novel, the American colonial mission serves as a metaphor for Bea's career advances, although since the colonizer is always already male as well as white, Bea must repress her female body to best fit the role. As if acknowledging the lack of female precedents for Bea's career, Hurst employs masculine metaphors of colonial conquest to describe Bea's trailblazing successes as she engineers a real estate development "a nose ahead of the gold rush," ushering in "militaristic years of expansion and growth" (190-92). Her business partner in this land development deal is Virginia Eden, a fabulously wealthy entrepreneur in the beauty business modeled after Elizabeth Arden. These "comparatively rare bird[s]," as Eden calls herself and Bea, are likened to explorers "who with their teeth into the wind were riding farther and farther into the uncharted seas of big business for women" (190-91). Eden is also associated with gold, further linking her to explorers in search of wealth in the new world: she carries a gold pencil, wears rings with jewels "of large carat" on her fingers with "sparkling tips to her nails," is "paged by a row of gilt buttons," and explains that a solid gold Aladdin's lamp is her business's trademark, which she presents as a gift to Bea upon their first meeting (191-194). As Berlant points out, even Virginia Eden's name suggests the colonial, in its Jeffersonian/Virginian connotations (121). Eden envisions building an idyllic colonial residence that echoes Monticello in its American colonial utopian promise, but she also has in mind an urban East Coast utopia rather than a pastoral one, modeled after British metropolitan town houses along the Thames.

During this meeting they discuss Eden's business proposal to buy up a city block of riverfront tenements and "start a colony" of socialites in new townhouses (198). Bea envisions transforming the "pock-marked tenements into a row of Colonial houses along what Miss Eden described as 'the London Embankment all over again, what with Blackwell's Island across the river bed, giving a House of Commonsy effect'" (196). They decide to form a real estate venture together, enticing wealthy New Yorkers to buy into it: they only need "the right ten or twelve people to make it the smart thing to up and move away from the beaten old trails" (198). When they encounter ethical differences and Bea buys out Virginia's interest, they both recognize that "where two men might be able to afford to publicly agree to disagree without further comment, let us so much as yea the other's nay, and they'll have our hairpins flying" (243). Gender considerations influence their public business decisions and personas, as Virginia and Bea continue to enjoy media attention because of their unique identities: wealthy and successful women in a male-dominated business world. Their joint venture not only blazes new "trails" in the male business world, it literally breaks new ground in New York City, claiming a formerly working-class street for the upper classes: Bea is an American pioneer, despite her avocation of traditional domesticity and her female body, which she masks behind the corporation of B. Pullman and its "mammy" trademark, Delilah.

The colonial trope surfaces again in descriptions of Bea's favorite architectural and decorative style. Her fixation with Colonial style began early, when she hired Frank Flake to "devise something new and novel in the way of china" for her shops: she settles on "Americana," white glass "harkening back to Colonial wares" (239). This choice resonates for Bea with the "beautiful general design" of Fishrow, which "restrict[s] each plot-holder to conform to a certain unanimity of Colonial scheme" (239) She has plans for her own Colonial style house in Fishrow, which will house the furniture Bea has already purchased, including "a fine example of Duncan Phyfe tea-table, a museum-piece maple candle-stand on tripod, a six-legged burl-walnut highboy, a Hepplewhite sideboard with a knee-hole front, and a pair of Sheraton inlaid knife urns to adorn it" (251). And for daughter Jessie's room, "an early American girl's room that was to look out upon a plane tree, flagstones, and a pair of stiff knickerbocker garden benches beside a river, a spool bed and a tambour desk beautifully inlaid with satinwood in the original patina" (251). Bea's affinity for traditional American decorating styles and for traditional domestic lifestyles only partially come together in her consumerism: she has bought the furniture and envisioned the house, but she continually delays construction and will never inhabit it when it is finally completed.

As she describes the house, Bea displays her romantic attachment to Americana: "Colonial pillars down the front [...] tall stone gate-posts topped with stone pineapples that I've already bought from a house in Charleston that was built before the Revolution" (261). The heady mixture of nostalgic domesticity with the colonial aesthetic of Americana betrays Bea's own insecurities about her appropriateness as a woman and mother: as a businesswoman she spends almost no time in a what she sees as her traditional feminine role—mother and homemaker, but rather attempts to create a domestic refuge by purchasing furniture that for her symbolizes colonial America and the cozy home she doesn't really have. Her vast wealth allows her to buy the symbols of that which she hasn't been able to acquire through accepted channels: marriage to a breadwinner and a lifetime of running a home. The trouble is, she can't escape the markers of her business world conquest narrative in the colonial style she thinks represents domesticity, but which also bears the traces of the conquests she was not supposed to have made in business. Ironically, her daughter will move into the house after marrying Bea's beloved Frank Flake, whose name is a contradiction since he isn't quite frank at first with Bea about his love for Jessie, and he turns out to be quite cold, like a snowflake, again echoing the chill that follows Bea through life—"snowy napery," "Arctic Avenue," "ice-fields of business." Frank and Jessie marry and their children scamper the hallways and garden while Bea travels the world overseeing her business's global expansion.

## GEOGRAPHIES OF LIFE: RACE, SPACE, AND PLACE

Bea's domestic ideal is completely enveloped in the colonial mobility narratives, and her obsession with class mobility is likewise rooted in the domestic and in imperialist tropes of racial superiority. Bea's romantic attachment to Americana has roots in her childhood, when her mother inculcates rigid class and gender norms. Hurst makes sure to point out that Bea grows up in her parents' house on Arctic Avenue in Atlantic City, between Mississippi and Georgia Avenues (2). The street name, Arctic, as mentioned earlier, suggests extreme cold and her parents lack of passion bears out the association; the cross streets mark the Chipleys class location, lower middle class, with the stigma of two of the poorest Southern states, Mississippi and Georgia. The other ocean in their address, the Atlantic, fixes them firmly on the East Coast with ready access to England and its social traditions—in fact, Bea's father is English. While the Chipleys are not poor, they are forced to take in a lodger, and Bea's mother often behaves as though she feels out of place in her neighborhood, so close to the Boardwalk. After both parents and her husband die, Bea is faced with the possibility of real poverty, the kind that even lodgers can't avert, and when she finally succeeds enough to move away from the old house to New York City, she leaves it happily as if she were leaving Mississippi and its rural poverty, as well as Atlantic City, with its connotations of British colonies and traditional early American society. The Arctic chill follows her, however.

As a girl, when she fantasizes about marriage, Bea imagines in detail what her house would look like: "Curving white staircase, such as they were building into those adorable new Ventnor cottages. Bow window in the dining-room, looking out, over geraniums, at ocean," nothing like her parents' house and nothing at all about her future husband (26). From her childhood, Bea associates location with class, and has almost no interest in sex or romantic love. After Mr. Pullman proposes, she considers that her life with him would be safe, "perhaps someday a bungalow in Ventnor, with a brace of bow windows that overlooked the ocean. Security!" (33). Her abstract attraction for marriage and home life strikes one of her neighbors, who asks her, "Are you marrying marriage or Mr. Pullman?" to which Bea replies that marriage is the symbol of Mr. Pullman (42). More likely, Mr. Pullman is merely the vehicle for the stability that Bea wants so badly, representing a safe, secure home life. For Bea the house represents these qualities more than the man, and the house of her dreams is in a more upscale area than her parents' home on Arctic Avenue.

The street names and neighborhood geographies in *Imitation of Life* further articulate the importance of place and adjacency, particularly in terms of class. Bea learns early in life that certain areas are reserved for certain kinds of people: streets, neighborhoods, beaches, even rooms in a house are zoned for one class rather than another. As a child, Bea learns to associate England with upper class values and aesthetics. She learns about father's English heritage from her mother, who tells her that he comes from a Leeds family that "had seen better days" (9). But to his wife's chagrin, his sister had immigrated to America, too, after her ironmonger husband died, and Bea's memories mark her as decidedly déclassé: Aunt Chipley had "drunk coffee from her saucer in great soughing movements and gone stocking-footed about the house" and once had "yelled at Father that he was born a little clark, was a little clark at heart, and a clark would live and die" (9). Bea's mother models class-conscious behavior for her daughter even in her preference for isolated beaches over the bustling working-class entertainments of the Boardwalk, the "unpeopled waters" around the Inlet over the "peanut whistle, popcorn smells, or shouts of bathers" on the Amusement Pier (24). The reserved matriarch can only occasionally bring herself to stroll the Boardwalk with her family, "seating herself rather stiffly on a bench in front of Clabby's Baths, or on the Steel Pier for a band concert" (22). Mrs. Chipley's stiffness conveys her sense of incongruity in such an unseemly situation, and Bea inherits some of her self-identification as a middle-class "lady" who clings to class differences. Her later insistence that the napkins for her shop must be "stiffly white" echoes her mother's rigid notions of class and propriety.

Bea's adult knowledge of Atlantic City far exceeds her mother's narrow parameters, since in her financial necessity she must traverse poorer streets selling maple syrup. The need to earn her own money forces Bea to expand her geographical knowledge of the city, leading her into poor areas populated by recent immigrants. After her dreams of economic security evaporate with her husband's death, Bea ventures into previously unexplored parts of Atlantic City, "certain streets along which Mr. Pullman would no more have walked with her, much less have permitted her to walk alone!" (87). Bea's geographical sense of the city is inflected with her own WASP aesthetic and feelings of class superiority:

Greek restaurants poured greasy odors, kosher hotels buzzed with the activities of stout matrons in machine-stitched wigs. Nationalisms flared along these side streets, each country to its odor, complexion, and often as not, its hoisted flags. (87)

The emphasis on scent, repeated twice in these two sentences, makes the non-WASP areas of town sound like foreign countries, exotic, overwhelming, and not especially appetizing. Bea brags of her new knowledge of the city: "'Lead me blindfolded through Atlantic City,' she would tell her father, […] 'and I can tell the streets by the smells. I can tell Jewish garlic from Italian'" (87). Later the novelty wears off, and Bea returns home to Delilah from her travails smelling of the poor neighborhoods, of poverty itself: "Stench from fish-frys, shore dinners, hamburger-wagons, of bathing-suits as they dried over porch railings, roasting peanuts, sour alleys and streets where the poor, in a dreadful kind of finery, aped the Boardwalk" (112). Ever the sympathetic domestic, Delilah exclaims, "I kin tell de smell of a white-trash fish-fry wid mah both eyes shut," never explaining how she can distinguish that smell from any other kind of fish-fry, just as the novel never explains how Bea can tell Jewish garlic from Italian (112). The descriptions of Bea's journeys into poor sections of town underscore the fact that she, as a white middle-class woman, doesn't belong there. But her increased mobility in the city streets does lead to her economic mobility, despite the seeming impropriety. Her forays into "ethnic" areas inhabited by recent non-Protestant immigrants parallel the imperial mission of the colonizers, and Bea's motivations for her travels are similarly grand: financial gain through the spread of her fetishized white napery and commodified domesticity.

Bea's colonial aesthetic is a specifically WASP aesthetic, and it plays out in her relations with other women, both white ethnic[8] and African American. These relationships are hierarchically structured in Bea's mind in terms of her middle-class superiority as well as her racialized notions of non-WASP ethnicity. Implicitly Bea links Italian and Jewish[9] women with classed and raced inferiority, which then helps to naturalize to her overtly

---

8   I use this term to refer to women of Southern or Eastern European descent, in this case, Italian American and Jewish women.

9   Abe C. Ravitz's book traces Hurst's career from its beginnings in the 1910s through the late 1920s, when much of her published fiction was set in the Lower East Side, chronicling the lives of immigrant Jewish women and families. Ravitz's careful study of Hurst's life, work, and personal correspondence from these early decades links her conservative German-Jewish roots with her interest in the recent immigrants of the New York ghettoes, whom her parents had frequently referred to as "kikes" (5). He quotes her from a 1924 interview: "Hurst went on, too, to underscore her conscious ethnic focus, insisting that 'her success in writing stories with Jewish characters' emanated from the 'racial urge she felt to speak for the Jewish people'" (84).

racist perceptions of Delilah. The slippage between class, ethnicity, and race frequently takes root in Bea's colonial aesthetic; for example, walking back streets the Italian and Jewish cultures take on racialized overtones, as do her complex and eroticized relations to Delilah and Virginia. As long as Bea can distinguish herself from Jewish, Italian, and African American women, she can remain asexual and superior; meanwhile, her relationships with these other women often borders on the erotic. She admires Virginia's alluring good looks, she collapses into Delilah's warm embraces, and her female employees are sternly rebuked when Bea receives anonymous love letters.

As a white Protestant, Bea's encounters with white ethnic women demonstrate perceived class differences, from her Atlantic City neighbors to her adult friendship with Virginia Eden. Throughout her life, Bea distinguishes herself from these women through what she perceives as cultural, physical, and class differences. At her wedding, Bea's Italian American next-door neighbor who had known her since she was a baby, Mrs. Vizitelli, "would not hear of coming into the parlor, but insisted upon viewing the ceremony from the pantry" (36). The self-imposed exile in the pantry, phrased as her own insistence rather than any social barriers having to do with class or ethnicity, demarcates the spaces in Bea's home that Mrs. Vizitelli feels authorized to inhabit: the kitchen, the pantry, places where women's domestic labor transpires, rather than the parlor, where social events take place. Like Bea's feelings of discomfort walking in immigrant neighborhoods, the WASP and non-WASP cannot meet socially without some barriers and distinctions. Always present is her awareness of class divisions, which often slip into racial or ethnic differences as well.

Bea doesn't feel the same geographic restrictions as Mrs. Vizitelli, however, since Bea occupies the position of relative social power and therefore greater mobility. She feels nothing to prevent her entering the realm of the "other," as her father and husband hold the wedding party in a Jewish hotel where they both know the chief steward. As she arrives at the "showy Boardwalk hostelry, catering [...] to a wealthy Semitic clientele," Bea observes the Jewish women thoughtfully: "heavy-busted, Oriental-eyed girls in heavy authentic jewelry" and "plump, pretty, clucking mothers" (44). She is, however, not completely at ease, since that would imply that she is a social equal; she is momentarily self-conscious as "everyone stared when the wedding party walked through the dining-room," and imagines what the "slightly greasy lips of the stout and pretty young Hebrew mothers of un-married daughters" would say of her conservative New England groom, probably "as so much oatmeal" compared to their exoticized, racialized characters (44-45). Everyone appears to know that the wedding group are not Jewish, but that knowledge only causes a brief awkwardness; instead of insisting on segregating herself from those different from herself as Mrs. Vizitelli had done, Bea seats herself and enjoys the dinner. Bea displaces pleasure, sensuality, and maternity onto Jewish women, "strangely alive" and spicy, in contrast to her own pallid "oatmeal" WASP husband; she has no living adult female role models of her own ethnicity, and she can only recall her mother's repressed and formal relationship with her father, whom she always called "Mr. Chipley" in front of Bea. Her association of sensual-ity and passion with white ethnic women carries over into her friendship with Virginia Eden, who is described as Bea's opposite in many ways: she is sexual, emotional, and self-consciously feminine.

Even as an adult, Bea's friendship with Virginia Eden never crosses the boundaries of ethnicity and class that Bea perceives as major differences between the two wealthy businesswomen. Born Sadie Kress in Jersey City, the young Virginia Eden was compelled by circumstances to develop an "aggressively eager" ambition so that she could earn enough to support her family: "shiftless parents," "paralyzed sister," and "gang-running brother" (245). Her Jewishness didn't change with her name and class status, how-ever, as Bea constantly notices in Virginia's relationships with her employ-ees, husbands, and children. For example, Bea is amazed by Virginia's management style, which contradicts Bea's notions of propriety: from her household servants, Virginia "enjoyed neither their deference nor what might be termed their respect," but they "adored her," and they "left in fre-quent huffs, only to return on a more intimate and more firmly entrenched basis" (242). Bea's amazement stems in part from her fusty New England affectations, fostered by her late mother, but also from a growing sense of wistful yearning for the emotional fulfillment that Virginia seems to derive from her stormy relationships with everyone in her life. Virginia, as an up-wardly mobile Jewish woman from Jersey City, is allowed to have "a household of excitements, waste, easy intake, easy outgo" that so bemuses Bea, who herself feels empty and alone when she looks at her own life (243).

Similarly, Virginia's private life is contrasted with Bea's: she has been married three times, twice to the same man, and lives with various in-laws, children, and step-children. Bea sees herself as "cold" compared to Virginia, whom she sees as feminine and fertile, "a woman toward whom life flowed like sunshine over the fields and meadows it was fructifying" (247). Indeed, the title of the novel stems from Bea's comparison of her own life to Virginia's: "Love and happiness, as [Virginia] said them, made what had been going on through years of a petty and mundane routine seem imitation of life" (195). Bea's own life, described by newspaper articles as fabulously successful, seems to her an imitation of life, as her family is a celibate imitation of a real one, in which she represents the father and Delilah the mother. While Virginia "regarded life as her debtor, she its relentless paymaster, [...] she made B. Pullman to herself, seem its slave" (194-95). As a Jewish woman, Virginia seems to Bea more naturally inclined to love and emotional excesses, whereas Bea imagines herself, "where the intimate aspect of life were concerned, [...] a wooden Indian" (245). Bea's constant distinctions between herself and Virginia only serve to amplify her sense of isolation and failure as a woman: unfeminine, asexual, and minimally maternal. Because Eden is racialized as Jewish, Bea sees her as sexual and domestic as well as extremely successful in business; as a WASP, however, Bea cannot allow or reconcile such a seeming contradiction in herself. Bea also never considers the privileges that come with her white identity that Virginia, no matter how wealthy and assimilated, is denied. Similarly, Bea sees Delilah as a perfect mother and domestic, but she cannot identify with such an overtly racialized character; seeing herself as deficient in domesticity, Bea manages to ignore the racial inequalities in her relationship with Delilah.

## SELLING DOMESTICITY: DELILAH AND BEA, INCORPORATED AND INTERNATIONAL

In contrast to Bea, and like Virginia in some ways, Delilah is the epitome of the domestic, in both senses of the word: she is a maternal homebody who cooks, cleans, and thinks only of the comfort of her "family," and she is also an African American domestic servant who works for a white woman. Their relationship is represented as one of opposites: masculine and feminine, commercial and maternal, public and private, middle-class and work-ing-class, master and servant, white and black. In an echo of a colonial rela-tion, too, Bea is masculinized as the white master while Delilah is femi-nized as the inferior non-white other. Further complicating their relation-ship, Bea and Delilah are frequently figured as a married couple in the text, Delilah's "huge smile [...] the glowing heart of that furnace" representing the home to which, "sore and weary, Bea nightly dragged herself, wanting to be enveloped into the limitless reaches of its warmth" (99). After a long day's work, Bea comes home to Delilah's loving hands: "those warm pale-palmed fingers kneading and soothing and cooling the tortured soles of her feet" and "kneading as if into dough" Bea's "burning shoulder blades" (99-100). In the kitchen, of course, Delilah reigns supreme, "who had not only the palate and the capacity of the gourmet, but the grand old Southern skill to prepare dishes fit for a daily company of them," including "steaming mountains of griddle cakes of fluff and no weight" (95-96). Delilah is Bea's angel in the house, enabling her to venture into the "ice-fields of business" knowing she can return to the warm hearth where Delilah presides over the household. While Bea constantly professes to idolize domesticity, she never actually participates in it, leaving the raising of Jessie, the care of her inva-lid father, and the running of her home to Delilah.

Bea's business successes represent her creativity and hard work, and she consistently explains her ambition as motivated by her domestic long-ings, fantasizing about retiring to a cozy home with her daughter and Deli-lah. On the other hand, however, Bea is described as cold, masculine, and lacking maternal and sexual instincts alleged to be "natural" for a woman. For example, as she sells domesticity and home cooking for huge profits, Bea undergoes a transformation into a soldier, a direct parallel to the doughboys who were some of her most loyal customers: "unloosing what must have been latent dogs of war within her, she seemed to have tasted the blood of big business" (177). Instead of actually leading a domestic life, Bea markets and sells it, even though that participation in the public sphere of business makes her ineligible for the domestic life she professes to crave. Ironically, metaphors of domesticity describe her business acumen throughout the novel, likening her new shops to children being born and business failures as still-born babies (161). Flake compliments her on "the fecundity of her copy" as they write advertisements together, exclaiming that Bea "mix[es hokum] almost as well as Delilah does her batter" (176).

Her only claim to domesticity is through metaphors comparing her business acumen to Delilah's ability to make a perfect pancake batter.

The most valuable thing Bea gains from Delilah's domestic skills is a product that she can sell that makes people feel comfortable, homey, and spoiled: Bea translates her love for the domestic atmosphere of Delilah's household into a booming business in waffle shops that appeal to World War I doughboys, the "troops of boys marching through cold city streets these days, on their strange embarkations for war" (149). But Bea also profits from her position of privilege which allows her to appropriate Delilah's domesticity and transform it into a product for sale. Bea's vision brings the domestic (as in home and as in servant) into the business world, and she brings to the business the contrasts of warm and cold that mark her difference from Delilah and her separation from the private sphere, selling "for a little pocket change, a delicate-lipped cup from which to drink good coffee" (149). The waffle shops feature Delilah or her look-alikes serving up home cooking to lonely people who crave a homey place to relax: "akin to the kennel warmth and brightness she so passionately wanted to pour around herself and little family in the house on Arctic Avenue" (149). Selling Delilah's cooking and mammy image, Bea realizes that her success lies in her ability to "surround people for a few moments out of a tired day, with a little unsubtle but cozy happiness of body and perhaps of mind" (152).

The popularity of the waffle shop with young soldiers going to and from the First World War lends the business a kind of patriotic aura, while providing the huge profits that enable local, national, and then global expansion: "those boys, eager to be off, and on the return, desperately anxious and eager to forget [...] had helped bring it all about" (170). The personal contacts she and Delilah make during the war carry over into their New York apartment, as the women invite the lonely young soldiers to come over after the shop closes; Bea "puffed [...] up like a mother hen" and Delilah, "not to be coaxed out of the rear end of the apartment, would consent to sit in her dark kitchen [...] and sing through the open doorway" (230-31). Like Mrs. Vizitelli's self-imposed exile in the kitchen during Bea's wedding, Delilah voluntarily enforces the racial and class divisions that keep her relationship with Bea acceptable; as a black servant, she can live with Bea in a socially acceptable kind of intimacy, providing the domesticity Bea requires without the romantic and erotic entanglements of a sexual relationship.

Her chaste husband role is not without its price, however, and Bea feels uncomfortable imagining herself in a feminine sexual role. Always complicating Bea's enjoyment of success is her feeling of failure as a woman, both sexually and maternally. She is in love with Frank Flake, her manager and advisor, who is eight years younger, and as she contemplates telling her teenage daughter about her feelings, Bea is acutely aware of the "inappropriateness" of her sexuality for a woman her age: "Dared she risk revolting the high-strung youth of [her daughter] Jessie with desires which all these years must have lain squirming in the damp cellar spaces of the vast structure she had erected?" (318). If her business is her substitute for domesticity, her "house" and her "child," sex has been locked "squirming in the damp cellar." Bea's discomfort and inexperience with romance is clear in her dealings with Frank and her awkward attempts to tell him her feelings. When she proposes marriage to Frank, who will eventually reject her and marry Jessie, Bea uses the language of the British corporation that wants a merger with her company: "like the Imperial Chain, I should say to you, 'We do not press you for an immediate decision. Give yourself six months time'" (311). She cannot recreate herself in the image of a demure woman in love, coyly waiting for her beloved to propose; Bea the businesswoman proposes to him first, and can only phrase her offer, albeit jokingly, in terms of a business merger.

Rather than recognize that her professional persona conflicts with her notions of domestic bliss, which no WASP woman in the novel lives up to, Bea chastises herself for being too old for romance. Instead of acknowledging that her ambition and aggression have altered her personality so that she cannot live up to the feminine ideals her mother passed on to her, Bea sees herself as a perverse older woman chasing a younger man. Bea sadly recognizes the "travesty of herself," a woman in her thirties who has never been in love, but she also feels a "sense of revulsion against something old and predatory within herself" (282). Although a pioneer in the business world must be a predator, Bea can only see herself in the most conventional kind of partnered relationship: "I'm a curtain-hemmer at heart. A toter of some man's carpet slippers for him when he comes home of an evening" (344). She seems unaware that the only woman who comes close to that characterization (caricature) is her black maid Delilah, and the slippers are no man's but her own. Bea instead fixates on the fact that Flake is younger, making her feel like "[a]n older woman" (282), as if she is unnaturally and aggressively "spreading her net for bright youth" (285). Her acquisitive business strategies have earned her huge successes, but she finds that they cannot coexist with traditionally feminine qualities: passive, domestic, romantic, maternal. The novel demonstrates what is at stake for a WASP woman who wants to live up to an ideal domestic feminine role as well as succeed in the world of big business, and Bea misses out on most of her daughter's childhood, loses the man she loves, and ends up traveling the world alone, the sound of her "failures" echoing in her mind.

Like the colonial United States, Bea's business expands westward and then abroad. But, also like the nation, her business's expansion is predicated upon the strict separation of spheres: public and private, WASP and white ethnic, white and black, middle class and working class. The symbolism invested in the images of mobility—the motif of the train with its snow white napery—alludes to the rapid class mobility Bea achieves personally as well as the global success of her business, even as she envisions her life as more and more meaningless and unfulfilled. The company moves from its Atlantic City origins, first to New York and other East Coast cities, then across the United States, and by the end of the novel, "the world literally this time, an oyster to be pried open from Rome to Monte Carlo" (279). Bea's capital has geographic mobility: expansion signals success. Even as her concern may be bought out by the Universal Sales Association, or partnered with aptly named British Imperial Chain—"There was Canada yet to be invaded"—Bea can only think about the married bliss she could have if Frank, the general manager of Bea's company, accepts her business-like marriage proposal (280).

In spite of her business successes, however, Bea ends up unsatisfied because she has seen her business as only a means to a happy domestic life which she suddenly finds herself unable to live: her daughter grows up and marries the man Bea had fantasized about marrying, Frank. Thus finally Bea considers herself unsuccessful as a woman: she feels masculinized by her life of work and also by her age (she is in her thirties!), sexually inadequate because of her long celibate widowhood and unfulfilling marriage, and maternally deficient because she took almost no part in raising her daughter. At the end of the novel, Bea lives "years of strange dark foreign nights" in hotel suites in Paris, Deauville, London, and Sydney, as "her enterprises joined hands to almost literally encircle the world, Madrid to Rome, to Vienna, to Berlin, to Paris, London, Sydney, Shanghai" (348-49).

But in spite of her enormous wealth and success, her world travels, Bea can't attain true happiness because Flake has married her daughter Jessie; it is her enterprises that join hands, not Bea and her beloved. By showing her as a failed mother and a successful businesswoman, the novel suggests that Bea is ruined for domesticity by her business because of her whiteness, her racial purity; non-WASP women—for example, Virginia Eden—can succeed and work and still be feminine, sexual, and domestic, but as a WASP woman Bea can't because of her class and race privilege. Her imperial successes don't mix with her notions of femininity and thus she is a domestic failure.

## IF HE HOLLERS LET HIM GO: MAPPING MALE PRIVILEGE AND RACIAL EMBODIMENT

> All I had when I came to the Coast was my height and weight and the fact I believed that being born in America gave everybody a certain importance. I'd never had two suits of clothes at one time in my life until I got in this war boom.
>
> CHESTER HIMES/*IF HE HOLLERS LET HIM GO* 153

*If He Hollers Let Him Go* centers on the daily life of Bob Jones, an African American leaderman at a Los Angeles shipyard during World War II. The novel looks at Bob's responses to the racism that surrounds him and affects his own personal ambitions for success and happiness. Dealing with racism on the job, Bob loses his temper when Madge, a white woman from Texas, refuses to work with him and calls him "nigger." He curses her, which earns him a demotion and he becomes obsessed with hurting her. Bob's interactions with Madge are charged with sexual tension and racial hostility, and although she is interested in him sexually, he finally rejects and insults her. This prompts her to seek revenge, which she does by locking him in a room and screaming "Rape!" so that her white male co-workers break down the door and beat Bob almost to death. After fleeing the scene, he is arrested and beaten again by police. When a doctor reports that she hasn't been raped, Bob is forced into the military and told he is lucky not to go to jail.

Outside the workplace, Bob wants to marry his middle-class girlfriend Alice, whose parents are members of the African American bourgeoisie and sadly out of touch with the "race problem" that faces working blacks in the city. Alice urges him to become a lawyer and create a comfortable secure family home as insulated as possible from everyday racism: "I want a husband who is important and respected and wealthy enough so that I can avoid a major part of the discriminatory practices which I am sensible enough to know I cannot change" (97). But although Bob aspires to a private, middle-class existence, he knows he won't be satisfied to publicly "adjust himself to the limitations of his race," in Alice's words (97). He knows that the struggle against white supremacy takes place in his thoughts and feelings as well as in the streets and workplaces, and he doubts he could be happy. Bob realizes that his own constant anger and resentment hurt him: "I knew that unless I found my niche and crawled into it, unless I stopped hating white folks and learned to take them as they came, I couldn't live in America, much less expect to accomplish anything in it" (150). Interior monologues and dream sequences, along with Bob's daily activities and interactions with others, portray his dilemma as it manifests itself in all areas of his life: home, work, public places, love, self-esteem, masculinity, sexuality, class identity.

The novel details the ways in which racism impacts every aspect of Bob's life, both public and private, but the primary conflicts that drive the novel take place at work, where he supervises a crew of African American workers. Before the war, Bob could never have been a leaderman in the shipyard, and he would have had far less contact with whites on almost any pre-war industrial job. During the war years, Americans at home had to face massive changes in the workplace as African American men and women joined the defense industries in unprecedented numbers: "twice as many blacks held skilled positions at the war's end than did so when it started. In all, over one million black workers became part of the industrial work force during the war years" (Lipsitz 73). Bob Jones works at a shipyard in Los Angeles County, where the wartime industrial boom brought 662,225 new residents (McWilliams 372). Many of the migrants were Southerners, both white and African American, men and women. These migrants had to adjust to the vast differences between the segregated Jim

Crow South and the legally enforced desegregation of the defense industry after President Roosevelt's Executive Order 8802, issued in June 1941, banning discrimination, *de jure* if not *de facto*, in the war industries. The setting of the novel in the shipyards of wartime L.A. allows Himes to explore the changing relations among workers and how those relations are grounded in, and often defined in, the specific spaces of Los Angeles: at work, on the streets, in movie theaters and restaurants, and in private homes.

Bob knows the geography of race and class in Los Angeles neighborhoods: affluent African Americans owned homes in isolated areas separate both from the white middle class and from the black working class. As he drives to his girlfriend Alice's house on the West Side, he thinks about her tony address: "When you asked a Negro where he lived, and he said on the West Side, that was supposed to mean he was better than the Negroes who lived on the South Side; it was like the white folks giving a Beverly Hills address" (48). Arriving in her neighborhood, Bob surveys the streets: "The houses were well kept, mostly white stucco or frame, typical one-story California bungalows, averaging from six to ten rooms [...] The lawns were green and well-trimmed, bordered with various local plants and flowers. It was a pleasant neighborhood, clean, quiet, well bred" (48-9). His description is charged with his class-conscious criticism of middle class well-kept, well-trimmed, well-bred African Americans and his suggestion that they are out of touch with the majority of blacks and too concerned with fitting in to white society. The ironic undercurrent comes through in the context of the next paragraph: "I felt like an intruder and it made me slightly resentful" (49). Bob knows the city (and his own unmarried working class status) well enough to know he *should* feel out of place in Alice's neighborhood, but he resents such class divisions and Alice's family's place in such a conservative social world, where the "talented tenth" rhetoric of the 20s still held sway along with solid capitalist family values.

Bob feels uncomfortable in Alice's neighborhood because of class differences, but he feels most unwelcome in poor white areas of the city. The neighborhood where Madge lives makes him nervous, and he worries that since it's more working-class, he could run into trouble. He sits in his car waiting for her, smoking and listening to the radio, and endures suspicious looks: "People passed, glanced at me, then turned to stare with hard hostility when they saw I was a Negro. It was a rebbish neighborhood, poor white; I'd have felt much better parked in Beverly Hills" (139). Although he wouldn't fit in with a rich white neighborhood like Beverly Hills, Bob fears the "rebbish" Southern poor whites more. He thinks they are more likely to cause him trouble, especially since many poor whites in Los Angeles during the war years were Southern migrants seeking defense jobs. The combination of their legacy of racist Southern culture and the false perception that they were competing for jobs frequently leads the poor whites to harass black workers. Bob's feelings of unease in Madge's block are confirmed when he sees "several faces peering furtively around the corners of the curtains in the front room" of a rooming house near where his car is parked (139). The geography of the city has an axis of class as well as an axis of race, and for Bob the most dangerous combination of those is poor white.

The limitations in his position as worker-consumer are everywhere apparent to Bob in Himes's novel: his awareness that he has only restricted access to the American Dream, which he clearly desires, makes his daily experiences of racism more painful. Bob connects his consumerism to his citizenship, particularly regarding his new car. His pride as a consumer shows in the way he describes his car, connecting his buying power with racial pride as well:

a '42 Buick Roadmaster I'd bought four months ago, right after I'd gotten to be a leaderman, and every time I got behind the wheel and looked down over the broad, flat, mile-long hood I thought about how the rich white folks out in Beverly couldn't even buy a new car now and got a certain satisfaction. (10)

When he fantasizes about beating up his boss after he is demoted, the thought of losing his car stops him, rather than the knowledge that he'd suffer a police beating, a fine, and some days in jail: "I'd lose my car. I think that was what made me decide that my pride wasn't worth it. My car was proof of something to me, a symbol" (30-31). His car symbolizes his masculinity and his status as an American worker and consumer: it is his source of mobility in literal geographic terms as well as figuratively speaking his purchasing power and his ability to move into the middle class.

## GOING PUBLIC, GOING WEST: AFRICAN AMERICANS IN WARTIME LOS ANGELES

But the consumer power Bob feels behind the wheel of his Buick is constantly problematized in the novel by his lack of social power as an African American in the public sphere. His anger and resentment toward white drivers and pedestrians and his painful anticipation of their racism mark his drive to work, as the stresses of rush hour are exacerbated by racial tensions. When Bob nearly hits a pair of white pedestrians, the exchange of looks between them and him explains the power relations: "I sat there looking at the white couple until they had crossed the sidewalk, giving them stare for stare, hate for hate [...] My arms were rubbery and my fingers numb" (13). His visceral reaction to their cold hostility sets the tone for the novel: Bob is excruciatingly aware of the myriad effects of racism on the way he is treated in his daily life, driving from home to work to Alice's house. He realizes that even though they are on foot and he is behind the wheel, the white couple has more power; they realize their privilege as well, and they take their time crossing against the light in morning rush hour traffic because they know he can't act.

The racial and class-based geographies of Los Angeles affect Bob's sense of personal style, as well; when he dresses to go out with Madge, Bob contemplates where they might go together. He needs clothes that can move with him from black social circles to white, to "look sharp" and "feel comfortable" in either: "I could wear an outfit over on the Avenue and feel strictly fine, but if I went downtown in it I felt gaudy" (136). He decides that his "beige gabardine pumps, grey flannel slacks, camel's-hair jacket" and "aqua gabardine shirt" will make the transition easily without making him feel overdressed or tacky (136-37). Work attire has a classed dimension for him as well, making him proud to be a working-class man. Bob's "coveralls," "tin hat," "leather jacket" and "high-heeled, iron-toed boots" make him feel masculine and strong: "Something about my working clothes made me feel rugged, bigger than the average citizen, stronger than a white-collar worker—stronger even than an executive" (8-9). His masculine identity as a worker makes him feel superior to those wealthy white men whose labor is less physical and commonly perceived as feminized, and Bob revels in his "rugged" work outfit, feeling "a swagger in [his] stance" (9). Depending on what he wears and the public spaces where he wears it, Bob alternates between masculine pride and racial self-consciousness, his gender privilege vying with his racialized embodiment. Even at work in his tough clothes, Bob and other African Americans negotiate the shaky ground gained during the war boom.

The everyday lives of many African American workers in the novel bear the marks of their recent past in the South, and they often interpret the geographical location—the South—as the site of the worst kind of American racism. Southern racism has a specific place for these workers, but it is also usually located in a particular time—the past. For example, Bob's carpool riders chafe under the memories of the South, as Pigmeat explains when Bob calls him "buddy": "When I escaped from Mississippi I swore I'd lynch the first sonabitch that called me 'buddy'" (11). The term has a demeaning connotation for Pigmeat, who insists that where he comes from "a 'buddy' drinks bilge water, eats crap, and runs rabbits. That's what a peckerwood means when he calls you 'buddy'" (11). Another black Southerner jokes that he'll go back to Arkansas "when the horses, they pick the cotton, the mules, they cut the corn; when the white chickens lay black eggs and the white folks is Jim Crowed" (22). Life on the West Coast is an improvement over the South for Pigmeat and other black war workers, primarily because they have well-paid jobs and enjoy at least *de jure* protection from discrimination in the workplace. Their daily lives on the job, as the novel illustrates, still present innumerable challenges, and in order to keep their jobs, the African American defense workers must negotiate every confrontation patiently. But their perception of the nation allows them to perceive a degree of progress in racial attitudes that accompanies their geographical migration, leaving the ultra-racist South for the relatively permissive West Coast.

Still, white workers resent African Americans at the shipyard, and in Himes's novel most of the racist antagonism comes with a Southern accent, thus allowing Bob and other African Americans to "place" racism as a Southern phenomenon and thus as out of place here in L.A. For example, when Bob and his riders arrive five minutes late for work the gatekeeper says, "What'd y'all do las' night, boy? I bet y'all had a ball down on Central Avenue" (15). As Bob walks toward his crew's dry dock, a guard tells him, "Put out that cigarette, boy. What's the matter you coloured boys can't never obey no rules?" (15). The gatekeeper's drawl and "y'all" and the guard's "boy" and double (triple?) negative mark them as racist Southerners requiring extra tolerance and restraint. Similarly, Bob knows that Hank, a white tacker leaderman from Georgia, gives his tackers to any white mechanics who ask, but he makes "the coloured mechanics wait until a coloured tacker was free" because white tackers won't work for black mechanics (24). Bob knows that if anyone complains about this racist and inefficient policy, Hank put on "his special smile for coloured" and "gave them a line of his soft Southern jive" (24). In these Southern white accents, Himes portrays the overt racism in wartime industry that even legal protection didn't prevent. The pervasive hostility of virtually every interaction between Bob and white Southerners eventually causes him to lose his temper and sets the machinery of retribution in motion, specifically when he has conflicts with poor whites.

More covertly, however, a connotation of class pervades the insults directed at many of the white racists in the novel, who are portrayed as poor and called "Okie," "Arky," "peckerwood," "cracker," and "white trash." The geographical references to Oklahoma and Arkansas originated with the first waves of Dust Bowl refugees and gradually applied to anyone who appeared to be a rural white Southerner—Bob refers to a young white woman getting drunk in a predominantly African American bar as "the Arky Jill" (76). Bob's association of geographical origin, the South, with white racism combines with his stereotype of poor Southern whites as "trash," thus not only detestable because of their Southern white racism but also because of their poverty. The poor white women, like "the Arky Jill," are portrayed as sometimes cruel and often sexually forward, as class and racial identity meld with assumptions about gender and sexuality. At work, Bob takes pride in his position of responsibility, which places him above many white women workers in the hierarchy of the shipyard; his descriptions of interactions with white women suggest that many of them recognize and resent his gender privilege, perhaps thinking that their racial privilege should afford them authority over him.

As a leaderman, Bob has authority over women, white and African American, and he earns more money than they do. He sometimes flirts playfully with young black women on the job, but Bob's workplace relations with white women are strained with racial and sexual tension barely below the surface of their interactions. In an interesting reversal of the male gaze, he notes how they watch him: "Whenever I passed the white women looked at me, some curiously, some coyly, some with open hostility. Some just stared with blank hard eyes. Few ever moved aside to let me pass; I just walked around them" (18). He notices the range of responses his bodily presence generates among white women, from the coy who might be interested in him sexually, to the openly hostile, whose racism can barely be restrained. Bob values his job, which provides him with a good paycheck and a position with leadership responsibilities, so he does what he can to keep the peace among white and black workers.

When he needs to borrow a tacker for a few hours, Bob asks the tacker leaderman Hank, who claims that the four white women tackers "lounging" around the deck and "gabbing" are busy (25). Bob then asks another white leaderman, Don, who suggests he take Madge, a Southern white woman, who refuses: "I ain't gonna work with no nigger!" (27). Bob has encountered Madge before around the workplace, and he has noticed that whenever she sees him she "deliberately put on a frightened, wide-eyed look and backed away from [him] as if she was scared stiff, as if she was a naked virgin and [he] was King Kong" (19). But in the run-in with Madge when she refuses to work with him, Bob loses his cool and curses her: "Screw you then, you cracker bitch!" (27). Bob's perception of Madge is overtly linked to her class, and although he is a worker too, Bob disdains the poor whites who in turn resent him for his good job and nice car and fear his over-embodied black sexuality. Their mutual hatred is not simply racial, nor is it an equal measure of class and race prejudice. Bob also calls Madge a "bitch," and his feelings for her vacillate from extreme disgust to involuntary lust; her behavior with him indicates that she sees Bob not just as a "nigger" but as an African American man with more economic power than she has and the supposed tendency to rape white women. The sexual is inseparable from race and class in their interactions and perceptions of one another.

After the confrontation with Madge, Bob is summoned to the superintendent's office and demoted to mechanic effective the following Monday, when an underqualified white man will take over responsibility for his work crew (30). Bob's employer tells him that he was supposed "to help me keep down trouble between the white and coloured workers" and that he thought Bob was qualified because he doesn't have "a chip on [his] shoulder like most coloured boys" (29). Appealing to his intelligence, breeding, and chivalry, Mac chastises Bob for his outburst: "I figured you were too intelligent to lose your head about something like that. I figured you had better manners, more respect for women than that" (29). Mac's assumptions about Bob slip from racial to class markers, first suggesting he's better than most "coloured boys," but then appealing to his "manners"—as if white racism is merely the rudeness of uncultured white trash, Mac suggests that, even though he is African American, Bob is exceptional and he should know better than to let the poor whites' hostility affect his polite demeanor.

Bob had anticipated some disciplinary action resulting from his confrontation with Madge, but he didn't realize he'd be downgraded; he thought that his boss would fear the backlash of African American workers: "I thought he'd be afraid of the coloured workers making trouble. It shocked me to find out he didn't give a goddamn about the coloured workers, one way or the other" (30). Based on the information in George Lipsitz's study of wartime wildcats and hate strikes, perhaps Bob's boss should have been afraid of the effects of his demotion: during World War II, African American workers frequently protested racism on the job with wildcat strikes and mass demonstrations (73). For example, janitors at a Detroit Chrysler plant "wildcatted in March 1943 in protest against the company's failure to promote blacks and to pay them adequate wages. One month later they walked off the job again because management demoted a black supervisor and placed the janitors under the authority of a white man" (Lipsitz 77-78). Bob's surprise at his supervisor's actions suggests that Bob is aware of the unrest in the defense industry and the power that African American workers were beginning to harness to better their workplace.

In fact, when he approaches his union steward Herbie Frieberger, demanding that he tell Madge that she has to work with African Americans, the white hate strike is a main concern, and Herbie replies, "This is dynamite. If we tried that, half the workers in the yard would walk out" (113). When Bob loses his temper with Herbie's attempts to stall, the union man calls on the unity rhetoric of the war effort: "This isn't any time for private gripes. We're fighting fascism—we're not fighting the companies and we're not fighting each other—we're all fighting fascism together and in order to beat fascism we got to have unity" (114). Echoing African American workers all over the country, Bob challenges the unity rhetoric with its own logic: "Get these crackers to unite with me. I'm willing. I'll work with 'em, fight with 'em, die with 'em, goddamnit. [...] What the hell do I care about unity, or the war either, so long as I'm kicked around by every white person who comes along?" (114-15). Herbie's resort to rallying round the anti-fascist cause and Bob's angry challenge play out the larger arguments taking place around job discrimination at the time: government agencies, including the War Manpower Commission, "placed a higher priority on wartime efficiency over non-discrimination, fearing the consequences of white walkouts in protest over black hires" (Boris 83). Bob's retort fails to convince the union steward, however, and Bob stands gazing out over the harbor, remembering that the military effort he is working to strengthen also enforces institutional racism in its ranks: "A cruiser was silhouetted against the skyline. The white folks are still going strong, I thought; then I thought about the black sailors aboard waiting on the white" (115). The cruiser, symbol of American military might, global mobility, and the fight against fascism, also represents for Bob the inequalities upon which the nation is founded. Bob notes the irony that he and other African American shipyard workers helped to build the cruiser, which, like the nation, still operates on a system that discriminates against them.

## WHITE PRIVILEGE, MALE PRIVILEGE: BODIES, SEX, AND LANGUAGE

In rare moments, outside the institutional restrictions of work, Bob manages to connect with white men around their shared gender privilege, when their racial identities temporarily recede into the background. But the two terms of identity come into conflict eventually, on one occasion when Bob gives two white sailors a ride across town: Bob's car, his favorite symbol of his prosperity and mobility, is their first subject of conversation. The sailors are still in their teens, in uniform, and from San Francisco and Memphis. They both sit in the front seat and converse with Bob casually about cars, as if there were no major social divisions between themselves and him. The freshness and candor of the two sailors starts Bob thinking about whiteness:

I began wondering when white people started getting white—or rather, when they started losing it. And how it was you could take two white guys from the same place—one would carry his whiteness like a loaded stick, ready to bop everybody else in the head with it; and the other would just simply be white as if he didn't have anything to do with it and let it go at that. (41)

Whiteness is compared to a weapon in Bob's thoughts, which can be used to hurt him if the white person chooses. Geography again comes into consideration, as Bob is careful to compare "two white guys from the same place," ostensibly the South. He acknowledges the importance of place to a white man's sense of identity, but he wants to investigate the other factors, since place alone cannot determine whether or not a white man will use his race as a weapon.

Bob's perception of whiteness as potentially non-threatening, embodied by the two sailors, one of whom is a Southerner, contains within it a seed of hope, since he realizes that there is a possibility that a person can be white without wanting to "bop everybody else in the head with it." Enjoying his conversation with the boys, Bob relaxes and they start talking about the women on the sidewalks as they drive past, speculating whether or not they are married, mothers, cheating on their husbands, and so on. But they all fall silent when they see an older African American woman:

a dark brown woman in a dark red dress and a light green hat carrying a shoebox tied with a string, falling along in that knee-buckling, leaning-forward, housemaid's lope, and frowning so hard her face was all knotted up. I wanted to say something to keep it going, but all I could have said about her was that she was an ugly, evil-looking old lady. If we had all been coloured we'd have laughed like hell because she was really a comical sister. But with the white boys present, I couldn't say anything. I looked straight ahead and we all became embarrassed and remained silent for a time. (42)

An unspoken taboo prevents Bob from making fun of a black woman in front of whites, and the white sailors realize it as well; they cannot say anything about her, either. She exists for them only as a pathetic body, as opposed to the younger women they had been ogling just before. The silence has altered their demeanor, and when the conversation picks up again, they can no longer occupy the unmarked disembodied male perspective together: "we were all a little cautious. We didn't talk about women any more" (42). Bob suddenly realizes that, even among friendly white men, his racial identity binds him to the woman, even though she is "an ugly, evil-looking old lady," in a deeper and more intimate way than his gender identity binds him to the men in the car with him, although they are bonding by talking about women as sex objects under their collective male gaze. This fear of even speaking, which all three men seem to feel, paralyzes their conversation and closes off the common ground that they had been able to find earlier. The white men are suddenly aware of their whiteness, which limits what they can say about the woman without offending Bob, while Bob's racial embodiment has come between them because he identifies with the woman in spite of his powerful desire to exist only in terms of gender. In this scene, as in others in the novel, relations of oppression supersede relations of privilege.

Another sexual situation leads Bob to think about racial conventions in terms of gender, again with a white man, when he tells the white leaderman Don about what happened with Madge. Bob describes to Don the angry exchange of insults, but then a strange thing happens: Don gives Bob her home address, saying "Maybe you can cure her" (119). Bob isn't sure how to interpret this: maybe Don thinks he wants to ask her out, or rape or beat her "to get even with her," or maybe Don wants to prove to Bob that "all men of his race didn't approve of that sort of thing [Madge's racism]" (119). The address puts Bob in a precarious position with Don:

I wanted to tell him I didn't want to go to bed with her, I wanted to black her eyes; but just the idea of her being a white woman stopped me. [...] I couldn't tell him I *didn't* want her because she was a white woman and he was a white man, and something somewhere way back in my mind said that would be an insult. And I couldn't tell him that I *did* want her, because the same thing said that that would be an insult too. (119)

These conflicting impulses lead to nervous laughter and Bob gets out of the situation, but he still wonders "what a white man and a Negro could talk about that wouldn't touch at some times or other on one of those taboo subjects that would embarrass one or the other, or both" (119). He realizes that the two hypothetical men would need to have the same position on white supremacy, either fully against it or fully in favor, because every aspect of life would eventually bring up the issue of race. Since he cannot ever be sure that even friendly white men are fully against white supremacy, Bob falls silent in order to avoid conflict. As with the white sailors, Bob's racial embodiment limits his ability to conform to masculine social conventions. Black male sexuality occupies for Bob the contradictory space of gender power and racial oppression.

Bob's theory of whiteness takes into consideration performance as well as appearance, and his problems with whites arise from their racist behavior that he sees as "white." Whiteness can be used as a weapon, not only by hostile white men spoiling for a fight, but also by provocative white women like Madge who can accuse black men of rape. When he ponders his mixed feelings of attraction, anger, and disgust toward Madge, Bob tries to unpack the sexual and racial values surrounding their interactions: "it wasn't that Madge was white; it was the way she used it" (125). Bob senses that she entertains mixed feelings toward him as well. He imagines that "she wanted them [African American men] to run after her. She expected it, demanded it as her due. [...] teasing them with her body, showing her bare thighs and breasts. Then having them lynched for looking" (125). Bob decides that Madge is using her race and her sexuality as weapons to harm black men, that she is "luring [him] with her body and daring [him] with her color" (126). Considering how carefully Bob has analyzed his situation with Madge, it is even more harrowing when she is successful in all he suspects of her: he is drawn to her sexually but runs away before they have sex, she accuses him of rape at work and he is arrested, beaten, and forced into the military. The sense of Bob's inevitable doom pervades his interactions with Madge, culminating in his induction.

Unlike his unproblematic admission that he liked the white sailors, Bob constantly struggles with his attraction for Madge and his disdain for her "white trash" appearance—her overt racism is one obvious cause for this conflict, but his first person narration of Madge's age and class also seem to influence his mixed reactions. In one scene that shows how extreme his feelings for her are, Bob approaches Madge at lunch, hoping to settle their dispute somehow, and instead of pretending fear she flirts with him, momentarily unbuckling "the white armor plate she'd wrapped herself up in" and catching him off-guard (130). He asks her out and when he comes to her apartment that night, much too late for a date, he finds her ready for bed and obviously unprepared for a date. In a long descriptive passage, worth quoting at length for the sustained detailed scrutiny of Madge's appearance, Bob looks at her carefully from head to toe:

She had on a nubby maroon robe and her blonde hair, dark at the roots, was done up in metal curlers tight to her head. Without lipstick or make-up she looked older; there were deep blue circles underneath her eyes and blue hollows on each side of the bridge of her nose. Tiny crow's-feet spread out from the outer corners of her eyes and hard slanting lines calipered obliquely from her nostrils, dropping vertically from the edges of her mouth. Her mouth was big, hard, brutal, with lips almost colorless; and her eyes were wide, blue, staring, almost popping, but now there was a muddy look in them. Beneath her robe her breasts seemed lower, big and loose, and her hips lumped out from her waist like half-filled sacks. For bedroom slippers she wore a pair of worn-out play shoes that had once been red. She had big feet and her ankles were very white, laced with veins, and dirty on the bone. (145)

From his description, her whiteness is partly fake—like her hair with its dark roots and curlers, the blue shadows under her eyes—but she still uses it as a weapon. The hardness of her eyes and mouth, along with her curlers, big feet, and dirty ankles, mark her as a white trash woman whose minimal attractiveness is earthy—"dark," "muddy," and "dirty"—rather than a more pristine or pure femininity. Madge is big: her mouth, her eyes, her breasts, her feet are all "big" and "wide" in "worn-out" shoes, and the overall effect of the description is to portray her as a cartoonish older woman.

After he makes a pass at her, they tussle, and she taunts him with racist threats even as she propositions him. Finally, though, Bob turns her down; his lust for her has evaporated once she has admitted she wants him sexually. He refuses to play into her rape fantasy, and after she calls him "nigger" repeatedly and says "This'll get you lynched in Texas" during their love-play (if you can call it that?), Bob storms out (145). She chases him, threatening to get him lynched if he leaves her, which only further angers him. Again he comments on how unattractive she is: "She looked like hell. She was a real beat biddy, trampish-looking and pure rebbish" and tells her "go wash your face [...] you look beat" (146). After he gets in his car, with her chasing him outside with threats, he tells her, "You look like mud to me, sister, like so much dirt. Just a big beat bitch with big dirty feet. And if it didn't take so much trouble I'd make a whore out of you" (148). His disdain for her is a complicated combination of his sexist view of a mature woman (recall his discomfort when he and the white sailors saw the older African American woman) and his class-biased attitude toward poor whites, geographically linked to the South in his expression "rebbish."

Bob's calling Madge "beat" and "rebbish" further mark her as Southern white trash, a woman far beneath him in power relations of both class and gender. Bob associates Madge with dirtiness and impurity through his constant references to "mud" and "dirt," and while his attitude is clearly sexist and classist as well as fueled by personal animosity, his constant recourse to the rhetoric of purity can be also read in the context of work discrimination. In fact, Bob reverses a commonplace complaint from whites working with African Americans for the first time. According to Boris, many wartime workplaces were disrupted by whites who refused to share toilet and locker facilities with African Americans, claiming that blacks were dirty, malodorous, syphilitic, and generally biologically inferior (94). The counter-argument from anti-discrimination handbooks pointed out that "black women and men not only cleaned public and private toilets but care for children, prepare food, and 'handle much of the linen and make up the beds of many white Americans'" (Boris 94). Nevertheless sharing sanitary facilities continued to generate protest, especially from white women, who threatened to walk out and sometimes did; many employers installed segregated facilities to silence resistance (Boris 94). White women's obsession with cleanliness operates on a racial level as a justification for segregation while at the same time privileging their own notions of white feminine purity. By describing Madge as white and dirty, Bob attempts, however offensively, to correct in his own mind the racist associations of blackness with dirt and impurity that were currently circulating in wartime industrial workplaces like his.

Madge is "dirty" in another sense, as well: her rough language and her sexual availability to Bob, which further seals her fate as "white trash" to be made into a "whore" if he chooses to sleep with her. In her apartment, they spar with one another, challenging each other sexually: Madge tells him, "You can't have me unless you catch me" and "All right, rape me then, nigger!" (147). The language he uses with her is also disrespectful and vulgar, using curses and harsh words. From the narrative of their encounter, it is clear that neither is interested in the other personally; they are using one another to work out their racial grievances in a sexual arena. The conflict is, she wants him to fulfill a rape fantasy and still maintain her white privilege, while he wants to sexually conquer her to dissolve her white privilege, make a whore of her. Unfortunately for Bob, his relative gender and class privileges don't trump her white racial privilege, and she wins the power struggle in the end. As when he and the white sailors saw the older African American woman, Bob's racial body takes precedence over his masculine identity.

Madge contrasts with Alice, who is very attractive and at the same time chaste—she is middle-class, marriageable, and ostensibly worth the wait. Indeed, Bob describes Alice in a way that starkly contrasts with his descriptions of Madge. He compares Alice to Bette Davis twice in the novel, an appropriate description since Davis was a star famous for her petite, intelligent beauty and sophistication, for her eyes more than her secondary sex characteristics such as hips or breasts. Bob describes Alice as she makes her entrance,

like Bette Davis, big-eyed and calisthenical and strictly sharp. She was togged in a flowing royal-purple chiffon evening gown with silver trimmings and a low square-cut neck that showed the tops of her creamy-white breasts and the darker disturbing seam down between; and her hair swept up on top of her head in a turbulent billow and held by two silver combs that matched the silver trimmings of her gown—a tall willowy body falling to the floor with nothing but curves. Black elbow-length gloves showed a strip of creamy round arm. (53)

Unlike Madge, whose whiteness is ugly or faked or both, Alice's fair skin is "creamy" and her curves are appealing because she is "willowy" rather than lumpy. Alice's skin is light enough for her to pass for white when she goes out with white friends, and in this passage Bob clearly finds her "whiteness" appealing, twice calling her skin "creamy." In fact, the only hint of earthiness or sex is the "darker disturbing seam" between her breasts, which Bob notes but then skips up to describe her hair. While he clearly finds her beautiful and attractive, Bob describes Alice as a delicate movie star or a queen. Her purple evening gown with silver trim marks her in terms of class as well: it sounds expensive and it is the color of royalty, with silver suggesting wealth, coins, fine jewelry. Alice symbolizes Bob's desire for upward class mobility, but he frequently argues with her over the issue of race, worrying that the ascent into the middle class requires him to tacitly accept the racism of the hegemonic white culture.

Overall, Alice is young, rich, and thin, while Madge is wrinkled, trashy, and dumpy. Alice is likened to Bette Davis, while Madge is racialized white trash. With this ironic reversal of common racial stereotypes, Bob's own racial identity becomes more scrambled: although they are both African American, he worries that he doesn't deserve Alice because she is middle-class, and he feels superior to working-class, white trash Madge. His attraction to both women makes him question his own racial and class identity, and his volatile relationship with Madge leads to violence, rejection, and at the end of the novel, involuntary induction. The fact that he is faced with the choice between two women only further underscores Bob's fixation on his masculine identity and the conflicts it causes for him in his work and personal life. But he also must contend with the violence of masculine and African American embodiment in the wartime social milieu of Los Angeles so arrestingly captured in Himes's brusque prose style.

Working in the hard-boiled style of the Los Angeles *noir* writers, epitomized by Raymond Chandler, James M. Cain, and other writers of popular fiction targeted at male audiences, Himes chooses his words for maximum impact, often supplying gory details of Bob's psychic suffering. Bob's embodiment in the novel is not an attribute of his gender or sexuality per se; rather, it is because of his vulnerability to and fear of violence. His fantasies of killing a white man he fought at work, of beating and/or raping Madge, and of other passing daydreams are an ironic foreshadowing of the beatings he will sustain at the hands of his co-workers and the police after Madge's rape charge. Violent language also peppers the novel in Bob's narration and dreams. Bloody metaphors regularly evoke the psychological effects of racism in graphic physical detail, whether in response to his own subconscious imaginings or his experiences in the public spaces of Los Angeles. Bob narrates a dream in which he lies on the sidewalk in front of the Federal Building, being beaten almost to death by "two poor peckerwoods" with rubber hoses, but they want to stop, saying "It ain't right to beat this nigger like that. What we beating this nigger for anyway?" (69). They are ordered to continue by the "hard cultured voice" of the president of the shipyard "dressed in the uniform of an Army general" as two laughing policemen look on (69). Bob's dream graphically portrays the way the racial and class conflicts between (Southern) white and black workers are exacerbated by the captains of the war industries, whose primary concerns are production, not worker welfare or racial harmony.

His violent metaphors also describe his experiences in public and at work. After walking out of a Hollywood movie because of a stereotyped mammy character, Bob laments, "The sons of bitches were grinding me to the nub, to the white meatless bone" (79). Bob imagines the pain of racism in his body, and equates it with mutilation; when he pictures Madge's hard brutal mouth saying "nigger" he feels as if "something took a heavy hammer and nailed me to the bed" (101). When he has to endure a racist joke in Mac's office, he feels it as "a gut punch and my stomach was hollow as a drum; it took all I had to keep standing up straight, to keep on looking at him" (123). As he loses his nerve trying to talk to Madge, his experience is profoundly gendered as well as raced, and he alludes to the lynching that he feels convinced Madge would demand if she could: "I felt castrated, snake-bellied, and cur-doggish, I felt like a nigger being horse-whipped in Georgia" (126). Bob's reaction to this humiliation and fear is to lash out with equal violence, thinking, "what I ought to do is rape her [...] That's what she wanted" (126). As Boris points out, Bob's blackness negates his masculinity, making his body vulnerable to violent attack and undermining his self-confidence and peace of mind (78). His resentment often builds up to the point where he no longer feels in control, and almost gives in to his own violent urges.

Bob muses in a more cynical moment, after waking up from two consecutive nightmares to the sound of his landlady Ella Mae's baby crying, that if she "really wanted to give him a break they'd cut his throat and bury him in the back yard before he got old enough to know he was a nigger" (4). He is immediately ashamed of this angry thought, but only because he knows how much the baby's parents love it. More interestingly, however, Bob ascribes the wrong gender to the baby, a girl named Emerald. He finds it easy to identify with Ella Mae's child as an African American born into a racist society if he thinks of the child as male. Later when he's flirting with Ella Mae about marrying her, she replies that then he'll have to raise Emerald. Bob doesn't understand what she means, asking her, "Emerald what?" and then catching himself: "I forgot her name was Emerald" (47). He admits that he is always startled by the unusual name, but doesn't admit that he thinks of the child as male. In his slip about Ella Mae's baby and in other dilemmas throughout the novel, Bob cannot pose the same challenges to gender norms that he can to racist conventions: he "naturalizes gender even as he questions the significance of racial difference" (Boris 78). His racial affinities for women of color conflict with his sense of gender privilege, as his masculinity is not as threatened from all sides the way his racial identity is.

## "DOMESTIC" DILEMMAS: HURST AND HIMES

Hurst and Himes chronicle the careers of Bea Pullman and Bob Jones, two workers in the public sphere who face constant resistance in their attempts to earn a living and to advance within their fields. The less than sanguine endings of the two novels help to spell out the implications for white women and African American men who challenge restrictions of the public sphere. Bea ultimately sees herself as a "domestic" failure because although fabulously wealthy, she is alone without husband or child; because of white sexual anxiety about African American masculinity, Bob loses his job, his fiancée, and possibly his life as he is coerced into joining the armed services during the World War II. The theme of incorporation/embodiment runs through both novels, as Bea's masculinization through work and Bob's excessively embodied racial identification mark them as improper for their public roles, particularly at work. In other words, as a white woman Bea feels she should be more domestic: she envies women who have husbands and families and measures her own success by that social scale. Bob, on the other hand, feels empowered by his masculinity until, in many situations, it is superseded by his physical vulnerability to racism or his affinity with other racialized victims of injustice.

The shipyard's exploitation of Bob's "domestic" wartime labor, as opposed to foreign military service, without the benefit of civil rights allows his contribution to the war effort to be nullified at the whims of a white woman he sees as beneath him; his racialized labor isn't rewarded or recognized when Madge calls attention to his embodied black masculinity. Although Bob continually insists on his male privilege at work and in public spaces of Los Angeles, it is always undermined when his raced and often sexualized body enters the discourse. Similarly, Delilah's domestic labor enables Bea to escape her own white female body by hiding in her corporation—her masculine role in the company and in the household depends on Delilah's overdetermined black female body in the kitchen and on the product, what Berlant calls Bea's "prosthetic body" (119). In both novels, the white body relies on the African American body, as (domestic/industrial and domestic/house servant) labor, as site of displaced sexuality, and as an escape from white physicality.

White women's fetishization of cleanliness, like Bea's repeated references to "white napery" in *Imitation of Life*, operates on a racial level as a justification for segregation while at the same time privileging their own notions of white feminine purity. Bob's association of dirt and impurity with the white woman Madge demonstrate the degree to which his own thought processes are influenced by the discourses of racial purity that were currently circulating in wartime industrial workplaces like his, demonizing African Americans as unclean. The subtext of empire pervades both novels and affects both characters, troubling the parameters of the word "domestic" as it pertains to both the family home and the national home. White and African American roles in both these "homes" come under close scrutiny, as do the power relations between men and women. The two texts illustrate the vast changes in American social space taking place between the wars, as white women and African Americans attempted to move out of the private sphere and into the privileges of the public world of big business and industrial wage labor.

## WORKS CITED

Berlant, Lauren. "National Brands/National Body: *Imitation of Life*." *Comparative American Identities: Race, Sex, and Nationality in the Modern Text*. Ed. Hortense J. Spillers. New York: Routledge, 1991. 110-40. Print.

Boris, Eileen. "'You Wouldn't Want One of 'Em Dancing With Your Wife': Racialized Bodies on the Job in World War II." *American Quarterly* 50.1 (1998): 77-108. Print.

Crooks, Robert. "From the Far Side of the Urban Frontier: The Detective Fiction of Chester Himes and Walter Mosley." *College Literature* 22.3 (1995): 68-90. Print.

Diawara, Manthia. "*Noir* by *Noirs*: Toward a New Realism in Black Cinema." *Shades of Noir*. Ed. Joan Copjec. New York: Verso, 1993. 261-78. Print.

Findlay, John. *Magic Lands: Western Cityscapes and American Culture after 1940*. Berkeley: U of California P, 1992. Print.

Fine, David, ed. *Los Angeles in Fiction*. Rev. Ed. Albuquerque, U of New Mexico P, 1995. Print.

Gilbert, James. *Perfect Cities: Chicago's Utopias of 1893*. Chicago: U of Chicago P, 1991. Print.

Himes, Chester. *If He Hollers Let Him Go*. 1945. New York: Thunder's Mouth, 1991. Print.

Hurst, Fannie. *Imitation of Life*. New York: Harper, 1933. Print.

Kaplan, Amy. "Manifest Domesticity." *American Literature* 70 (1998): 581-606. Print.

Lipsitz, George. *Rainbow at Midnight: Labor and Culture in the 1940s*. Urbana: U of Illinois P, 1994. Print.

McClintock, Anne. *Imperial Leather: Race, Gender, and Sexuality in the Colonial Contest*. New York: Routledge, 1995. Print.

McWilliams, Carey. *Southern California Country: An Island on the Land*. New York: Duell, Sloan and Pierce, 1946. Print.

Ravitz, Abe C. *Imitations of Life: Fannie Hurst's Gaslight Sonatas*. Carbondale: Southern Illinois UP, 1997. Print.

Skinner, Robert E. "Streets of Fear: The Los Angeles Novels of Chester Himes." Fine 227-38.

Trachtenberg, Alan. *The Incorporation of America: Culture and Society in the Gilded Age*. New York: Hill and Wang-Farrar, 1982. Print.

Walters, Wendy W. "Limited Options: Strategic Maneuverings in Himes's Harlem." *African American Review* 28 (1994): 615-31. Print.

# 3 Who's Got the Car Keys?

Geographic, Economic, and Social Mobility in the

Magic Kingdom of Los Angeles

> By the mid-twentieth century, if not soon-
> er, virgin cities had begun to replace virgin
> land in the minds of many Westerners as
> the key image in defining the region.
> JOHN FINDLAY/*MAGIC LANDS*

In his study of Western U.S. cities, John Findlay identifies a way to read
the twentieth-century American cities of the West as "magic kingdoms," of
which Disneyland is the primary example. According to Findlay's use of
term, a magic kingdom is a specially designed public site within a Western
U.S. city, and upon which the city relies for its own identity, that attempts
"to exclude diversity and misery from their idealized settings, substituting
in their stead a world indexed to the middle-class standards of an affluent
society" (9). Consciously setting themselves apart from older Eastern cities,
these magic kingdoms conceived of themselves as "refuges from the aesthetic and ecological realities of cities," such as minority and working-class
residents (Findlay 9). Extending Findlay's argument to the earlier part of
the century, this chapter will demonstrate that Los Angeles was constructed
by city "boosters" and Los Angeles novels as a magic kingdom free of the
"problems" of the public sphere created by the immigrant and poor residents of other large American cities. The Los Angeles novels of the 1930s
build upon those images of Los Angeles as a magic kingdom, erasing the
pasts and presence of Indian, Mexican, and other communities of color
while at the same time depicting the successful upward mobility of the Jew-

ish immigrants who founded the Hollywood studios. Findlay's magic kingdom is a useful way to read the city of Los Angeles as it functions in the novels and culture of the 1930s because it illuminates the utopian "magic" city's dependence on the elision of racial and class differences, represented as private issues that have no place in public space or discourse. I will use Findlay's term to refer to the specifically Western character of the utopian city of Los Angeles, as it is imagined in the novels and in the rest of the country, and to contrast it with the lack of attention paid to the lived reality of Native and Mexican Americans in the city. The magic kingdom devises a way to include Native and Mexican Americans without having to actually engage with them socially: by creating commodified "Old West" and "Spanish" styles for white consumption in the public spaces of the city, specifically its commercial sphere.

Los Angeles played a crucial role in the production of U.S. public culture in the period from 1930-45, as a geographical location and as an imaginary site. During the Depression and the war years, moving into the middle classes became more of an obsession than ever before, and when work and food were scarce the country looked for inspiration to images of people who were "going places" and the technological innovations that would carry them into a brighter future. Los Angeles texts of this period, along with the history and geography of the city, provided those images and articulated the national desire for class mobility as well as the consumer desire for physical mobility in the form of the automobile. Recurring tropes of mobility in the fiction and film of the period also figure prominently in the economic and social developments in Hollywood and the wider national culture between 1930 and 1945. This chapter offers ways to read the presence of multiple colonial pasts in fictional texts that center around the "magic land" of Los Angeles, including the city's public and private spaces—architecture, decor, industries, and urban planning. In Los Angeles novels, the city's history links into three discernible narratives of mobility: geographic, in terms of urban expansion, migration, and immigration; economic, in terms of the rags to riches myth that beckoned immigrants from all over the country and the world; and social, in terms of acceptance and assimilation into the dominant culture. These texts not only circulate images of mobility, they also provide the scene on which thwarted desires for mobility are played out. Images of mobility in Hollywood films and Los Angeles novels participate in the ways in which class and geographic movement operate in the national imagination. Ironically, the images of the highway and the automobile (a strange combination of privacy within public space) in many of these texts signal negative mobility and lack of access to the highways of modernity, even in the freeway city of Los Angeles.

The literary phenomenon known as the Los Angeles novel has its origins in Helen Hunt Jackson's 1884 novel *Ramona*, but David Fine dates its birth in the 1930s, when the movie studios attracted writers from all over the country to furnish scripts for the newly introduced "talkies" (Introduction 2). These writers, including James M. Cain, Raymond Chandler, Nathanael West, and F. Scott Fitzgerald, not only created treatments, dialogue, and screenplays for studios, they also "wrote novels that gave the city its metaphoric shape, [and] established a way of reading the Southern California landscape" (Fine, Introduction 2). Cain's and Chandler's novels are set in Los Angeles without specifically centering around Hollywood, while West, Fitzgerald, and Budd Schulberg (a Hollywood native) use the setting and metaphors of the movie capitol to describe the corruption and falsity of the city and of the nation as a whole. For the purposes of this chapter, I consider a Los Angeles novel one that is set in the city; a subset of this genre is the Hollywood novel, which takes as its primary subject the film industry of Los Angeles, located in the popular imaginary site of Hollywood. Thus, a Hollywood novel is by definition a Los Angeles novel, but a Los Angeles novel may or may not be a Hollywood novel.

The first section of this chapter examines the ways in which twentieth-century white Angelenos in Los Angeles novels romanticize their "magic" city's past as a "Spanish colony," eliding the history of Southern California as a Native American settlement and later a territory of independent Mexico, while Native and Mexican American residents are invisible or severely stereotyped in Los Angeles novels and marginalized geographically and economically in the public spaces of the city itself. The second section considers the Los Angeles novels' representations of mobility narratives pertaining to the Hollywood Jews, the immigrant founders of the major studios and their particularly Los Angeles-based, and often self-consciously public, experiences of Americanization and assimilation, in contrast to the experiences of the Mexican Americans in Los Angeles at the same time period. The chapter concludes with an explication of the mobility trope as it pertains to whites living and working in Los Angeles. The city represents for many of them the pinnacle of Western expansion, modernity, and speed—a trope concentrated in recurrent images of public mobility in the form of automobiles and freeways. But for others, Los Angeles also embodies the corruption and contradictions at the heart of the American Dream.

## "SPANISH STYLE": COLONIAL PASTS AND PRESENCE IN 1930S LOS ANGELES

The history of Los Angeles is marked by mobility narratives, from the conquistadors to the Okies. The geographic movements of people from Europe, other regions of the U.S., and Mexico to the "magic land" of Los Angeles are represented quite differently in the Los Angeles novels of the 1930s and 40s, ranging from heroic and steadfast to malevolent and corrupt. Predictably, all of the positive representations of migrants depict white Europeans and Americans, including assimilated Jews, although some representations critique the Midwesterners who dominated Los Angeles's social and political life in the 30s. The less flattering images are reserved for raced and classed "others" including less assimilated Jews and Native and Mexican Americans, when they are represented at all. The parallel experiences of Jews compared with Native and Mexican Americans afford interesting contrasts when they attempt to participate in the dominant culture of Los Angeles, and the Los Angeles novels provide numerous examples of these contrasts. The virtual absence of fully developed Mexican and Native American characters in the Los Angeles novels speaks to their invisibility in the city's wider culture, while the commodification of "Spanish" or "Old West" architecture and decorating trends for white consumption illustrates the elaborate distancing techniques needed to excise them from the "magic" city's identity.

The Pierces' red tile roof and stucco facade in James M. Cain's *Mildred Pierce* and Homer Simpson's galleon-motif living room decor in Nathanael West's *The Day of the Locust* promote the illusion that California's past was populated by white Spanish missionaries, cowboys, and happy converted Indians, erasing the racial violence and labor exploitation of that earlier time as well as the continued marginalization of the city's Mexican population into the 1930s, when repatriation of thousands of Mexicans was subsidized by the Los Angeles city government. Bert and Mildred Pierce have a "Spanish" style living room with a "crimson velvet coat of arms," "drapes, hung on iron spears," and paintings of western scenes including "a butte at sunset," a cowboy, and a covered wagon (Cain 104). And although Homer Simpson's "Irish" cottage has "New England Farmhouse" style bedrooms, the living room is "Spanish" with a model galleon on the mantel, "wall fixtures in the shape of galleons with pointed amber bulbs projecting from their decks," and a table lamp "that had several more galleons painted on it" (West 287). The reduction of history, even mythologized history, to a decorator's fad on such a massive scale that Cain's narrator calls it "the standard living room sent out by department stores as suitable for a Spanish bungalow" still contains in its symbols an unquestioned imperialism (104). The galleons, covered wagons, cowboys, iron spears, and coat of arms simultaneously connote past European colonialism and the continued colonization of North America by the United States. The actual historical background for the "Spanish" bungalows in Los Angeles was the armed conquest and subsequent settling of the Western United States by systematic movements of "explorers," troops, and colonists across oceans, deserts, and permeable national boundaries.

The prominence of these symbolic motifs from three different centuries of Los Angeles history in middle-class living rooms in the 1930s affirms what Gesa Mackenthun calls "an asynchronous temporality in which the present is shot through with memories of a past that keeps encroaching upon the living" (269) and, furthermore, articulates a desire to assimilate the past into innocuous mass-produced decoration. In Cain's novel *Mildred Pierce*, Bert Pierce built his "Spanish" bungalow on land he developed into a residential subdivision during the real estate boom of the 1920s; up until 1848, when most of the large ranchos were subdivided, the land was probably a part of land grants to Mexican settlers. But the tenacity of the "Spanish" myth in 1930s California popular culture and architecture attests to the strength of the symbols of colonial mobility and power: the galleon and the covered wagon carrying the white race and nation to its manifest destiny in the West. At the same time, less appealing and picturesque forms of mobility, such as that of displaced Native and Mexican Americans remain underrepresented in the Los Angeles novels and invisible to the residents of the city at the time. White European and American geographical movements are noble acts of Manifest Destiny, whereas Mexican border-crossings are altogether more threatening. Some Los Angeles novels represent white migrants—usually Midwesterners—to the city in a critical light, often caricaturing them as unsophisticated and conservative, but Mexican American characters come across as far less sympathetic.

One of the few Mexican American characters in a Los Angeles novel of the 1930s is Mig in Nathanael West's *The Day of the Locust* (1939). He is first described by the narrator as "toffee-colored with large Armenian eyes and pouting black lips," although the reader infers that he is Mexican because of his nickname, short for Miguel, and the Spanish greeting he uses (328). He raises birds for cock fighting, drinks tequila, and eventually has an affair with Faye, the femme fatale in the novel. As the protagonist, Tod, watches him around a campfire, he realizes that Faye and Miguel are flirting. Tod's perception of Miguel's sexual threat is expressed in racial terms:

[...] the Mexican sat full in the light of the fire. His skin glowed and the oil in his black curls sparkled. He kept smiling at Faye in a manner that Tod didn't like. The more he drank, the less he liked it. (331)

Miguel's racial difference is clearly stressed in these passages: his "toffee-colored" skin that "glowed" in the firelight and his sparkling black curls attract Tod's notice as well as Faye's. The only Mexican American character in the novel, Miguel conforms to racist stereotypes of Mexicans, and his sexual power only increases the hostility of the white men who already dislike him. Although a minor character with little development, Miguel's facial features are described in painstaking detail—much more so than other more central characters—and in terms that draw attention to his ethnicity. The narrator refers to Miguel as "the Mexican" interchangeably with his name, as though he were only an embodiment of his national or racial origin, an archetype of Mexico. Miguel has named his cocks for figures in Mexican national history, including Villa and Zapata, but his transient presence in the novel doesn't allow his character to develop any real identity.

Apparently homeless and unemployed but not seeking work, Miguel lives in a camp in the Hollywood hills with a cowboy named Earle, although they later move into Homer Simpson's garage with the birds. Homer finds the situation distressing, especially the hen: "You never saw such a disgusting thing, the way it squats and turns its head. The roosters have torn all the feathers off its neck and made its comb all bloody and it has scabby feet covered with warts and it cackles so nasty" (372). Homer then compares the hen to Miguel: "He's almost as bad as his hen" (372). Homer's distaste for the hen is linked to his discomfort around Miguel, who in turn taunts Homer because he knows he dislikes the hen: "he tries to make me look just for spite. I go into the house, but he taps on the windows and calls me to come out and watch" (372). Homer is intimidated by the implications of sexual violence that the hen represents, and Miguel enjoys tormenting him with the spectacle of the bloody hen; for Homer, Miguel comes to stand for the repressed sexual aggression he fears in himself. Like the Mexican American residents of white-dominated Los Angeles in the 1930s, his main function in the novel is local color and confirming the stereotypes of whites—he is a homeless cockfighter with oiled hair who seduces white women.

The only Native American character in *The Day of the Locust* ironically parrots white attitudes toward Mexicans, arguing in the most blatantly racist language in the novel that "they were all bad" (405). As Tod listens to this debate, another character argues that "he had known quite a few good ones in his time" (405). After the Indian cites "the case of the Hermanos brothers who had killed a lonely prospector for half a dollar," the other man replies with an anecdote about "Tomas Lopez who shared his last pint of water with a stranger when they were both lost in the desert" (405). Tod wants to find out about Miguel and Faye, so he interjects his opinion that "Mexicans are very good with women" (405). To his dismay, the Indian answers that they are "better with horses" and follows that tangent instead (405). Eventually Tod coaxes more information from them, discovering that Earle claims he fought Miguel because "the Mex robbed him while he was sleeping" (405). The Indian replies, "The dirty, thievin' rat" and spits (406). The Indian character is a convenient vehicle for displacing anti-Mexican sentiment away from whites and onto a comic, archaic figure. West plays up the irony of the Indian's racism by describing him as similarly typecast and marketing his own caricatured cultural identity. Although the Indian hates Mexicans and he refers to Miguel as a "dirty greaser," he wears a sandwich board advertising "Tuttle's Trading Post for Genuine Relics of the Old West" and laughs when introduced to Tod as "Chief Kiss-My-Towkus," to which he answers frankly, "You gotta live" (405). At the trading post he sells souvenirs, including "Beads, Silver, Jewelry, Moccasins, Dolls, Toys, Rare Books, Postcards" (404). Like the city of Los Angeles creating an "Old Mexico" tourist attraction on Olvera Street, the only Native American character makes his living literally selling emblems of his commodified culture to tourists. His "relics of the Old West" suggest a mythological Californian past, but the real past and present of Native Americans in California is invisible in the novel.

Although there are few Native or Mexican American characters in the other Los Angeles novels, the city's mythological Spanish past comes up frequently. Al Manheim, the narrator of Budd Schulberg's Hollywood novel, *What Makes Sammy Run?*, explains his attraction to the idea of Hollywood:

I was anxious to investigate the persistent rumors that the 'streets paved with gold' which the early Spanish explorers had hunted in vain had suddenly appeared in the vicinity of Hollywood and Vine. I was half convinced that Southern California was really the modern Garden of Eden its press agents claimed it to be. (32)

Manheim's musings refer to the ways in which twentieth century Los Angeles "boosters" played up the romantic historical past of Spanish colonialism without reference to either the area's past Mexican political rule or the Mexican American communities still resident there. Like the European colonizers, Al contemplates Los Angeles as an empty space, a "Garden of Eden," that could be a source of personal wealth rather than as a place that has been home to an indigenous population of Indians for 20,000 years and Mexican Americans for nearly two centuries.

The European colonization of the Los Angeles area officially began when Spain claimed the area with explorations in 1769 and the first colonists in 1781 (del Castillo 4-5). Many of the most successful early "Spanish" settlers, known as Californios, were farmers from the northern Mexican desert who saw themselves as nominally Mexican but isolated and largely cut off from the rest of the Mexican state. After failed attempts to lure more colonists to the dry, distant California outpost, the Spanish colonial government forced the immigration of convicts and orphans in 1825, 1829, and 1830, much to the chagrin of the comfortable, class-conscious Californios, who were by then concerned with maintaining their large ranchos and the purity of their "Spanish" blood in the midst of the newly arrived Mexicans, whom they saw as *cholos* (low class) and thieves (del Castillo 6-10). While the Californios had maintained a distinction between themselves and the resident Native American tribes, collectively named Gabrielinos after the mission established there, the dividing lines became more rigid as the area grew in population. The Indians had first arrived 20,000 years earlier; by 1770, there were approximately 5000 Indians living in the Los Angeles basin (del Castillo 1-2). Although the first Mexican settlers often intermarried with the Indians and adopted aspects of their cultural knowledge, particularly medicine and agriculture, by 1836 they forced the Indians into segregated villages increasingly distant from the Mexican town (del Castillo 3). After conversion to U.S. statehood in 1850, Indian prisoners, who were often arrested randomly or for the slightest infractions, were sold to the highest bidder for private service in weekly public auctions; the practice continued through 1869, when high death rates had finally decimated Indian population (Robinson 45-46).

In his letters of 1852, Hugo Reid describes the effects of the breakup of the missions on the Indians of the Los Angeles area during the transition from Mexican colony to American territory and then statehood (Heizer). His perspective on the Indian situation is clear in his assertions that the Indians suffered, not because of the abrupt political and economic changes or maltreatment by whites, but because of the Mexicans, "Sonoreños" who exercised a bad influence on them in the absence of beneficent white missionaries:

These Sonoreños overran this country. They invaded the rancheria, gambled with the men and taught them to steal; they taught the women to be worse than they were, and men and women both to drink. Now we do not mean or pretend to say that the [Indians] were not previous to this addicted both to drinking and gaming, with an inclination to steal, while under the dominion of the church; but the Sonoreños most certainly brought them to a pitch of licentiousness before unparalleled in their history. (qtd. in Heizer 99)

Reid's racial hierarchy apparently places Mexicans below Indians, although he sees that he is skirting self-contradiction by almost claiming the Indians were innocents; since they were only recently Christianized their morality was fragile, but the Sonorans "overran" the area like an army of pests and unraveled the limited victories of the church, corrupting the Indians. Unwilling to acknowledge the impact of American expansion on the Native American tribes of the Los Angeles area, Reid prefers to interpret the social problems in the Indian community as a result of an outside influence—he projects that bad influence onto Mexicans in order to maintain his superiority and avoid any accountability for his presence in California.

## WHITE CITY: LOS ANGELES IN THE 20TH CENTURY

It is ironic, then, that the romantic nostalgia for Old Spain pervades the white culture of Los Angeles throughout the booming first third of the twentieth century, in spite of the fact that the city's history complicates such a misreading of the past. The historical basis for the "Spanish" founders myth crumbles when we consider that of the 23 adults who founded Los Angeles in 1781, eight were Indian, ten were of African descent, and one was Filipino; of the 21 children, 19 were mixed race and two were full-blooded Indians (Ríos-Bustamente and Castillo 33). The enforced homogeneity of the magic Los Angeles cannot reconcile the "Spanish" past with the Mexican realities of the twentieth century city, so it transforms the living culture into a commodified "style." Nevertheless, as George Sánchez points out, "it was the middle-class midwesterner . . . who dominated the public culture and politics of the city during the early twentieth century," and who preferred the "Spanish" motif in architecture and decor (91). The substitution of a contrived "Spanish" style for economic and social acceptance of real Mexican Americans illustrates the enduring imperative for homogeneity and the increasing consumerism of the white elites in 1930s Los Angeles. As Monroe Stahr in *The Last Tycoon* explains the business of the movies, "we have to take people's own favorite folklore and dress it up and give it back to them," white Los Angeles dressed up Mexican culture and put it up for sale (Fitzgerald 105).

Meanwhile the city's population had quadrupled between 1910 and 1930, leaping from 319,000 to 1.24 million (Sánchez 71). Among the newcomers were eugenics enthusiasts who flocked there hoping to found a white enclave far from the growing immigrant populations of the East coast, where the warm sun would "reinvigorate the racial energies of the Anglo-Saxons" (Davis 27). As Perley Poore Sheehan's 1924 book *Hollywood as a World Center* makes clear, Los Angeles represented a new kind of American city, without the cross-cultural complications of older, more ethnically mixed East Coast cities: "They are pleasant folk, these neighbors of yours in Hollywood. They speak English. [...] They keep their own places beautiful and are concerned with the beauty of the street. They are lovers of flowers and birds" (37). Writing as if slum-dwellers in New York or Boston don't love flowers and birds, Sheehan constructs a race-inflected class distinction between "Aryan" Angelinos and residents of other cities who don't speak English and who are presumably less "concerned with the beauty of the street" than with daily survival of their families. The city represents "the end of the trail" for the "last great migration of the Aryan race" (Sheehan 1). Sheehan's Hollywood participates in the identity maneuvers of Findlay's magic kingdoms: Los Angeles is described as a Western utopia consciously different from other U.S. cities, where immigrants and the poor inhibit the magic new city from evolving. Sheehan's magic city, where people speak English, conforms to Findlay's definition of a magic kingdom, which is "less troubled by urban problems and more open to improvements in metropolitan design, social relations, and styles of living," including the elusive flowers and birds (Findlay 2). The connection between livable new urban spaces and racial and class homogeneity marks the history of the American Western city, beginning well before Findlay's chosen time period of the 1950s; the founders of Los Angeles had it in mind as early as the 1880s, and the population explosion of the 1920s and 30s only exacerbated the competing identities of the city, as the self-styled magic kingdom, but also as a real-life multicultural amalgam of American, Mexican, and other cultures.

The gradual whitening of Los Angeles continued throughout the 20s and 30s as thousands of Midwesterners moved to sunny single-family homes in and around the city, bringing with them their "Aryan" and Puritan values: temperance, religious conversion, and strict social mores (Sánchez 91). Nathanael West satirizes the Midwestern flavor of 1930s Los Angeles in *The Day of the Locust*, in which Homer Simpson is a Midwestern migrant whose gold-digger girlfriend leaves him for Miguel, the heavily stereotyped Mexican cockfighter. The apocalyptic ending of the 1939 novel stages a riot at a movie premiere in which the "lower middle classes" go on a rampage, providing Tod with a perfect experience upon which to base his painting, "The Burning of Los Angeles" (410). He muses that the Midwesterners who move to Los Angeles are not "harmless curiosity seekers," but actually "arrogant and pugnacious" and "savage and bitter" (411). Playing on the Edenic images of California, West paints a vivid picture of the disillusionment that awaits the retirees, who had "slaved at some kind of dull, heavy labor, behind desks and counters, in the fields and at tedious machines of all sorts, saving their pennies and dreaming of the leisure that would be theirs" (411). All the years of delayed gratification build up to a disappointment of epic proportions, as the migrants move to California but cannot adapt to a life of leisure: "They get tired of oranges, even of avocado pears and passion fruit" (411). The boredom turns the Midwesterners mean, and they begin to feed on violence in the news and movies: "lynchings, murder, sex crimes, explosions, wrecks, love nests, fires, miracles, revolutions, war. [...] Nothing can ever be violent enough to make taut their slack minds and bodies" (412). The disillusionment of the retirees and their thirst for sensationalist images are ultimately responsible for the riot, since the crowd originally assembles to try to glimpse the stars attending a movie premiere. West's dark vision of the city centers on the corruptions of Hollywood, but he refuses to make a false distinction between the movie industry and a mythical idyllic Midwest. Indeed, the riot is the result of those people who "come to California to die; the cultists of all sorts, economic as well as religious, the wave, airplane, funeral, and preview watchers—all those poor devils who can only be stirred by the promise of miracles and then only to violence" (420). Unlike Hugo Reid's scapegoating of the Sonoran Mexicans, West ascribes the ugliness of Los Angeles to white Americans, culminating in a violent mob scene.

In 1930, 37 out of every 100 American-born Angelinos were from the Midwest; the majority were from Ohio, Indiana, Illinois, Iowa, Nebraska, Missouri, Kansas, Michigan, and Wisconsin (Sánchez 88). Newly transplanted Iowans, for example, established "state societies" that held picnics to help one another adjust to their Los Angeles lives and maintain their Midwestern identities; many midwesterners from other states followed suit (Sánchez 92). As West sarcastically writes, "Did they slave so long just to go to an occasional Iowa picnic?" (411). His character Homer Simpson comes from "a little town near Des Moines, Iowa, called Wayneville, where he had worked for twenty years in a hotel" (286). After a bout with pneumonia, Homer moves to California on the advice of his doctor and rents an inexpensive "Irish" cottage in Pinyon Canyon—the realtor explains that "the people who took cottages in that neighborhood wanted them to be 'Spanish'" rather than Irish, so Homer's rent is low (287). The effect of the waves of Midwestern migrants on the culture of Los Angeles is far-reaching, as Carey McWilliams writes in his landmark 1946 study, "One could make a book of the Iowa jokes heard in Southern California. [...] On meeting in Southern California, strangers were supposed to inquire: 'What part of Iowa are you from?'" (170). But the impact of such a large Midwestern contingent also affected the city's Mexican American communities, usually adversely.

In addition to their religious and cultural differences with the prior population, the influx of American Protestants also intensified the suburbanization of the city: "ruralize the city; urbanize the country" was the motto of the head of city housing as early as 1910 (Sánchez 92). In the process of developing the magic city of Los Angeles into a utopian white middle-class enclave, medical metaphors of sickness and ailing health came into play, as editorials described the poor and non-white neighborhoods in terms of traffic fever, urban blight, and tooth decay whose remedy was removal and thorough antiseptic cleaning (Klein 14). One such campaign led to the construction of the Union Station next to the Placita in 1934, necessitating the demolition of parts of Chinatown and the Mexican American neighborhood. Another 1930s urban "restoration" involved the movement to create an "Old Mexico" tourist area on Olvera Street. As Sánchez describes it, "the restoration was completed at the very moment when thousands of Mexicans were being prodded to repatriate" (226). For Mexican residents, the Union Station project and the Olvera Street development clearly delineated their role in the city: "Mexicans were being assigned a place in the mythic past of Los Angeles—one that could be relegated to a quaint section of the city destined to delight tourists and antiquarians" (Sánchez 226). These projects had mixed results for the Mexican American community: their residential neighborhoods were forced farther from the central downtown area and farther from racially mixed and Anglo neighborhoods, while their culture was commodified for tourists and at the same time ignored and marginalized by white fellow residents of Los Angeles. Like Miguel in *The Day of the Locust*, Mexican Angelenos were minor characters in the story of the city, only acknowledged in the most patronizing and least respectful ways and only when it benefited the white city officials and residents.

## "FROM POLAND TO POLO IN ONE GENERATION": MOBILITY NARRATIVES OF THE HOLLYWOOD JEWS

Fitzgerald's Hollywood novel, *The Last Tycoon*, tries to negotiate between anti-Semitic stereotypes and the real Jews who created the Hollywood system. His narrator Celia, daughter of an Irish-American industry executive, describes a minor character, Manny Schwartz, as visibly Hollywood because he looks Jewish and greedy: "a middle-aged Jew" (4), who "stares with shameless economic lechery" at Monroe Stahr (6). Celia further describes Schwartz's appearance more specifically, how his "exaggerated Persian nose and oblique eye-shadow were as congenital as the tip-tilted Irish redness around my father's nostrils" (7). She ascribes his Jewishness to his appearance but she also reads his greed, his "economic lechery," as a Jewish characteristic, playing into the anti-Semitic rhetoric of Jews as not only greedy but also sexually deviant or lecherous. Schwartz's character commits suicide in the childhood home of a former U.S. president, and Celia balks at the connection of the two men: "Manny Schwartz and Andrew Jackson—it was hard to say them in the same sentence" (13). Jackson, symbol of the Gilded Age, might actually be an appropriate figure for a Hollywood executive, but Celia seems reluctant to consider Schwartz a real American: instead she focuses on his immigrant identity, assuming that "he had come a long way from some ghetto to present himself at that raw shrine" (13). Again Schwartz is described in religious terms, as if he has embarked on a pilgrimage to the "raw shrine" of Andrew Jackson. However, as Celia's narrative of Schwartz amply demonstrates, the financial success of an immigrant Jew in Hollywood was no guarantee of acceptance as an American, or even as a member of the middle class. Schwartz represents the first generation of Hollywood Jews, whose foreign accents and mannerisms marked them as outsiders in American culture; their children and successors, the second generation, were much more assimilated and Americanized.

The theory that American Jews, particularly the second generation, are somehow different from European Jews arises in several Hollywood novels, including *The Last Tycoon* and Budd Schulberg's *What Makes Sammy Run?* Both novels attempt to invalidate anti-Semitic stereotypes while at the same time exploring what Schulberg and Fitzgerald imply is a new type of Jew: the Hollywood Jew. In Schulberg's novel, Sammy Glick isn't simply the ambitious, money-hungry Jew of the anti-Semites, although he can be read according to that stereotype; rather, he is described as a truly Americanized, capitalist Jew, who denies his Jewishness if it will help him get a job. In *The Last Tycoon*, several Jewish characters, including Manny Schwartz, do conform to stereotypes although the protagonist Stahr does not; exposed to this range of Jewish characters, other characters ponder the inflexibility of anti-Semitic stereotypes, wondering if American Jews really are a departure from the stereotypes of European Jews. Both these novels raise the problem of anti-Semitism in the context of the Horatio Alger myth of American Dream: to be a successful American, an immigrant must work hard and save money, but if a Jewish immigrant displays this ambition, it is seen as greed. The challenges both novels present are not only to anti-Semitism but to the contradictions inherent in the American Dream itself. In the 1930s, the Hollywood Jews were uniquely positioned at the intersection of assimilation, financial success, and "Americanness" on the one hand, and the powerful image-making and nation-building industry of the movies on the other. Neal Gabler has shown that the early Hollywood Jews had a "ferocious, even pathological, embrace of America" due in part to their incomplete acceptance as immigrants (4). His study of the "empire" created by the Hollywood Jews explores the paradoxical relation between immigrants and America in the movie business: "that the movies were quintessentially American while the men who made them were not" and that nevertheless "American values came to be *defined* largely by the movies the Jews made" (7). One of Gabler's most convincing examples of this paradox is the "small-town America" series of Andy Hardy films made with Mickey Rooney and Judy Garland, which were the brainchild of Louis B. Mayer, the Russian Jewish immigrant and founder of MGM (215-16). My reading of the 1930s Hollywood novels works through a similar paradox—that the values considered to be definitively American were inextricably linked to the qualities that informed anti-Semitic images of Jews, and that both these sets of values were to a large degree fueled by class anxieties. Interestingly, however, the mobility narratives of the Hollywood Jews in *What Makes Sammy Run?* and *The Last Tycoon* rarely acknowledge the fact that the American Dream they embrace also drives the expansionist imperialism that founded Los Angeles and disenfranchised Native and Mexican Americans in the process, even when one character's class consciousness develops through his association with the embryonic union movement for Hollywood writers.

In Schulberg's novel, Al Manheim struggles with his feelings for Sammy Glick, trying to figure out what makes him run, how he got to be so ambitious and driven. At the root of Al's concerns about Sammy is his own Jewish identity: he wants to differentiate himself from Sammy without falling into anti-Semitic rhetoric, so he finds other differences between them, namely class. Al's initial opinion of Sammy is clearly rooted in class antagonism, based on what he sees as Sammy's residue of working-class immigrant coarseness. He continually judges Sammy in terms of class: he is "cheap" and tasteless, son of European Jews who settled in Rivington Street tenements on New York's Lower East Side, in contrast to Al, who grew up in New England with his middle-class rabbi father. Retreating into class prejudices, Al attempts to explain Sammy's nature as a result of his ghetto childhood, but when Al's involvement with Hollywood labor struggles awakens his class consciousness he realizes that poverty isn't fully responsible for shaping Sammy. He discovers that Sammy is the quintessential modern American businessman, and his Jewishness and his working-class origins are only secondary markers—they don't explain him.

Al, a theater reporter, first meets Sammy when he is an office boy at Al's New York newspaper. He is horrified by Sammy's blind lust for power and wealth, which Al identifies with Sammy's street-urchin manner and "dog eat dog" ethics (75). Al grew up in New England, son of a Reformed rabbi, attended a Methodist college, and doesn't go regularly to temple. His father's kindly middle-class morality and sense of fair-play still influence him, though without specifically religious ramifications. In fact, in an ironic construction, Al refers to his father's character as a "Christ-like gentility" (20). Al is repulsed by Sammy's "cheapness," the way his class origins in the tenements mark him as inferior to more assimilated, middle-class Jews like himself. When Sammy engineers a publicity stunt to get his name in the paper, Al's rhetoric echoes the class-centered discourses of the 1930s: "Don't be cheap. Cheapness is the curse of our times. You're beginning to spread cheapness around like bad toilet water," to which Sammy replies, "Sure it was cheap. [...] After all, I got better publicity free than you could have bought for big dough" (22). The word "cheap" has different meanings for the two men from such different class backgrounds: for Sammy, cheap is good—it means affordable, while for Al it means the ugliness of poverty, tasteless. Indeed, Gabler describes the Hollywood Jews as "aggressively tasteful rather than boorish," and Sammy strives to achieve tastefulness as his career takes off (240).

Soon afterwards Sammy begins to recognize the importance of class-based "taste" that Al tries to teach him and manifests his class mobility through his constantly upgraded shoes, which tie in with the controlling metaphor of the novel, "running," as in the novel's title, *What Makes Sammy Run?*. His class mobility, which he attains by "running" non-stop, making deals, and exploiting everyone he can, is symbolized by his shoes throughout the novel. Sammy tries to change his class identity the way he changes shoes, from the "new pair of $7.50 black flanged shoes" he buys with his first windfall (18), to the trendy Mexican *huaraches* given to him by his first director (37), to the elaborate procedure in his bedroom where a custom fitter measures his feet and suggests making a plaster cast so that his "designers can draw up any style shoe you wish and you're sure of getting a one-hundred-percent perfect fit" (205). By the time Sammy is a studio executive, he buys the most expensive shoes he can find because he believes that they mark him as successful and powerful. He recognizes that his public consumption is a register of his class status, as Al comes to understand witnessing Sammy's outrageous public spending. One night in a chic nightclub, Sammy buys everyone champagne and "blew five hundred bucks at the crap table (and told everyone it was a thousand)" (94). Al is mortified by this gross show of affluence as his companion analyzes Sammy's actions in a sociological perspective: "Kit tried to explain that it wasn't really a loss because a guy called Veblen said we make our reputations by how much money we publicly throw away" (94). Sammy's intuitive understanding of consumerism and class perception keeps him "running" through his money, knowing that earning a reputation as a big spender is as much about social power as it is about mere cash money. Al's middle-class taboos against conspicuous consumption add to his desire to distance himself from Sammy, but Kit pushes him to see Sammy in a wider social context.

In his attempts to distinguish himself from Sammy, Al constantly compares Sammy to other Jews, including himself, trying to find out what makes him run. The comparisons never yield a satisfying answer, however, since Sammy represents the top of the evolutionary pyramid in Al's version of social Darwinism. After witnessing Sammy call an agent in Hollywood and finagle a reading for a story out of thin air, Al compares himself to Sammy: they are "both columnists, both Jewish, both men, both American citizens" but they live in what Al sees as completely separate worlds (27). Moreover, Al needs to distance himself from Sammy's "dishonesty, officiousness, bullying," because those qualities contradict his idealistic notion of a good American, one who plays fair and succeeds by following the rules. But class distinctions often play into anti-Semitic stereotypes, as second generation Hollywood Jew Betty Lasky illustrates in her description of the older Warner brothers: "They were very animalistic types. I wasn't used to types like that—the ghetto types. [...] They were so ugly-looking but so ghetto ugly. [...] It was like a child going to a circus and looking at a freak" (qtd. in Gabler 239). Lasky, whose father raised her with a French governess in a completely sheltered aristocratic existence, devises a simile that suggests the specular nature of the relationship: she is the normal "child" at the circus looking at the "freak," who is ostensibly as human as she is, yet so utterly deformed as to be almost unrecognizable, causing her to doubt or deny any kinship. Growing up in relative comfort, far from the tenements, middle- and upper-class Jews like Lasky and Al Manheim are aware of the differences between themselves and "ghetto types" but have difficulty explaining it to themselves except through references to "types" and class.

Al's visit with Sammy's mother and brother in the old neighborhood suggests to Al "the irony of the fascist charge that the Jews have cornered the wealth of America" (179). The traditions of the old Eastern European Jewish communities translated slowly into American market capitalism, and Al associates the traditional Jews with age and obsolescence. Compared to his brother Sammy Glick, Israel Glickstein is another kind of Jewish man, devout, caring, and community-minded, but he also seems to Al "like an aged Jew in prayer. [...] like an old, bent man with a young face" (181). Israel has stayed true to the old traditions and works at a settlement house trying to keep the Lower East Side community together. Marking his difference, Al notices that he speaks "without an accent but with the wailing tone and cadence of the Jewish chants" (184). The old-fashioned character of Sammy's family also extends to his mother, who speaks more comfortably in Yiddish than English. Al recounts her ideas about Sammy: "In the old country there may have been Jews who were thieves or tightwads and rich Jews who would not talk to poor ones, but she had never seen one like Sammy" (194). The new American Jew doesn't fit the old definitions—he isn't religious and feels no loyalty to other Jews—but he does subscribe to the American mobility myth that hard work brings success. Al concludes that, in order achieve success in America, ambitious Jews like Sammy reject the traditions that are

> withering away in America, for the customs and the traditions that the Glicksteins brought over at the end of the nineteenth century may have been inherited by Israel, droning in his *yarmolka* at my side, but were thrown overboard as excess baggage by anyone in such a hurry as his younger brother. (184)

Employing the metaphor of the immigrant's ocean voyage, Al describes the modern ambitious Sammy as hurrying, willing to jettison any and all of his culture to speed his success. The geographical metaphor of immigrants on ships represents Sammy's class mobility, which Al sees as his "running" after profit at the expense of those middle-class values Al holds dear: civility, modesty, sensitivity.

Al's reading of Sammy also emerges through his knowledge of poor Jews who fail to succeed—men who share many of the core values Al sees in himself and whose scruples prevent them from attaining the kind of success that Sammy claims for himself. Al compares Sammy to ghost writer Julian Blumberg, who is "just about the same age, [...] probably brought up in the same kind of Jewish family, same neighborhood, same schooling, and started out with practically the same job. And yet they couldn't be more different" (96). Julian represents for Al the proof that anti-Semitic stereotypes are untenable: he is one of those "Jews without money, without push, without plots, without any of the characteristics which such experts as Adolph [sic] Hitler, Henry Ford, and Father Coughlin try to tell us are racial traits" (96). There are simply "too many Jewish nebs and poets and starving tailors and everyday little guys, to consider the fascist answer to What Makes Sammy Run?" (96). But when Al can't explain Sammy the individual simply by his Jewish identity or his ghetto roots, he turns to sociological explanations.

By the end of the novel Al decides that Sammy is only the logical result of the American capitalist system that fosters ghettoes like Rivington Street, which are "allowed to pile up in cities like gigantic dung heaps smelling up the world, ambitions growing out of filth and crawling away like worms" (203). Sammy isn't an anomaly, he's the natural product of the competitive market:

I realized that I had singled him out not because he had been born into the world any more selfish, ruthless and cruel than anybody else, even though he had become all three, but because in the midst of a war that was selfish, ruthless and cruel Sammy was proving himself the fittest, the fiercest and the fastest. (203)

Al recognizes that Sammy isn't Sammy just because he was born a poor Jew—his brother is nothing like him although from the same family. He rules out Hollywood as a bad influence, since Julian works for the studios, too, and still has a conscience. Finally, Al attributes Sammy's ruthless "running" to the values at the root of American free enterprise. The notion that the harder you work the more successful you will be has become in Sammy a pathology that has blocked his abilities to experience what Al sees as "human" existence—love, happiness, generosity—in any terms other than profit-oriented. As this realization dawns on him, Al remarks that he "could almost hear the motor in [Sammy] beginning to pick up speed again" (246). Sammy's "running" carries him up the ladder in the studios to executive status, but ultimately, for Al, this "running" forms a "blueprint of a way of life that was paying dividends in America in the first half of the twentieth century" (247). As Sammy points out to Al, "going through life with a conscience is like driving your car with the brakes on," whereas Sammy chooses to go at top speed (55). The metaphor here operates not only as a representation of class mobility, but as a particularly modern American kind of movement: driving a car. Sammy's mad dash to success isn't described only in terms of shoes and running, but also in terms of driving fast: upward mobility is linked here with that quintessentially American status symbol, the automobile.

In the history of the Hollywood studios, Louis B. Mayer represents one mobility narrative in which a young immigrant strives to become "American," which he takes to mean middle- or upper-class and successful. As Gabler points out, Mayer provided through his movies, such as Andy Hardy, "reassurance against the anxieties and disruptions" of the 1930s—reassurance he knew was needed because he himself felt its need (119). Mayer's fantasy of America came from his own need to join, as an upwardly mobile Jewish immigrant, the comfortable middle classes that kept Jews from joining their country clubs and schools. His desire to belong, finally, to American society was the driving force behind his studio's success. In fact, according to Gabler, a "native born, white, Anglo-Saxon, Protestant" American couldn't have accomplished what Mayer did: to invent MGM's picture of America, "one would have needed the same desperate longing for security that Mayer and so many of the other Hollywood Jews felt" and few native-born Protestant Americans could feel, as Mayer did, "so fearful of being outside and alone that one would go to any lengths to fabricate America as a sanctuary, safe and secure, and then promulgate this idealization to other Americans" (119). In other words, the urge to assimilate gave Mayer the motivation to model an on-screen nation, which came to influence how Americans imagined their country.

His cultivation of American-ness suffused his private life as well, and Mayer took up horseback riding and betting on races as part of his new aristocratic American persona. He was "one of the most successful racehorse owners in the country," which Gabler points out was one more arena in which he learned to circumvent anti-Semitism: he and a group of other Jewish movie executives built their own track after Santa Anita refused them (265). Listening to Hollywood moguls, clearly patterned after Mayer, talking about race horses, Fitzgerald's executive Monroe Stahr muses to himself that the Jews in Hollywood differ from European Jews of the past: "for years it had been the Cossacks mounted and the Jews on foot. Now the Jews had horses, and it gave them a sense of extraordinary well-being and power" (74). Stahr describes the reversal literally, in which Jews own horses, but also the metaphoric shift in which Jews now have power in the form of cultural and financial capital. To attain that capital, the Hollywood Jews had to establish their own institutions because they were excluded from existing middle- and upper-class social and economic structures: their own country club, their own race track, their own schools, and as Gabler's title indicates, their own movie empire and their own screen version of America. Becoming American meant more than living in the United States—it also meant making money and participating in prestigious social events.

Because of anti-Semitic American conventions, upward class mobility for the Hollywood Jews didn't always translate into social status, although class identity was extremely important. Leaving behind the taint of the ghetto was crucial for the first generation of Hollywood Jews in the 1920s, and the second generation is often described as more effortlessly assimilated and Americanized: as Gabler extrapolates, "who needed the suit cutters, junkmen, and bouncers when they could have bright assimilated Jews like Thalberg" (230). But even that first generation of movie executives, including Mayer, saw themselves as more American than their fathers, most of whom were adult immigrants while their children grew up in the United States. The narrative of progressive Americanization from one generation to the next only amplifies how distant "true American-ness" really was for the Hollywood Jews, who hoped that their children would "give the lie to the anti-Semitic stereotype of the Eastern European Jew" by appearing cultured and tasteful, embodiments of the "new Hollywood Jew" (Gabler 241). The second generation were better able to assimilate into American society, but often with the class biases and internalized anti-Semitism of Al Manheim and Betty Lasky, who associate certain mannerisms and physical characteristics with poverty and "ghetto Jews." Becoming American also meant becoming middle-class; mobility means leaving something or someplace behind, as Sammy Glick throws his Jewish baggage overboard in Al's metaphor.

Los Angeles offered the Hollywood Jews a perfect place to become American: the relatively young city, still resembling a frontier town at the turn of the twentieth century, housed the even younger movie industry, which yielded the enormous growth and subsequent profits to allow the immigrant founders to propel their children and successors into wealthy and assimilated American society. The presence of more physically marked "others" in the form of Mexican Americans doubtless also contributed to the relative ease with which the Hollywood Jews joined the mainstream of American culture: reforming or giving up their religious practices, subscribing to conservative and "patriotic" social and political values, and educating the American in what it really means to be American. Unlike Mexican Americans, whose cultural links to Mexico were more immediate and harder to refute, both because of geography and physical appearances, the Hollywood Jews were able to "pass" for, and gradually become, American on their journey across national, social, and economic boundaries.

## WHITE PEOPLE IN CARS: DRIVING AMBITION, AVENUES OF SUCCESS, AND DEAD ENDS

In many texts of the time, the city planning as well as the interior decoration of Los Angeles represented the new American city. As the city grew in the 1930s, the single family bungalows and wide clean suburban streets in strictly segregated neighborhoods were held up by realtors as a pleasant alternative to the crowded, dirty, immigrant-populated cities of the East Coast. Presented as a new modern city, Los Angeles was both more ordered and, to many, more restrictive: during a sightseeing drive around town, Celia, a rich producer's daughter in *The Last Tycoon*, calls it "a perfectly zoned city, so you know exactly what kind of people economically live in each section, from executives and directors, through technicians in their bungalows, right down to extras" (Fitzgerald 70). As the daughter of a producer, she grew up with an insider's awareness of studio power relations that she could read directly onto the city's built environment. Like Celia, Carey McWilliams documents the "rigidly stratified community" of the motion picture industry as it can be mapped onto the city: in the actual neighborhood of Hollywood "live the hangers-on of the industry; its carpenters, painters, and machinists; its hordes of extras," while "the elite live outside Hollywood in Beverly Hills, Brentwood, Bel-Air, Santa Monica, the Hollywood Hills, and San Fernando Valley" (334-35). In the racially segregated city, class further divided neighborhoods. A study of city housing in 1940 illustrates the segregation facing African Americans: while prosperous children of European immigrants could move to better neighborhoods, upwardly mobile blacks were simply not allowed to buy houses in "white" middle-class neighborhoods (Marchand 82). Instead, affluent African Americans lived in isolated areas separate both from the white middle class and from the black working class.

In ever-present details such as the iron spears, galleons, and the Spanish bungalow, Hollywood in the 1930s and early 40s created images and stories that attempt to make sense of the history of the western U.S. and of Los Angeles's pasts in ways that can be recuperated into an American racial and geographic home. Hollywood novels and films incorporated national and social concerns about race, class, and mobility into the cultural imaginary, participating in the construction of American identities while occasionally also questioning them. Segregation in Hollywood wasn't limited to housing, however; in the film studio on- and off-screen jobs were subject to the same hierarchies as the city's residential neighborhoods. As white middle class writers flocked to the studio screenwriting jobs paying $75 a week, working-class women, many of them immigrants, competed for the lowest paid jobs on the lots: secretaries, film lab workers, and costumers earning $18 a week (Nielsen 175). The division of labor in costuming jobs for women was also racially hierarchized: white women worked as cutters and fitters, while the most difficult jobs, such as beading dresses, belonged to Mexican American women (Nielsen 166-68). African American women weren't allowed to work in costuming at all in the 40s, as seamstress Grace January's experience at Paramount proves: "she quit after a week because they would either not give her any work at all or just give her dirty work to do" (Nielsen 168). The fleeting glimpses of African American and Asian American servants and workers in films and the paucity of starring roles for actors of color remind us that while white women were beginning to enjoy increasing mobility and visibility outside their traditional domestic roles, people of color and poor whites were needed to step into those roles. Along with the sought-after socio-economic mobility for white Americans came the symbols of wealth, which often translated onscreen into an Asian houseboy or African American maid, and of course, giant, streamlined, fast automobiles.

Selling relatively large homes and tracts of land to single families en- couraged the low urban density that was new even to a country famous for its wide open spaces and bolstered the already increasing reliance on the automobile that marked the first three decades of this century (Marchand 117). The increased personal space afforded by a single family home also made owning a car necessary, as it placed more distance between families and increased the distances between residential and business areas. Even in the 30s traffic was daunting for inhabitants of the "rich ghettoes" far re- moved from the business centers: Fitzgerald's tycoon, Monroe Stahr, often slept in his office suite at the film studio to avoid the daily drive across "the immense distances of Los Angeles County—three hours a day in an auto- mobile [was] not exceptional" (146). For the working and middle classes, for whom sleeping at work was not an option, owning a car was a needed guarantee of mobility, an assurance that they could get to work on time.

The automobile in American culture in the early twentieth century rep- resented all things modern, innovative, and above all, mobile. A car con-

veyed a person's consumer status and her endless personal mobility, allowing her to work, live, and shop in areas of town separated by vast distances
while also allowing her to avoid parts of town (and the people who lived
there) that were undesirable. Peter Ling argues that, in the 1920s, "Americans rejected mass transit in favor of the private motor vehicle" because of
a complex confluence of factors, including the desire for single family
housing, urban decentralization, corruption in transit companies, and the
desire for individual isolation due in part to racial and class hostilities (90).
According to Ling, the main attractions of automobility were its efficiency
as a "delivery system" that moves workers and consumers to more distant
markets and as a "social insulator" for the inhabitants of the diverse, rapidly
growing populations in sprawling cities such as Los Angeles (90). For example, the growing white Midwestern population of Los Angeles associated "mass transit with the lower castes," a prejudice that was reinforced by
"the practice of the Pacific Electric of housing its Mexican track workers in
labour camps along the tracks in suburban districts" (Ling 88). The automobile in Los Angeles gained primacy at the same moment when the public
transit system—streetcars and Interurban Railway—was dismantled: mass
transit declined steadily after the mid-1920s, while the proposal for the first
freeway came in 1937 (Kay 214). During the Depression, the notion of en-
hanced individual mobility also resonates in terms of socio-economic class:
taking control of one's own direction, leaving behind the crowds, the isolated automobile driver resembled an American pioneer, a rugged individualist who is faster, more prosperous, and more independent than the streetcar riders.

The streamlined Art Deco styles that automobile manufacturers market-
ed as "aerodynamic," a word that likens their cars to aircraft, became the
marker of modernity for those who could afford it. In the Depression,
streamlining connoted "technological progress as such and the program to
engineer recovery by the rational application of science and technology to
industry" (Gartman 102). Faith in modern technology and speed, embodied
by the new sleek cars, allowed consumers to focus more on superficial appearances than on underlying problems: the "spectacular unity, continuity,
and cleanliness of streamlined forms kept consumers thoughtlessly dazzled
and diverted from the Depression's historical realities of economic stagnation and class conflict" (Gartman 103). The scientific rationale behind
streamlining was specious, too, since the wind resistance was only signifi-

cantly reduced at very high speeds and the smaller windshield and more pronounced curves actually reduced visibility. Rather, the increased aestheticization of the automobile reified it, since the streamlining "kept the eye moving and prevented the concentration of thought on signs that testified to the fragmented process of production" (Gartman 127). During the 1930s, Americans loved to imagine themselves behind the wheel of a new streamlined car, even if it is bought on the installment plan, speeding along the highway, and no city was more automobile-friendly than Los Angeles.

At the same time as its modernity beckoned, Los Angeles also appealed to the American fascination with the West as the nation's frontier, its manifest destiny. When heavy industry began to lay off workers in the North and East, the so-called "postindustrial" landscape of California promised a different kind of economy, the pinnacle of which was "the movies" and stardom. Hollywood represented wildly divergent national fantasies: a modern utopia with orange trees and movie stars, but also an amoral frontier boom town. As Richard Lehan points out, Los Angeles is "the last major city to grow out of the idea of the West" while at the same time it is "the first city in the western world to take its dimensions from the automobile" (30). During the Depression, film audiences experienced Hollywood as the source of the movies and as a signifier of easy money, second chances, and a happy, prosperous white America. Going west to Los Angeles retained traces of the nineteenth-century imperative to young men seeking their fortunes, although instead of gold and the open frontier, wealth resided in the burgeoning movie industry.

The 1920s and 30s saw nationwide road improvement campaigns as the number of car-owners increased—in Los Angeles the numbers increased forty-fold to 800,000 in 1930 (Marchand 117)—and "roads replaced train tracks as the nation's circulatory system and in its metaphoric vocabulary" (Marling 58). In the Los Angeles novels of the 30s and early 40s, driving takes up a larger proportion of the action than in novels set in other cities or regions. In Fitzgerald's *The Last Tycoon*, Monroe Stahr meets his date Kathleen in a parking lot. They drive to Santa Monica, stop at a roadside restaurant but don't go in because its parking lot looks "forbidding with many Sunday drivers" (81), drive on to dine in a drug store, then back to her house, where Stahr says "let's jump in the car and drive somewhere" (86). After the awkwardness of trying to say good-bye at her door, Kathleen seizes the offer:

she caught at the exact phrasing—to get away from here immediately, that was ac-
complishment or sounded like it—as if she were fleeing from the spot of a crime.
Then they were in the car, going downhill with the breeze cool in their faces, and
she came slowly to herself. (86)

Only through constant movement, driving around the city, can the characters in the Hollywood novels find a sense of self. Often the female characters enjoy particular pleasure in cars, as does Mildred Pierce in James M.
Cain's novel of that name. For her, the car also symbolizes freedom from
her marriage and a new-found self-determination. Mildred wrangles the car
away from her estranged husband and drives it home, speeding down Colo-
rado Avenue: "the car was pumping something into her veins, something of
pride, of arrogance, of regained self-respect, that no talk, no liquor, no love,
could possibly give" (164). The power to drive fast, to escape a bad situation, to control the direction of her life, makes the automobile a potent
symbol of freedom for women in these novels.

The automobile plays a lead role in the relatively new genre of detective
fiction, much of it made into films, particularly that of Raymond Chandler.
In the first Philip Marlowe novel, *The Big Sleep*, published in 1939, Chandler portrays the Los Angeles cityscape as a series of urban avenues and
quiet canyon roadways, with the lone private eye on the prowl and on the
stake out in his car as he works on the Sternwood case. The *noir* city of *The
Big Sleep*, in the novel and the later film, is embodied by the rich oil-baron
Sternwood family as decadent, immoral, and corrupt, from the frail patri-
arch in the wheelchair to the two sleazy sisters who love to gamble, drink,
and use drugs. The image of the solitary tough guy driving around Los Angeles easily translated onto the movie screen in the 1946 film of Chandler's
novel, with Humphrey Bogart cruising the murky *noir* city making an in-
delible visual and metaphorical impact on the American imagination. Marlowe exemplifies the individualist who cannot survive without a car of his
own: we can't picture him on the streetcar. The car chases and get-aways so
vital to the hard-boiled detective novel and the *film noir* thriller depend on
the private automobile, as do many of the distinctive visual images and descriptions: "rain drummed hard on the roof of the car and the burbank top
began to leak. A pool of water formed on the floorboards for me to keep my
feet in" (19), "six more bright lights bobbed through the driving rain" (20),
"the filaments of its [head]lights glowed dimly and died" (20), "the car was

dark, empty, warm" (121), "silent, rain-polished streets" (125). Marlowe lives his life in the car, kissing women, kidnapping criminals, tailing suspects, and meeting informants in automobiles.

In a telling section of *The Big Sleep*, Marlowe meets a woman informant, Agnes, who leaves town immediately after their meeting. The meeting takes place in her car, a gray Plymouth, after which Marlowe gets out and she drives away; the narration exemplifies both Marlowe's misogyny and the central role of the automobile in the novel. Agnes opens the chapter with her demand, "Give me the money," and after he hands her the bills she "bent over to count them in the dim light of the dash" (109). Marlowe describes the sounds that punctuate the conversation in the car: "[t]he motor of the gray Plymouth throbbed under her voice and the rain pounded above it" as she tells him the crucial information he needs to crack the case (109). The sensory experience of sitting in the car in the rain, with the "dim light of the dash," typifies the feeling of transitory and mobile Los Angeles existence in the novel as a whole. Agnes recalls going Sunday driving on Foothill Boulevard with her boyfriend and spotting Marlowe's missing person in a car—"a brown coupe"—as they passed it (109). They followed the car to a "small garage and paintshop", a "[h]ot car drop, likely," where the missing woman was being held (110). Marlowe waits until Agnes finishes and then "listen[s] to the swish of tires on Wilshire" (110). After the meeting he returns to his own car and watches as "the gray Plymouth moved forward, gathered speed, and darted around the corner on to Sunset Place. The sound of its motor died, and with it blonde Agnes wiped herself off the slate for good" (110). He tallies the situation so far: "Three men dead, Geiger, Brody and Harry Jones, and the woman went riding off in the rain with my two hundred in her bag and not a mark on her. I kicked my starter and drove on downtown to eat" (110). Every detail in this brief but important section depends on the primacy of the car in Los Angeles culture: the transience and intimacy of a clandestine meeting in a car in the rain, the coincidental spotting of a missing woman on a Sunday drive, the secluded hideout as a garage, and the understated lyricism of Chandler's urban setting punctuated by the "swish of tires" and the throbbing motor of Agnes's Plymouth. Agnes, like Mildred Pierce, has her car and her freedom as she drives off down a Los Angeles street; indeed, Marlowe resents her freedom in light of the carnage he has seen so far investigating the case, and perhaps also his reliance on her for this important information.

Often, however, driving around never really leads anywhere, as many characters in Los Angeles novels discover. David Fine points out how important driving is, particularly in the 1930s novels of James M. Cain: "the fast-moving car fosters both a sense of power and control over one's destiny and, at the same time, a feeling of separation or insulation from the influence of others and a constraining social environment" ("Beginning" 50). Fine describes the ways in which Cain's protagonists, from Mildred Pierce to Walter in *Double Indemnity* to Nick and Cora of *The Postman Always Rings Twice*, live and die in the roadside restaurants and on the highways around Los Angeles. In their struggles for financial security and true love, these characters play out their lives against the unique landscape of Southern California, "foothill, canyon, shoreline, desert," which "provided regional novelists with ready-made images for fluidity, mobility, and a deceptive sense of freedom" (Fine "Beginning" 51). Speeding across the landscape, Cain's characters seek more than geographic mobility—driving their cars they can imagine what freedom feels like, whether freedom from a spouse, the police, poverty, or just their mundane lives.

During the Depression and into the 1940s pleasure driving was a cheap form of entertainment that involved sightseeing and stopping at restaurants and service stations along the highways. The American Dream of setting up a successful business out of a minimal investment and lots of hard work was easily translated into highway economics: in Robert Sherwood's 1935 play *The Petrified Forest* and Cain's 1934 novel *The Postman Always Rings Twice* the survival of the restaurants depend on their locations along highways and the drivers who stop in for snacks, coffee, and a tank of gasoline. In the Michael Curtiz film of Cain's *Mildred Pierce*, Mildred chooses a building on a busy intersection to start her restaurant, which will give her family an economic boost into middle class. Selling the idea to her friend Wally, she exclaims, "it's good for drive-in trade—I clocked 500 cars in an hour!" Mildred's restaurant idea blossoms into a booming chain of drive-in restaurants, each with its own parking lot and located near busy intersections; she offers home cooking to hungry motorists and commuters who haven't the time or energy to cook at home, a precursor to the fast-food industry. The high traffic represents a potentially lucrative restaurant market to Mildred Pierce, but her own car is a symbol of more than customers—the automobile represents the social mobility that she desires for herself and her daughter.

Her daughter Veda, however, isn't happy with a roadside pedigree no matter how many middle-class trappings it buys her: "You think that just because you made a little money you can get a new hairdo and some expensive clothes and turn yourself into a lady. But you can't because you'll never be anything but a common frump whose father lived over a grocery store and whose mother took in washing." Even Mildred's overcompensation in gifts isn't enough for the voracious Veda: when she spends too much on a dress for Veda, she tosses it away scornfully, saying she "wouldn't be seen dead in such a rag." When she gives Veda a posh Buick convertible for her birthday, Veda grabs the keys and speeds away from her mother as fast as she can. The filial relationship between Mildred and Veda prompts Mildred's employee and confidante, Ida, to remark, "Personally, Veda has convinced me that alligators have the right idea. They eat their young."

Mildred's ambitions have influenced Veda to the point that she interprets the world only in terms of class; unlike her mother, who has experienced the hard work of upward mobility and respects working people, Veda is a snob. When her younger sister Kay behaves like a tomboy, Veda tells her, "You act like a peasant." Describing her father's girlfriend, Veda sneers, "she's distinctly middle class." But Veda's most powerful rejection of her mother's class origins comes in the angry outburst when she shouts her intentions to leave home at the horrified Mildred:

I can get away from you! From you and your chickens and your pies and your kitchens and everything that smells of grease! I can get away from this shack with its cheap furniture and this town and its dollar days and its women that wear uniforms and men that wear overalls! [...] You think that just because you made a little money you can get a new hairdo and some expensive clothes and turn yourself into a lady. But you can't because you'll never be anything but a common frump whose father lived over a grocery store and whose mother took in washing.

Veda condemns her mother's restaurants—chickens, pies, and kitchens—and her attempts to look the part of the successful businesswoman. The kind of upward mobility Mildred works so hard for on the busy intersection is debased currency to Veda, who becomes a perverse embodiment of her mother's social and economic class ambitions. Like the second generation of the Hollywood Jews, she has absorbed the values of the middle- and upper-class world that her mother worked for, only to then reject her mother's poor origins and lack of "taste."

For the upwardly mobile businesswoman in Cain's (and Curtiz's) *Mildred Pierce*, Los Angeles is the setting for social and economic progress from a dreary lower middle-class existence to fabulous wealth, but at a personal cost of both Mildred's daughters—Kay dies while she is at rich Monty Beragon's beach house and Veda is banished for her affair with her stepfather, Monty (in the film, Veda goes to prison for murdering Monty when he refuses to marry her). The novel ends with Mildred back together with first husband Bert, who says of Veda, "to hell with her. [...] let's get stinko!" (366). Similarly, if not as sordidly, film ends with a beautiful sunny day, as Mildred and Bert leave the police station together, walking past a pair of scrubwomen and into the glaring California sunshine. All of Mildred's tearing around town in her automobile, enjoying her freedom and business successes, only served to land her right back with her first husband, safe and secure with a hard-working man.

As so many of the Los Angeles novels attest, upward mobility is attainable for whites with ambition, such as Mildred Pierce, and for immigrants who can shed their "foreign" cultural identities, such as the Hollywood Jews. The prosperous careers of Mildred and Sammy have their high costs, but by the superficial standards of wealth and power, they are completely successful. Upward mobility for countless other Angelenos was not so accessible: the Midwesterners of West's dystopia in *The Day of the Locust* and the lost souls and two-bit crooks of Chandler's *The Big Sleep* exemplify the wrong turns and dead ends that await many of the white Americans who sought the American Dream in Los Angeles. The magic city has predicated its image on the utopian Western metropolis, attempting to elide the history of Native and Mexican Americans who founded and settled the town and who still live on the margins of the Los Angeles novels such as West's, in the form of caricatures and parodies that reinforce the sense that they don't belong. The symbols of mobility that permeate the Los Angeles novels of the 1930s signal the elisions that cannot be completely successful: the "Spanish style" and the automobile are potent symbols of Los Angeles and they contain the traces of histories with which the magic city's imaginary origin stories are continually at odds.

## WORKS CITED

Cain, James M. *Mildred Pierce*. 1941. *Cain x 3*. New York: Knopf, 1969. 101-366. Print.

Davis, Mike. *City of Quartz: Excavating the Future in Los Angeles*. New York: Vintage, 1992. Print.

del Castillo, Richard Griswold. *The Los Angeles Barrio, 1850-1890: A Social History*. Berkeley: U of California P, 1979. Print.

Findlay, John. *Magic Lands: Western Cityscapes and American Culture after 1940*. Berkeley: U of California P, 1992. Print.

Fine, David. "Beginning in the Thirties: The Los Angeles Fiction of James M. Cain and Horace McCoy." Fine *Los Angeles in Fiction* 43-66.

---, ed. *Los Angeles in Fiction*. Rev. Ed. Albuquerque, U of New Mexico P, 1995. Print.

---. Introduction. Fine *Los Angeles* 1-26.

Fitzgerald, F. Scott. *The Last Tycoon*. 1941. Scribner Classic. New York: Collier-Macmillan, 1986. Print.

Gabler, Neal. *An Empire of Their Own: How the Jews Invented Hollywood*. New York: Anchor-Doubleday, 1988. Print.

Gartman, David. *Auto Opium: A Social History of American Automobile Design*. New York: Routledge, 1994. Print.

Heizer, Robert F., ed. *The Indians of Los Angeles County: Hugo Reid's Letters of 1852*. Los Angeles: Southwest Museum, 1968. Print.

Kay, Jane Holtz. *Asphalt Nation: How the Automobile Took Over America, and How We Can Take It Back*. New York: Crown, 1997. Print.

Klein, Norman M. "The Sunshine Strategy: Buying and Selling the Fantasy of Los Angeles." *20th Century Los Angeles: Power, Promotion and Social Conflict*. Eds. Norman M. Klein and Martin J. Schiesl. Claremont: Regina, 1990. 1-38. Print.

Lehan, Richard. "The Los Angeles Novel and the Idea of the West." Fine *Los Angeles* 29-41.

Ling, Peter J. *America and the Automobile: Technology, Reform, and Social Change*. New York: Manchester UP-St. Martin's, 1990. Print.

Mackenthun, Gesa. "Adding Empire to the Study of American Culture." *Journal of American Studies* 30.2 (1996): 263-69. Print.

Marchand, B. *The Emergence of Los Angeles: Population and Housing in the City of Dreams 1940-1970*. London: Pion, 1986. Print.

McWilliams, Carey. *Southern California Country: An Island on the Land.* New York: Duell, Sloan and Pierce, 1946. Print.

Nielsen, Elizabeth. "Handmaidens of the Glamour Culture: Costumers in the Hollywood Studio System." *Fabrications: Costume and the Female Body.* Ed. Jane Gaines. AFI Film Readers Ser. New York: Routledge, 1990. 160-79. Print.

Ríos-Bustamente, Antonio and Pedro Castillo. *An Illustrated History of Mexican Los Angeles 1781-1985.* Monograph 12. Chicano Studies Research Center, Univ. of California. 1986. Print.

Robinson, W.W. *Los Angeles: A Profile.* Norman: U of Oklahoma P, 1968. Print.

Sánchez, George J. *Becoming Mexican American: Ethnicity, Culture, and Identity in Chicano Los Angeles, 1900-1945.* New York: Oxford UP, 1993. Print.

Schulberg, Budd. *What Makes Sammy Run?* 1941. New York: Bantam-Random House, 1968. Print.

Sheehan, Perley Poore. *Hollywood as a World Center.* Hollywood: Hollywood Citizen P, 1924. Print.

West, Nathanael. *The Day of the Locust.* 1939. *The Complete Works of Nathanael West.* New York: Farrar, Straus, and Cudahy, 1957. Print.

# 4 Black-Audience Westerns

Race, Nation, and Mobility in the 1930s

> How to be both free and situated; how to
> convert a racist house into a race-specific
> yet nonracist home? How to enunciate race
> while depriving it of its lethal cling?
> TONI MORRISON/ "HOME"

In *Midnight Ramble,* a 1994 documentary on early black cinema, actor-singer Herb Jeffries recalls his inspiration for the singing-cowboy role be made famous in black-audience musical westerns of the late 1930s. On tour in Cincinnati, Ohio, Jeffries saw a young African American boy crying in frustration. The boy explained that he wanted to play Tom Mix but that his white playmates insisted that he could not because Mix was white and there were no black cowboy stars. As a result of that encounter, Jeffries promoted the idea of black cowboy movies in Los Angeles and subsequently became the first African American singing cowboy in the movies. He was billed using various combinations of his first name Herb or Herbert, and his last name, Jeffrey or Jeffries (for consistency, this chapter refers to him as Herb Jeffries throughout) in a series of independently produced black-audience musical westerns and thus provided African American audiences with an on-screen role model of a black cowboy.[1]

---

1   I would like to thank Susan Jeffords and Steven Shaviro for their enthusiasm about the earliest version of this essay, which was a chapter of my dissertation. Revisions came easily, thanks to the critiques, comments, and suggestions of the North American Studies Colloquium of the Dresden University of Technology,

Jeffries's anecdotal story illustrates the primary importance of racial and national identification to the development and reception of the black western during the late 1930s. His recourse to the role-model trope is not an unusual rhetorical move either, given the genre in which he was working. According to *The BFI Companion. to the Western,* studies conducted during the first half of the twentieth century found a trend toward younger boys in the audience at westerns: "Westerns became less popular as children got older," and findings further indicated that "pre-teenage children preferred westerns most, that boys liked them more than girls" (Buscombe 36).

Unfortunately, there are no data specific to African Americans; indeed, we can probably assume that audience studies were conducted with white subjects only. But, as the remarks of Jeffries and other veterans of race movies indicate, the audience for black westerns was imagined to be primarily African American boys.[2] Even more important, the late-1930s cycle of black musical westerns embodies a unique cinematic intersection of race, nation , class, and gender that should be of interest to scholars in the field of African American cinema as well as those working on the western film genre.

In the 1920s, race movies tackled controversial issues affecting African Americans, such as lynching. interracial relationships, and anti-Semitism. Some of the most frequently studied films from this decade include the

---

my audience and fellow panelists at the MELUS-Europe 2000 conference in Orléans, and the challenging and encouraging reviewers for *Cinema Journal.* My best editor remains Anneliese Truame. The revisions for this version could not have been completed without the seemingly boundless resources of the Seattle Public Library and Scarecrow Video in Seattle.

2   The trope of the young male African American spectator of cowboy movies is still a current one: in an advertisement for the soundtrack of *Posse* (Mario Van Peebles, 1993), on the video version of the movie, a young black boy sits in front of a television watching an old Hollywood western. The ad posits the soundtrack as a way to rebel against the inaccuracies of the white Hollywood version of the West by consuming the music associated with a revisionist black western made by an African American director. For more on this ad and for an illuminating discussion of characters of color in recent westerns, see Hoffman.

work of the prolific writer, producer, and director Oscar Micheaux,[3] whose films are located within established genres such as the melodrama or detective story but center around specifically racial issues and other "social problems" of the African American community. In contrast to these explicitly political movies, the black-audience entertainment films of the 1930s consist of adaptations of popular white genre films that do not directly portray racism or white-supremacist violence. According to Henry Sampson, the black-audience "entertainment" films of the 1930s focused less overtly on racial politics and more on approximating the standard conventions of their genres and on generating cinematic pleasure. As Sampson notes, "Unlike the black features of the [1920s], they made no serious attempt to treat the unique aspects of the black experience in America" (13).[4]

Given these distinctions, the cycle of black westerns from the late 1930s cannot be studied using the same assumptions scholars have established in work on the 1920s race movies. First of all, black musical westerns appeared twenty years after Oscar Micheaux's first feature in 1919. The target audience for these movies was different as well, aiming for children and adults, unlike some of the more serious dramas of the 1920s. Another difference is that the focus of the black musical westerns is on spectacle— music and action—more than on the story, which is rather skeletal. Yet, for this very reason—their alleged effort to be entertainment that does not consciously engage in the contemporaneous discourses on race—these films reveal a different approach to African American audiences and identifications of their time than earlier, more deliberately political films.

Because the racial politics is less overt, the dozens of black-audience westerns, gangster movies, and comedies of the 1930s remain largely unexamined. As a cultural critic, I am fascinated by this loudly proclaimed ab-

---

3   A small explosion of Micheaux scholarship occurred in the 1990s. Some of the best-known and most fascinating articles and book chapters from that decade and earlier include Bowser and Spence; Butters; Cripps, "Oscar Micheaux"; Gaines, "Fire and Desire"; Green; Grupenhoff; hooks; Jones; Leab; Reid; Regester; and Sampson.

4   The historical data in this essay are drawn largely from two landmark studies: Sampson's exhaustively researched film history, *Blacks in Black and White*, and Jones's study, *Black Cinema Treasures*, inspired by the discovery in Tyler, Texas, of a cache of now-famous lost films.

sence of political intent and goal of being pure entertainment. This chapter will excavate the embedded meanings and traces of racial politics that even the westerns—or especially the westerns—as popular culture documents still bear.

Specifically, this chapter examines the complex negotiations necessary in the making of black westerns, across the conventions of genre, casting decisions, and path-ways of audience identification. The Herb Jeffries movies of the late 1930s,will be the focus: *Harlem on the Prairie* (Sam Newfield, 1937), *The Bronze Buckaroo* (Richard C. Kahn, 1938), and *Harlem Rides the Range* and *Two-Gun Man from Harlem* (both Richard C. Kahn, 1939), although I restrict my close readings to the latter three films because there is no existing print of *Prairie*. First, I survey key terms and concepts as defined within the current literature relevant to this study, particularly in the fields of African American cinema and the study of the Hollywood western. In the second section, after describing and summarizing the movies and their production, reception, and exhibition, I look at their negotiation of and roots in preexisting genres, the western and the singing-cowboy movie in particular. In the third section, I examine representative sequences to better delineate the operations of race and nationality in black westerns, including the role of the "coon" character and the ramifications of having an all-black cast. The fourth section addresses the striking anachronisms and geographical juxtapositions in the films and the methods by which they encourage contemporaneous cultural identification through the deployment of gender roles as well as specifically African American social and cultural identities.

## CRITICAL APPROACHES TO BLACK-AUDIENCE MUSICAL WESTERNS

Black-audience movies, also called underground black movies, black-cast movies, and race movies, were made in the first half of the twentieth century—most in the 1920s and 1930s—and distributed to all-black cinemas. According to Sampson, in 1939, there were 430 "all-Negro" theaters in the U.S. (Sampson 642). Some critics have defined narrower categories to distinguish "black independent" films from those made by white-controlled production companies, so as to better discuss the different degrees of creative control, for example (Reid 17). For my purposes, however, I use the term "black-audience" to emphasize the movies' reception by their intended viewers; I am less concerned with the possibilities of African American auteurism or the quasi-essentialist notion that an all-black team made more "authentic" race movies than black-white partnerships. After all, there is little "authenticity" in any singing-cowboy movie.

Another issue that has continued to interest scholars is whether race movies constitute a "separate cinema," to echo the title of Kisch and Mapp's 1992 collection of race-movie posters and a 1998 Turner Classic Movies film series. Certainly, race movies were excluded from the Hollywood studio system, awards competitions, and publicity machines. If black-audience movies do constitute a "separate cinema," how can we discuss them in their multicultural, albeit racist and segregated, national context?

I would like to state my position within this debate by first rejecting what sounds like naiveté: how could any American making movies in the late 1930s not be affected by Hollywood cinema in some way? Moreover, how could film professionals hope to market movies while completely disregarding the reception of similar Hollywood products? Thus, I suggest that we took at 1930s race movies as a discrete but not isolated component of American cinema, of which Hollywood is also a part. Indeed, race movies borrowed from Hollywood, particularly in their improvisations on existing Hollywood genres, and, conversely, Hollywood stole from them (witness the all-black casts of King Vidor's *Hallelujah!* and Paul Sloane's *Hearts in Dixie* as early as 1929). This is not to say that race movies were not an important aspect of African American culture, although white Americans completely ignored them. Race movies, at least those of the late 1930s, cannot he studied without considering their context in both African American communities and the national culture of the United States, permeated as it was by Hollywood movies.

African American community support for race movies was unabashedly politicized and directly linked the success of black-audience films to the push for social and economic independence. Like many performers in the race movies of the 1930s, African American actor Theresa Harris, the female lead in the black-audience gangster film *Bargain with Bullets* (a.k.a. *Gangsters on the Loose,* Harry L. Fraser, 1937), went back to playing maid and waitress roles in Hollywood movies in the 1940s. Here she explains why black audiences should support the struggling black film industry:

We have tolerated so many rotten pictures made in Hollywood. [...] I do not see why our own people cannot be tolerant of the pioneering stage of this company. [...] I never felt the chance to rise above the role of a maid in Hollywood movies. [...] Hollywood has no part for me. (qtd. in Sampson 490-91)

Not only did black-audience films give African American talent a chance to play lead roles, but, Harris contends, the quality of these productions was not so far below that of the cheap Hollywood genre films that American audiences of all races attended. The popularity of the black-audience movies of the early twentieth century testifies to their value to their audiences, as Thomas Cripps has argued: "A plausibly rendered anatomy of black life often meant more to black audiences than aesthetic considerations" ("Oscar Micheaux" 72).

The debate over their technical "inferiority" and tower production values continues to interest scholars of race movies. While it is certainly true that they had lower budgets than Hollywood films and thus more uneven production values, this economic consideration must not serve as the basis for blanket value judgments. That is, by comparing black-audience movies to Hollywood movies, I do not mean to imply that the work of African American artists should be measured by specifically white standards; indeed, the departures from and improvements on Hollywood conventions in black westerns interest me most. I concur with Jane Gaines's assessment of Micheaux's style and believe it also applies to the movies I examine in this chapter:

Micheaux should be situated in the classical Hollywood tradition which, after all, he so carefully studied and emulated. It is not so much that he broke with Hollywood conventions [...] or even that he fell short of mastering them, but that he played 'fast and loose' with classical style. ("Fire and Desire" 63)

Black musical westerns can be read as creative interpretations of Hollywood B-westerns (star Jeffries called them "C-minus westerns"), with many of the same kinds of budget-inspired improvisations that are celebrated today in the movies of Val Lewton. The significance of these westerns in the history of American cinema is not that they were technically flawed or radically innovative, as Micheaux scholars have argued over in numerous publications, but, rather, that they challenged the prevailing function of race as a signifier in American cinema, albeit in different ways from Micheaux.

For American audiences of Hollywood movies, as Manthia Diawara points out in his important revision of Laura Mulvey's thesis on visual pleasure, "the dominant cinema situates Black characters primarily for the pleasure of White spectators ( male or female)" ("Black Spectatorship" 66). This race-specific pleasure in Hollywood cinema is often created by representing African American characters as nonthreatening, usually "deterritorialized from a Black milieu and transferred to a predominantly White world" (66). It follows from Diawara's thesis that, because black-audience westerns enact a reterritorialization of African American characters back into a predominantly black milieu, they at least attempt to sidestep this major hallmark of Hollywood cinematic representation.

Furthermore, this reterritorialization often took place within a physically and geographically reterritorialized theater setting, in which African Americans could watch black-audience films with positive images of black people in an audience of other African American viewers. Thus, an additional inducement to attend black-audience films may have been the chance to watch a movie without being constantly reminded of Jim Crow realities: at theaters catering solely to African American audiences, often the ushers, ticket takers, managers, and concessionaires were all black (not just the porters and maids as in white theaters), and unlike white theaters, entrances and seating were not restricted by race (Streible 227). At a time when most African Americans could not see a first-run Hollywood film except from balcony seats or at after-hours "midnight rambles," black-audience movies, including singing-cowboy features, created an on-screen America in which African Americans had access to all locations in life, both high and low and even tall in the saddle.[5]

---

5   According to Streible's study of African American film exhibition in Austin, Texas, first-run white theaters exhibited "colored midnight shows" and "admitted Black patrons on a regular basis, though customers there were limited to balcony seating and made to use a separate entrance." The alternative required some compromise, too, since "Black theaters were usually considered last-run possibilities for the major Hollywood studios' product," often running films one to two years after their initial opening. See Streible 224-26, for more on segregated exhibition practices; see also Sampson 11-12.

The battle over racial representation within her own writing that Toni Morrison describes in her essay "Home" expresses the dilemma implicit in these films as they struggled over the question of "how to convert a racist house into a race-specific yet nonracist home" (5). Black-audience westerns attempt to convert the house of the American western into a race-specific but nonracist home for African American audiences. Employing the metaphors of space and home, Morrison's question touches the heart of the matter: the house, the cinema, and the nation are at stake for black audiences of these westerns. The question of ownership, entitlement, and citizenship is quite literal at the story level in the ever-present motif of land disputes, as well as implicit in the genre itself, which has often been a vehicle for expressing not only whiteness but also white supremacy. The visual and spatial transgressions in black westerns, picturing black men in the preserve of the white Hollywood cowboy, enact a geographic reterritorialization in addition to a cinematic one.

Yet, despite what this cycle of movies has to offer the field of black cinema studies, books by Ed Guererro, Nelson George, and Mark Reid make no mention of the black musical westerns. Only Daniel Leab's *From Sambo to Superspade,* Henry Sampson's *Blacks in Black and White,* and G. William Jones's *Black Cinema Treasures* discuss these movies; in addition, Donald Bogle provides an entry on *The Bronze Buckaroo* in his 1988 *Blacks in American Films and Television* and mentions black musical westerns in other books. But these represent just a few mentions, and none is a full-length study of the cycle.

The recurring theme and setting of the American West in early African American cinema, most obviously in black westerns, suggests an embrace of the positive values associated with that region, values not typically ascribed to black characters in movies or for that matter in white-supremacist American culture: freedom, individualism, mobility, masculinity, and a patriotism rooted in a love of the land itself. Micheaux's first silent feature, *The Homesteader* (1919), was an adaptation of his 1913 autobiographical novel with the same title. It is the story of a black American man establishing a homestead in South Dakota, a geographical and ideological location Micheaux portrayed as a promising alternative to the northern cities to which many African Americans moved during the decades of the Great Migration. According to Gerald Butters, Micheaux saw the West as a "fertile cinematic landscape in which [he] could demonstrate uncompromised

African-American manhood" (55). The land and home are also key issues in Micheaux's *The Symbol of the Unconquered* (1920), in which a black man fights to keep his oil-rich property despite efforts by the Ku Klux Klan to frighten him off. The next decade brought the Great Depression, when all Americans knew what it meant to fear poverty and homelessness and to value home and freedom; these issues come through in the recurring struggles over ownership of land in black-audience westerns.

Cowboys played a key role in the western expansion of the United States, and the male heroes in westerns provided Depression-era audiences with a model of the quintessential American man: independent, tough, and with a strong sense of justice. In his 1996 study of westerns and their constructions of American masculinity, Lee Clark Mitchell discusses an impressive assemblage of texts, from James Fenimore Cooper's and Zane Grey's novels to Sergio Leone's movies, arguing that the various incarnations of the western participated in creating the nation's imaginary picture of itself. Although the texts represent a wide chronological range, Mitchell convincingly shows that in each period of U.S. culture the reconfigured western models national fantasies of national and masculine identity. As the title of his book, *Westerns: Making the Man in Fiction and Film*, emphasizes, the western is about "making the man," building an ideal image of a distinctively American masculinity. Although his book includes readings of both high- and low-culture texts, Mitchell fails to mention the cycle of black westerns made in the late 1930s. Michael Coyne makes the same omission in his 1997 monograph, *The Crowded Prairie*, which opens with a discussion of John Ford's *Stagecoach* (1939), released the same year as Richard Kahn's *Two-Gun Man from Harlem*. These oversights are unfortunate because the authors could have provided a more complete account of raced characters as well as raced audiences.

*The BFI Companion to the Western*, published in 1988, has an entry entitled "Blacks" in its "Culture and History" section that provides a thorough overview of the history of the black West and its representation in movies, including three paragraphs on the Herb Jeffries movies. The entry includes some factual errors, such as the number of sidekicks the hero had, the name of his horse, and the names of directors, but the entry serves its purpose: to assert the presence of black cowboys in both the historical West and the cinematic genre of the western.[6] Unfortunately, in this same *Companion*'s sixty-five-page alphabetical filmography, called "A Select Guide to the Western Film," no black western is listed; nor are any of the directors or producers listed in the eighty-four-page section entitled "Dictionary of Western Filmmakers." Another egregious omission occurs in the 1994 book (that includes a CD) *Singing Cowboy Stars,* by Robert W. Phillips. Herb Jeffries is not among the twenty-five stars profiled, although the book bizarrely includes John Wayne, certainly a stretch considering that Herb Jeffries was a professional big-band singer who went on to sing with Duke Ellington's Orchestra.

Jeffries has also been ignored in collections of western music. The four-CD collection *Songs of the West* features a booklet that includes a number of short essays. Entitled "The Western: Through the Years on Film and Television," the booklet includes a color reproduction of the movie poster for *The Bronze Buckaroo,* with the caption "Herbert Jeffrey, Hollywood's only black singing cowboy," alongside posters for Gene Autry movies and photos of the Lone Ranger and Hopalong Cassidy, but the text never mentions Jeffries or his movies, and none of his songs is included on the CDs (Zwisohn).

From this initial research, one might conclude that the black westerns of the late 1930s are irrelevant or at best worthy of a footnote in the histories of African American cinema, the western genre, and cowboy music. That is the false impression that this chapter seeks to correct.

---

6   This is not to suggest that black cowboys did not exist. Rather, in the public imagination and in popular texts such as dime novels and Hollywood movies, cowboys were exclusively white. However, African American cowboy Bill Pickett was featured in a black independent film, *The Bull Dogger* (1923). For information about other black westerns, see the filmography at the end of this chapter. For an excellent history of African Americans in the West, see Katz.

## BLACK-AUDIENCE MUSICAL WESTERNS: THE CYCLE AND ITS CINEMATIC GENRES

The first in the series of black musical westerns, *Harlem on the Prairie,* was made in 1937; however, no prints remain. The movie was produced by B-western Hollywood independent Jed Buell, who also made *The Terror of Tiny Town* (1938), a western with little people in lead roles. Buell reportedly phoned a Dallas distributor who handled segregated southern theaters to ask whether there was a market for such movies; the distributor said, "I'll take all you have. You mean you've got some?" (Davis). Jeffries cast the movie and billed himself as Herbert Jeffrey: also appearing were his back-up singers, the Four Tones, Spencer Williams (who acted in all four movies), Mantan Moreland, and several African American actors who worked in Hollywood Tarzan movies. The film was shot on location at N.B. Murphy's black dude ranch in Victorville, California (Sampson 387).

*Harlem on the Prairie* premiered at top cinemas, including the Rialto on Broadway in New York and the Paramount in Los Angeles, and met with good reviews in the trade press. There was apparently a strong market for this new black-audience movie; according to the entry in the *BFI Companion*: it cost less than $10,000 to make and grossed more than $50,000 in its first year (Buscombe 69).

*The Bronze Buckaroo* of 1938 was a Hollywood Productions movie. Directed by Richard Kahn, it featured Lucius Brooks as the comic sidekick to Jeffries's Bob Blake. The story involves a plot to buy out or scare off the owner of a land rich in silver ore. The villain resorts to kidnapping and extortion in his attempts to get the land. Luckily, Bob Blake comes to help his friend and get the girl. A sub-plot involves sidekick Dusty (Lucius Brooks) getting duped into buying a mule be believes can talk. The musical interludes include the song "Almost Time for Roundup" as well as a cowboy tap-dance number.

*Harlem Rides the Range* (1939) also featured Lucius Brooks as Dusty, with Jeffries, Williams, and other familiar faces; once again, Hollywood Productions backed the movie and Kahn directed. The story again revolves around a struggle for natural resources, this time a radium mine owned by one of Bob's friends, and, once again, Bob saves the day and gets the girl.

Made in 1939 by Merit Pictures, *Two-Gun Man from Harlem* was the last completed movie in the series. The story departs from the previous movies in significant ways in that it is a contemporary western, with telephones, automobiles, and scenes set in Harlem as well as in an unspecified western locale. The generic conventions are also tweaked toward the crime melodrama: Bob Blake's employer, Mr. Steele, is murdered by his wife's lover, but she accuses Bob of the crime. He runs away to Harlem but then returns in disguise to solve the murder and bring the killer to justice. The story and plot are more complicated than in the earlier movies, and the camerawork is more daring: in one fight scene, the camera cuts from medium shots of the two men to several extreme close-ups of arms swinging and chins punched by fists. Some action scenes include a musical score, which is noticeably absent from the earlier movies. The sound in the three latter movies drops out in places during dialogue, and the editing is jumpy; these "problems" could be the result of the low budget or because the videos are copies of old and damaged prints.

A fifth movie, *Ten Notches to Tombstone,* was never finished, and no fragments remain. The most obvious reasons for ending the series had to do with the star's absence. As mentioned earlier, Jeffries began singing with the Duke Ellington Orchestra in 1939, recording his biggest hit song, "Flamingo," that same year. After the bombing of Pearl Harbor, Jeffries joined the American military and remained in France for ten years after the end of the war (Davis).

As discriminatory practices began to change, African American movie theaters suffered from competition with more accessible Hollywood movies and the market for black-audience films diminished. According to Mark Reid, the black independents also suffered because much of their talent started to appear in Hollywood movies, for which they were better compensated. Reid's example is Lena Horne, whose debut was in a black-audience movie but who then signed with MGM (16). The full history behind these movies does not sit comfortably, though, in the annals of African American race movies. There is another intersecting history crucial in this cycle: that of genre.

In "'Our Country'/Whose Country? The 'Americanization' Project of Early Westerns," Richard Abel argues that the westerns of the 1910s were represented in the press as a distinctive American genre, not least because of their white-supremacist and xenophobic ideologies. The press called the "Wild West subjects" the "foundation of an American moving picture drama" and noted the "educational (that is, ideological) potential" for the audiences, made up mainly of young boys (Abel 83). In the context of the new masculinity of Theodore Roosevelt and other proponents of patriotic, expansionist "Americanism," the western offered a white male hero who appealed to boys across class and immigrant distinctions, "something like a genre of their own to go along with the separate spheres of play, toys, and clothing that were becoming part of their training for manhood" (Abel 84). Abel does not theorize about whether African American boys might have felt included in this new genre, but he is very clear on the importance of American nationalist and racialist ideology in the iconography of early westerns.

The commercial success of the black westerns depended on their conforming to the western genre's iconography: costume, props, plots, setting, and characters. Bob Blake rides the range on his white horse, Stardusk, decked out in a tailored western shirt with fringe across the chest, high-heeled cowboy boots, a white hat, and a shiny pair of guns. The story always involves a struggle over land, as mentioned above, and a battle to punish the villain, usually in a shootout at the climax of the movie. But the black westerns are not only westerns. They also belong to a specific sub-genre, much neglected by film scholars: singing-cowboy movies. Exploring this subgenre is a crucial step in understanding the black musical westerns that are the subject of this chapter.

The *BFI Companion* informs us that the Herb Jeffries singing-cowboy movies were clear imitations of Hollywood westerns of the period, not only in their choice of hero—Jeffries's singing cowboy was very much in the Gene Autry/Tex Ritter vein—but also in their highly derivative stories and plot devices" (Buscombe 69). Not calling it imitation but rather admiration, Jeffries himself has said that "Gene Autry was a big hero of mine and the morality of our pictures was based on Gene Autry films," in that the hero, Bob Blake, "wouldn't shoot anyone unless it was in self-defense. And he'd never smoke or drink" (Griffin).

Black westerns do resemble Hollywood's singing-cowboy movies, which followed the mild-mannered, highly moralistic plots deemed appropriate for young children and included songs and action for spectacle. Jeffries admired Autry for his morality, which included the Ten Cowboy Commandments: the hero "(1) Never takes unfair advantage, (2) Never goes back on his word, (3) Always tells the truth ," and so on through "(10) Is a patriot (above all)" (Buscombe 35-36). Bob Blake is a walking example of this honor code, which Autry certainly did not invent but did much to popularize, especially among young audiences. Bob's theme song, "I'm a Happy Cowboy," opens several of the movies—"with my rope and my saddle and my horse and my gun, I'm a happy cowboy"—establishing him as a benevolent soul whose only desire is to work on a ranch, sing songs, and help people. Bob Blake succeeded in providing young African Americans with a brave, strong, and patriotic American hero by adopting many of the Hollywood conventions of the cowboy image.

While I do not want to suggest, as do many critics and historians, that the Jeffries movies are merely imitations of movies for whites, the decision to make black musical westerns must have been influenced by the enormous box-office success of the Hollywood singing cowboys, given that the western in its more serious versions was less popular at the time. White independent directors and white-owned production companies made the black musical westerns in the late 1930s, when Gene Autry was among the top-ten moneymakers in Hollywood for his musical westerns, including *Tumblin'·Tumbleweeds* (1935) and *The Singing Cowboy* (1937). African American audiences, like white audiences, loved westerns, despite their frequently racist subtexts and plots. Jeffries recalls touring the South in the 1930s, where he noticed "there were thousands of small movie theaters where blacks went to watch the cowboy pictures of Tom Mix, Buck Jones, Ken Maynard, and Duke Wayne because they weren't allowed in white theaters" (Davis).

Perhaps for some of the same reasons, including access to the nationalistic myths of individualism, bravery, and adventure, audiences of all races found something to like in westerns. During the Depression, certainly, their core values reaffirmed demoralized audiences. Black-audience westerns could have functioned in a similar way, providing a happy ending to a story of heroic struggle, as bell hooks believes Micheaux's movies did:

Addressing the black public's need to have race movies reproduce aspects of white mainstream cinema that denied their presence, Micheaux incorporates into his work familiar melodramatic narratives. Just as the white 'master' narratives of cinema insisted that plots be structured around conflicts between good and evil, this became the usual ground of conflict in race movies. (135)

It is also likely, however, that the music was more of a draw than the acting or the story, since, as black-audience film veteran Harrell Tillman has said, Jeffries's performances were uneven in the cowboy movies: he was "an outstanding singer but a bad actor" (qtd. in Jones 169). In any case, American audiences were accustomed to musicals with thin plots, even expected them. For example, according to a review of *Harlem on the Prairie* in *Film Daily:* "There is little to the story, but it makes no difference as pix is designed as a musical" (qtd. in Sampson 384). Indeed, the 1930s black-audience singing-cowboy movie is important because of its unique musical expressions: the black country-and-western music provides a rare glimpse at the real diversity of what is often assumed to be a very "white" musical form.

Although the cinematic genre I am calling the black-audience musical western was constructed at least partially based on the conventions of Hollywood westerns and singing-cowboy movies, the music in black westerns is not easily traced to popular mainstream trends. After all, the label "singing-cowboy movie" may conjure up images and echoes of Autry or Roy Rogers, but no viewer of the black-audience "horse operas" can dismiss the music as derivative. With excellent songs and a variety of other spectacle, including dance numbers, these films provoke the question of whether the cowboy song really was a "white" form at all. In *The Bronze Buckaroo,* for example, the song "Almost Time for Roundup" echoes the well-established black forms of the blues and the spiritual in its plaintive sound and the call-and-response structure. So is Herb Jeffries as the singing cowboy a mere imitation of white stars like Gene Autry, whose cowboy code of honor he admired? Or is the music in these black musical westerns distinct from Autry's in some way, perhaps a specifically African American cowboy music? I answer this question by first looking at the scholarship on the singing cowboy that currently exists.

As Peter Stanfield points out in his fascinating genealogy of Gene Autry's oeuvre, "Dixie Cowboys and Blue Yodels: The Strange History of the Singing Cowboy," cinema scholars and critics, including Robert Warshow and Jon Tuska, "have systematically ignored or vilified Autry" and the other Hollywood singing cowboys on grounds ranging from their inauthenticity to their insufficient masculinity and even for not conforming to the generic ideal established around movies like *Stagecoach* from the same decade (13-14). As a result of this gap in scholarship, the shared connections between black and white musical forms in country-and-western music, crucially popularized in the singing-cowboy movies of both Autry and Jeffries, have not been adequately examined; Autry's popularity rested on his singing, but how many fans of cowboy songs know that these songs' origins lie in blackface medicine shows of the rural South rather than ranch hands singing the dogies to sleep on the prairies of the American West?

Stanfield traces the history of the white singing cowboy, which is "intimately tied up in [the] process of making Country music respectable and therefore marketable" (100). He argues further that the cowboy image enabled the performers to escape the negative connotations of poor white rural southerners, "simultaneously suggesting a classless and uncontroversial image of white supremacy" (100). For the white southern musician, the cowboy stage persona was an escape from contemporary cultural conflicts over the rural/urban divide and the uneven results of the industrialization of the South:

The cowboy carried none of the overt racist or class connotations of the hillbilly or his white-trash cousin, [...] yet through deed and action the cowboy supported the concept of Anglo-Saxon superiority while also being incontestably of American origin. (Stanfield 104)

Retreating into an image of the mythical American hero, poor white country-and-western singers could smooth over their less-than-privileged origins by becoming cowboys.

The "white" form of the cowboy song has a more diverse origin as well, beginning in the medicine shows that toured the South selling snake oil and entertaining crowds with tales of the West; in fact, young Gene Autry traveled with the Field Brothers Marvelous Medicine Show and most likely performed in blackface (Stanfield 97). Moreover, by taking the role of the cowboy, country-and-western musicians avoided controversy over their poor white southern as well as their black southern musical roots, the evidence of·a common stock of influences that constantly challenges our idea of racial segregation in the South (Stanfield 104).

The Herb Jeffries musical westerns reinforce Stanfield's point: whereas the cowboy persona is an effective way to avoid the specificities of racial stereotypes—white trash, in the case of white southern musicians—in the case of African Americans, the cowboy image symbolized what Abel calls "the mantle of national identity" minus the limitations imposed on nonwhite Americans (Abel 83). Making an all-black musical western thus involved not only negotiation but also innovation: in negotiating the cowboy persona as a shortcut to American national identity and in blending the seemingly white musical form with its southern, African American roots via blues and jazz.

## RACE AND REPRESENTATION IN THE BLACK-AUDIENCE WESTERNS

While black-audience films overall portray a vastly wider range of African American characters, some stereotyped roles do exist. For example, the singing cowboy's sidekick in black-audience westerns was played up as a classic 'coon' by actors Lucius Brooks in *Buckaroo* and *Range* and by Mantan Moreland in *Prairie* and *Two-Gun*.[7] Bogle details Moreland's "daffy coon antics" in late-1940s "all-colored features that openly celebrated his wide-eyed manic energy" without the derisive edge of racism that pervades coon roles in white films (Kisch and Mapp xxviii). Bogle insists on recognizing the talent of African American actors even when they were hired to play stereotyped roles in Hollywood or in independents: "no one in his right mind could ever claim that the roles these performers played were anything other than flat-out deplorable. Yet no one can deny that the actors and actresses were significant talents" (Kisch and Mapp xxiv). My interest in the coon stereotype is not to categorize and thereby limit the interpretation of the character, or to discredit the endeavors of black-audience cinema in general. Rather, I propose to historicize the coon character in the specific context of the black western, encountering the following questions along the way: How might African American audiences at the time have read the coon character differently in race movies than in the context of Hollywood westerns, and what factors affected audience reception of this character within this particular context? What other racial issues did film makers have to consider in their scripting and casting decisions?

---

7    The entry for "Blacks" in the *BFI Companion to the Western* also makes this point, citing the "eye-rolling necrophobic negro" as its example (Buscombe 69).

For example, sidekick Dusty in *Range* and *Buckaroo* is always hungry, lazy, and joking, and he speaks black English. But the saving grace of the coon character in black-audience westerns is that he pulls in all the laughs. And instead of that laughter being associated with racist humiliation as it would in a white movie, in which the coon character was played by the only African American actor in the cast, audiences of race films could feel freer to enjoy the slapstick humor of the character without feeling betrayed, angry, or ashamed. During the 1930s, the presence of a coon character in a black-cast western that also featured a dashing cowboy hero, a villainous land grabber, and a beautiful damsel in distress must have been less traumatic for African American audiences than facing him as the only black character in a white-cast movie, as Barbara Bryant recalls: "In the black films, when a comic was being a comic, it was against a perspective which was balanced by the fact that he was being comical with other black people who were being sane, in control, and acting the roles of substantial citizens" (qtd. in Jones 170).

The complex forms of imitation and innovation implicit in these movies require a careful unpacking of the racial coding of the sidekick coon, demonstrating the negotiation of racial stereotypes involved in the task of scripting. First, the movie must replicate the authorizing aspects of the cowboy genre so that it appears to be legitimate within its genre and so that African American audiences can freely identify with the cowboy. Second, the movie must attempt to conform to the white genre in at least some respects, but without playing into its preexisting racial hierarchies. Caught in the middle of this negotiation, the coon character represents a vestigial racist film heritage that black-audience westerns want to escape but cannot completely avoid.[8] Further marking Dusty's behavior as stereotypical, the romantic leads are differentiated from him by speaking standard English and behaving like their counterparts in (white) Hollywood movies—that is, as though they were racially unmarked. Amplifying the racial codings, the coon character in these westerns is played by actors such as Brooks or Moreland, whose skin color is noticeably darker than that of the male and female leads, played by Herb Jeffries and Artie Young. What Bogle terms

---

8   The expression "vestigial racist film heritage" refers to Ella Shohat and Robert Stam's notion of "vestigial thinking," a Eurocentric, racist, and imperialist ideological inflection that persists after the official demise of colonialism (2).

"color coding" still reveals the marks of the racist culture in which these films were produced, even if there are no white actors and the movies were made in the spirit of race pride.

Yet, in many ways, the coon character is the star of the movie. In *Buckaroo*, for example, Dusty figures out how to trick the ranch hand who sold him a talking mule that will not talk. He also fires the shot that kills the villain during the climactic shootout, something that rarely happens in white westerns. Add to this heroism the fact that Bob Blake *is* very light-skinned, so much so that at first the star worried that black audiences would not believe he was African American (Davis). As Jane Gaines writes about *The Scar of Shame* (Frank Peregini, 1927),

> Black and white film stock registered too much truth—on the screen racially mixed actors looked white. Conversely, the dark-skinned blacks preferred by white producers [for stereotyped roles] were unacceptable in star roles in race films. They were not idealized (i.e., white) enough. ("*Scar of Shame*" 75)

Given the convention in race movies of casting light-skinned actors in lead roles, assigning the darker coon sidekick such an important role shifted some of the heroism away from Bob Blake, the lighter-skinned "star." Bob Blake is also the straight man to Dusty's clown; as Jeffries has said, this is one thing that distinguished black westerns from white: "It was real vaudeville [...] I was the straight man and he was the comic relief" (Griffin). The highlight of the movie for some audiences may well have been the laughs Dusty generated, rather than the upstanding morality of Bob, compounded by Dusty's heroic behavior in the shootout.

The paths of identification for other viewers of color were less clear, since the movies lack the usual western staple of Mexican and Native American characters. It is possible that the film makers neglected to include these characters for fear of reproducing negative Hollywood stereotypes for those roles. For a western, however, in which some degree of genre conformity is necessary for audience recognition, omitting the Mexican and Native American characters constitutes a risky move.

This omission is also significant because these stereotypes are crucial to a primary ideological function of the classical Hollywood western: to signify the consolidation of American identity at the frontier in which the white race dominates and incorporates all other nationalities and identities.[9] Indeed, as actor-director Ossie Davis pointedly recalls, "When we saw black folks in the [Hollywood] westerns at that particular time, usually the parts were so derogatory that we identified with the Indians rather than with the blacks!" (qtd. in Jones 167). The need to identify with a character of color enabled Davis to cross-identify with Native American characters rather than with the dehumanized African Americans, such as the coon in white westerns.

Given Davis's remarks, the absence of Mexican and Native American characters is obvious in the cycle of black musical westerns and signals a questioning or rejection of the stereotyped roles for these identities in Hollywood westerns. With the hero Bob Blake playing a racially unmarked cowboy hero on a white horse, the movies managed to negotiate the presence of the stereotyped and racially marked coon, but adding characters of differently racialized identities would have upset the all-black world that the films posit. Historically and generically, the raced identity of a Mexican or Native American character in the context of a black-cowboy movie would also necessarily (if unintentionally) signify their oppression at the hands of white America, represented by the cowboys, who are all played by African Americans.

The incongruity of African American actors portraying American imperialists and oppressors of other people of color may have struck the film makers as too difficult to negotiate. Cowboy roles were important vehicles for imagining black men as serious, masculine American heroes, but that could only work in an all-black milieu. Davis recalls the thrill of seeing a black cowboy character "in chaps and spurs and with guns on, who knew how to get on a horse and how to ride off and catch the villain and knock the living daylights out of him" (qtd. in Jones 168). Notice that Davis uses the word "villain" rather than "Indian" ; the villain had to be another black character rather than an Indian or a Mexican to maintain the illusion of a fictional all-black nation without the contradictions of overt racism.

Although black westerns performed an important function for their 1930s audiences—they invited black Americans to see black men as fully vested American citizens and as righteous heroes—this revision collided

---

9   For more on the role of the frontier in American national identity, see Slotkin. For more on the history of white supremacy in the West, see Drinnon.

with the function of race in the generic ideologies of the western as a representation of U.S. imperialism. As a nation-building narrative of "imperial-style adventures," the western legitimates the American nation's "manifest destiny" to permeate the borders of Indian and Mexican nations, while portraying any reverse movement as a ferocious attack on white civilized society, as symbolized by the sanctity of American land (Shohat and Stam 115). The geographical and historical displacements required for the black-audience western to succeed would have been overwhelmed if the overtly racist nature of U.S. western expansion were incorporated into the movies' already-precarious appropriation of the Hollywood cowboy genre. Because of this conflict, and despite the ready availability of Chicano and Native American actors in Hollywood at the time, black-audience westerns steered clear of the maze of racial power relations that casting actors of another ethnicity would have involved.[10]

For audiences of black westerns, political affinities with the victims of American racist and imperialist aggression might have complicated their identification with a cowboy character who kills Indians, even if he were played by an African American actor: hence the significant omission of cowboy/Indian battles in these movies. This omission is underscored by the sole mention of Mexico in *Harlem Rides the Range,* which indicates how awkwardly a Mexican character would have been positioned were he included. The ranch cook, Slim Perkins (F.E. Miller), is cajoled into a target competition, shooting cans off a fence rail. Slim is a coon character like Dusty, a cowardly but comical buffoon. His shooting skills are appalling at first, but then suddenly he hits a can with every shot. With his change in luck, Slim becomes boastful, claiming he was famous for his shooting tricks in Mexico, where he sat in the stands at bullfights and secretly shot the bull to help out the ineffectual bullfighter. His bragging comes to an abrupt end when Bob Blake reveals that he has been secretly shooting the cans to make Slim appear to be a good shot; all involved, except Slim,

---

10 In the "late 1930s and throughout the 1940s, an increasing number of Hispanic actors [...] appeared in Latin-themed films," thanks to the U.S. government's Good Neighbor policies, which encouraged trade with Latin America, including exports to enormous movie markets (Reyes and Rubie 15). According to Abel, Native Americans were cast in Hollywood movies from the earliest silents, although their roles were usually predictable stereotypes (85).

laugh heartily. Slim shifts from being entertaining and braggardly to being humiliated as he is exposed as a liar and a bad shot.

This scene performs two functions: it establishes the light-complected hero Bob as superior to the darker, more comic coon character Slim, while setting up a similar (fantastical) relation of superiority between Slim and an unnamed Mexican bullfighter. Although the film's color coding portrays Bob as better than Slim, it also allows Slim to position himself (however temporarily) as superior to someone else, the Mexican bullfighter, who is as bad at bullfighting as Slim is at shooting. The reference to a Mexican character, though imaginary, models the hierarchies that remain embedded in the western even in its black-audience version.

## STRATEGIC ANACHRONISM, GEOGRAPHICAL JUXTAPOSITION, AND CULTURAL IDENTIFICATION

In his exploration of shifting identity formations within a historically contingent and geographically diverse diaspora, Stuart Hall describes culture as "the terrain for producing identity, for producing the constitution of social subjects" (Hall 291). Black-audience westerns function as that terrain, particularly when we examine how their geographical and representational landscape first needs to be deterritorialized and unhinged from its white imperialist resonances and then reterritorialized as an African American national landscape.

To create believable black westerns, the movies employ several of what I call "strategic anachronisms," which would have most likely struck audiences as out of place yet somehow appropriate.[11] The explanation for these

---

11 This phrase alludes to Gayatri Chakravorty Spivak's much-debated conception of "strategic essentialism." Spivak's term works as a model for mine because she suggests that the relatively devalued concept of essentialism can be strategically employed as a basis for resistance in specific situations in which essentialist categories are mobilized as the basis for discrimination. In the world of cinema, anachronism is generally perceived as a flaw, as a lapse in the mimetic "reality" that the film attempts to create. I argue that these films strategically manipulate anachronism for purposes of cultural identification.

strategic anachronisms may lie in their common source: a publicly recognizable national black culture. While black audiences in the late 1930s may not have had full access to the histories of African Americans in the West—these histories having been largely suppressed until very recently—black audiences would have immediately recognized the twentieth-century signifiers of black culture that the films transpose into the western genre, particularly a black culture that was invisible to white movie audiences: the black middle classes. The anachronisms, along with the geographical juxtapositions of East and West, function as anchors for audiences to identify the movies and characters as "black." Standing with one foot in the historical American West and the other in the Harlem Renaissance, the black westerns thus perform an impressive balancing act.

According to Mark Reid, the first race movies were set in middle-class northern black communities (7-8). The prevailing emphasis on class also struck Thomas Cripps as significant: *"The Scar of Shame* and every other race movie of the 1920s retailed a black bourgeois success myth, a manual for those on the make, and a caution to the weak-willed who might be diverted from success by urban temptations" ("Race Movies" 50). *Scar* addresses serious issues, including class mobility, passing, and color consciousness in the African American middle class. Gaines points out that race movies such as *Scar* "were created by the black bourgeoisie, often in collaboration with whites, for the entertainment and edification of the group below them," a group that was divided along the lines of rural and urban environments and different levels of literacy (*"Scar"* 62). Many black-audience movies portray for national audiences the otherwise invisible world of middle-class African Americans. William Greaves, who acted in black-audience movies, including *Souls of Sin* (1949)[12] and *Miracle in Harlem* (1948), recalls: "You could see a black doctor, [...] a black lawyer, [...] a black gangster or a black whatever, and you could feel, 'That's right! We are people who can function in all walks of life!'" (qtd. in Jones 172).

One important function of the strategic anachronism in black-audience westerns is that they offered audiences representations of the contemporary African American middle class. In addition to well-spoken cowboy Bob, the characters who most clearly represent the middle class are the women—Miss Betty, Miss Dennison, and Sally Thompson—whose costuming and

---

12  The synopsis and stills from *Souls of Sin* appear in Jones 129-37.

appearance ground them firmly in the 1930s. For example, as Miss Dennison in *Range,* Artie Young has relatively little screen time and functions
primarily as a fantasy love object for Bob Blake, who has seen only Miss
Dennison's photograph when he falls in love with her. Later, when she finally appears in the flesh, Miss Dennison is the epitome of the beautiful
young 1930s woman: her short hair is marcelled and she wears a string of
pearls and a knee-length skirt. For an African American audience in the
1930s, the thrill of seeing a lovely black woman as a romantic lead, however abbreviated her screen time, must have been powerful, because the only
roles for black women in Hollywood films were small and narrowly conceived, mainly servants.[13] Not only is Young's character conspicuously not
a servant but she is portrayed as fashionable, well-traveled, and educated.
Furthermore, her fair skin contributes to the "color coding," as Bogle calls
it, that dominates the black westerns and conspires with the social conventions of the time, which marked lighter skin as more beautiful. This point is
underscored by the complete absence of any darker-skinned women in any
of the movies. Young's modern, fashionable appearance invited a 1930s
audience to identify with her precisely through the anachronistic incongrui-
ties of her costume and hairstyle.

Most likely, the low budget was a primary reason for the lack of period
costuming in *Range,* but the result is a western that creates a dual present.
The fictional characters appear to be in the classic western setting, in the
nineteenth century, but the anachronistic dialogue, the titles, and the costumes place the film firmly in the 1930s. To deterritorialize the western
from its imperialist bent and reterritorialize it as a "black" West, these films
employ anachronism and geographical displacement. Throughout the series
of black-audience westerns, the appearance of these strategic anachronisms
signals the need to ground the films in a contemporary 1930s black culture
in order to appeal to the audience. The constant references—verbal, visual,
and formal—to the films' fictional present as well as the contemporary dialogue and costumes constitute the dual present that allowed 1930s African

---

13 Also in 1939, Hattie McDaniel became the first African American woman to
   win an Academy Award, in the role of the domestic Mammy in *Gone with the
   Wind.* For an excellent discussion of how McDaniel and other African American
   performers brought dignity and humanity even to the most degrading roles, see
   Bogle (*Toms* 82-89).

American audiences to identify simultaneously with the western heroes of the nineteenth-century story and the cultural milieu of the Harlem Renaissance. This dual present extends the site of black western heroes as well as latter-day black heroes.

Twenty years after Oscar Micheaux's westerns, *The Homesteader* and *Symbol of the Unconquered,* African American audiences had been exposed to movies about black cowboys, including some with Bill Pickett in the early 1920s. But the incongruity, at least by Hollywood conventions, of African American ranchers and homesteaders in cowboy costumes feuding over valuable land is suggested even in the titles of three of the films: *Harlem on the Prairie, Two-Gun Man from Harlem,* and *Harlem Rides the Range.* These titles enact a geographical and temporal sleight of hand in which Harlem, the symbolic site of twentieth-century urban African American experience, is geographically transposed to the West, a place that in Hollywood movies is populated by land-owning whites, along with a handful of African American and Mexican laborers, cooks, and performers and by Indians whose main filmic function is to be shot at and killed. The "blackness" of the movies is proclaimed with the signifier "Harlem" in their titles, although the assumed time period of *Prairie* and *Range* predates any association of Harlem with black culture.[14] Although audiences were thought to have problems with Gene Autry's contemporary westerns because their expectations were that a western should be a nineteenth-century story, the box-office success of the singing-cowboy movies do not bear out this assumption (Stanfield 114). As Peter Stanfield points out, Gene Autry's contemporary musical westerns "addressed the difficulties his audience confronted in making the socioeconomic change from subsistence farming to a culture of consumption, from self-employment to industrial practices and wage dependency, from rural to urban living" (115). The timeliness of the dilemmas around land and home ownership in black musical westerns must have also appealed to audiences in the 1930s; indeed, Cripps suggests that black audiences were already experiencing some of the same economic and

---

14  *Two-Gun Man from Harlem* is a "contemporary" western, as noted in the plot summary; however, the generic blending of a western with a melodrama and murder mystery also distinguishes *Two-Gun* from the other movies in which Herbert Jeffries appeared.

geographical dislocations during the 1920s that Stanfield attributes to the audiences of Autry's movies ("Race Movies" 48-49).

None of the characters in any of the black westerns is actually from Harlem. In *Range*, Bob says he is from "down Amarillo way," in the Texas panhandle. But one of the effects of the Harlem Renaissance on the national black culture was that it provided a geographical and imaginary site that was known, even to those who had never been there, as the capital of black America—a neighborhood that existed literally in New York City and metaphorically as the center of black cultural production. Thus, black-audience westerns ironically enact an expansionist movement of their own, fulfilling the western's generic imperative to appropriate land in a westward direction by extending the geography of black America beyond the borders of Harlem and into the archetypal American West.

Another strategic manipulation of convention in the black western can be discerned in the geographical juxtaposition of Harlem with the West in *Two-Gun Man from Harlem*. In Hollywood westerns, the East is traditionally invoked as the site of culture and civilization, whether positive or negative in connotation, in contrast to the wild, untamed West. In *Two-Gun*, the East is mentioned in a reference to singer and bandleader Cab Calloway of Harlem's Cotton Club, but the reference functions differently. The comic coon character, named Mistletoe (Mantan Moreland), constantly brags about the merits of his cooking. After signifying at length on his steaks, which he says are as "tender as a mother's lullaby," Mistletoe claims his chili is the "same as a swing tune from Cab Calloway's band—red hot!" Like Dusty's clowning in *Buckaroo* and Slim's in *Range*, Mistletoe's comedy is one of the high points *of Two-Gun*. But his reference to Cab Calloway's swing tunes also functions to ground the 1930s audience in a black urban cultural milieu—the imaginary site of Harlem. After all, members of the African American audience had at least heard of Calloway, and most probably knew a great deal about him. Mentioning a swing tune by Cab Calloway in an all-black western invited audiences to identify not only with African American cowboys in the West but also with a beloved well-known musician of the current day, thereby spatially extending the realm of black culture from the metonymic site of Harlem into the West.

# HOME ON THE RANGE: MAKING SPACE FOR AN AFRICAN AMERICAN WEST

At first glance, the black westerns appear insignificant in the wider realm of film and cultural history; they are often formulaic and suffer from extremely low production values, and the performances and editing frequently lack the polish of Hollywood westerns. Nonetheless, I argue that the cycle of late-1930s black-audience musical westerns constitutes a unique moment in African American cinema: made during the Great Depression, they address the fears and insecurities of audiences facing national crisis. They also target a specific age group: young African Americans, primarily boys. This audience necessitated the heightened emphasis on spectacle, represented by the action and musical sequences. As perhaps another consequence of this younger audience, the movies had less overtly politicized subject matter: they did not thematize the kinds of "social problems" that many other race movies did, especially in the 1920s. That is not to say that they were not political, only that their politics was more implicit than explicit.

Because of these unique qualities, the cycle of black singing-cowboy movies calls for a slightly different critical approach from that taken toward other race movies, such as those of Oscar Micheaux. Black westerns are, unlike the work of an African American auteur like Micheaux, the collaborative effort of black singers, actors, and writers and white directors and producers. For this reason, terms such as "black independent cinema" and "separate cinema" do not apply. Whether or not auteurs such as Micheaux were influenced by Hollywood, the black-audience musical westerns definitely were. But that influence is only the beginning of the story, as I have tried to indicate. Perhaps because of their white backers and collaborators, or perhaps because they targeted a young audience and wanted only to entertain, black-audience westerns do not overtly—at the level of the story—challenge the imperialist racial hierarchies embedded in the Hollywood western. Rather than arguing that their collaborative origins make them less authentic or inherently compromised their political import, I maintain that black-audience musical westerns need to be placed in a wider context that accounts for their place in African American culture and in white American culture as well.

By arguing that black musical westerns imitate some of the generic conventions of singing-cowboy movies, I do not mean to suggest that the former replicated the subtext of white supremacy inherent in Hollywood fare; on the contrary, black westerns represent a complex negotiation between the pitfalls of the existing genre and the utopian premise of an all-black nation. They prove that imagining oneself as a real American is not the same as imagining oneself as a white American; on the contrary, these movies assert the rightful place of African Americans at the moment and the location of the nation's most heroic embodiments, the western frontier. The constructions of black masculinity in these films do not simply echo Hollywood's images of American national identity but actively participate in the formation of an identity that is uniquely African American.

## FILMOGRAPHY OF BLACK-AUDIENCE WESTERNS, 1919-1948

*Saddle Daze.* Wild West Rodeo. No studio or date.

*The Homesteader.* With Charles Lucas and Evelyn Preer. Written, directed, and produced by Oscar Micheaux. Micheaux Film Corp., 1919.

*The Crimson Skull.* With Anita Bush, Lawrence Chenault, and Bill Pickett. Norman Film Co., 1921.

*Shoot 'em Up, Sam.* No cast information. Black Western Film Co., 1922.

*The Stranger from Way Out Yonder.* No cast information . Tone Star Motion Picture Co., 1922.

*The Bull Dogger.* With Bill Pickett and Anita Bush. Norman Film Co., 1923.

*A Chocolate Cowboy* (short). With Fred Parker and Teddy Reavis. Cyclone Comedy, 1925.

*Black Gold.* With Lawrence Criner, Kathryn Boyd, Steve Reynolds, and "the entire all-colored town of Tatum, Oklahoma." Norman Film Co., 1928.

*Harlem on the Prairie.* With Herb Jeffries, Mantan Moreland, F.E. Miller, and Spencer Williams. Produced by Jed Buell, directed by Sam Newfield, and supervised by Maceo Sheffield. Toddy Pictures and Associated Features, 1937.

*The Bronze Buckaroo.* With Herb Jeffries, Spencer Williams, Lucius Brooks, Clarence Brooks, F.E. Miller, and Artie Young. Directed by Richard C. Kahn. Hollywood Productions, 1938.

*Rhythm Rodeo* (short). With Troy Brown , the Four Tones, the Jackson Brothers, Rosa Lee Lincoln, and Jim Davis. Produced by George Randol. George Randol Productions, 1938.

*Harlem Rides the Range.* With Herb Jeffries, Clarence Brooks, F.E. Miller, Lucius Brooks, Spencer Williams, and the Four Tones. Screenplay by Spencer Williams and Flournoy E. Miller and directed by Richard C. Kahn. Hollywood Productions, 1939.

*Two-Gun Man from Harlem.* With Herb Jeffries, Clarence Brooks, Margaret Whitten, Stymie, Spencer Williams, and the Four Tones. Directed by Richard C. Kahn. Sack Amusement and Merit Pictures, 1939.

*Look Out, Sister.* With Louis Jordan and His Caledonia Tympany Band, Suzette Harbin, and Monte Hawley. Directed by Bud Pollard. Astor Pictures, 1946.

*Come on, Cowboy.* With Mantan Moreland, Johnny Lee, F.E. Miller, Mauryne Brent. Toddy Pictures and Goldmax Productions, 1948.

*Sun Tan Ranch.* With Byron and Bean, Eunice Wilson, and Joel Fluellen. Norwanda Pictures, 1948.

## WORKS CITED

Abel, Richard. "'Our Country'/Whose Country? The 'Americanization' Project of Early Westerns." Buscombe and Pearson 77-95. Print.

Bogle, Donald. *Blacks in American Films and Television: An Illustrated Encyclopedia*. New York: Fireside, 1988. Print.

---. *Toms, Coons, Mulattoes, Mammies, and Bucks: An Interpretive History of Blacks in American Films*. New York: Continuum-Ungar, 1989. Print.

Bowser, Pearl, and Louise Spence. "Oscar Micheaux's *Body and Soul* and the Burden of Representation." *Cinema Journal* 39.3 (2000): 3-29. Print.

Buscombe, Edward, and Roberta Pearson, eds. *Back in the Saddle Again: New Essays on the Western*. London: BFI, 1998. Print.

Buscombe, Edward, ed. *The BFI Companion to the Western*. New York: Atheneum, 1988. Print.

Butters, Jr., Gerald. "Portrayals of Black Masculinity in Oscar Micheaux's *The Homesteader*." *Literature Film Quarterly* 28.1 (2000): 54-59. Print.

Coyne, Michael. *The Crowded Prairie: American National Identity in the Hollywood Western.* New York: Tauris, 1997. Print.

Cripps, Thomas. "'Race Movies' as Voices of the Black Bourgeoisie: *The Scar of Shame.*" Smith 47-60.

---. "Oscar Micheaux: The Story Continues." Diawara *Black* 71-79. Print.

Davis, David. "The Golden Buckaroo." *Los Angeles Times Magazine.* 6 Apr. 2003. Web. 17 July 2015.

Diawara, Manthia, ed. *Black American Cinema.* New York: Routledge, 1993. Print.

Diawara, Manthia. "Black Spectatorship: Problems of Identification and Resistance." *Screen* 29.4 (1988): 66-81. Print.

Drinnon, Richard. *Facing West: The Metaphysics of Indian Hating and Empire Building.* Minneapolis: U of Minnesota P, 1985. Print.

Gaines, Jane. "Fire and Desire: Race, Melodrama, and Oscar Micheaux." Diawara *Black* 49-70.

---. "*The Scar of Shame:* Skin Color and Caste in Black Silent Melodrama." *Cinema Journal* 26.4 (1987): 3-21. Rpt. in Smith. 61-82. Print.

George, Nelson. *Blackface: Reflections on African-Americans and the Movies.* New York: Harper, 1994. Print.

Green, J. Ronald. "'Twoness' in the Style of Oscar Micheaux." Diawara *Black* 26-48.

Griffin, Gil. "He was a Black Hero in a White Hat." *San Diego Union-Tribune* 20 Apr. 1999. Print.

Grupenhoff, Richard. "The Rediscovery of Oscar Micheaux, Black Film Pioneer." *Journal of the University Film and Video Association* 40.1 (1988): 40-48. Print.

Guerrero, Ed. *Framing Blackness: The African American Image in Film.* Philadelphia: Temple UP, 1993. Print.

Hall, Stuart. "Making Diasporic Identities." Lubiano 289-300.

Hoffman, Donald. "Whose Home on the Range? Finding Room for Native Americans, African Americans, and Latino Americans in the Revisionist Western." *MELUS* 22.2 (1997): 45-59. Print.

hooks, bell. "Micheaux's Films: Celebrating Blackness." *Black Looks: Race and Representation.* Boston: South End P, 1992. Print.

Jones, G. William. *Black Cinema Treasures: Lost and Found.* Denton: U of North Texas P, 1991. Print.

Katz, William Loren. *The Black West: A Documentary and Pictorial History of the African American Role in the Western Expansion of the United States*. New York: Simon and Schuster, 1996. Print.

Kisch, John, and Edward Mapp. *A Separate Cinema: Fifty Years of Black Cast Posters*. Foreword Donald Bogle. New York: Noonday-Farrar, 1992. Print.

Leab, Daniel J. *From Sambo to Superspade: The Black Experience in Motion Pictures*. Boston: Houghton Mifflin, 1975. Print.

Lubiano, Wahneema, ed. *The House that Race Built*. New York: Vintage, 1998. Print.

Mitchell, Lee Clark. *Westerns: Making the Man in Fiction and Film*. Chicago: U of Chicago P, 1996. Print.

Morrison, Toni. "Home." Lubiano 3-12. Print.

Phillips, Robert W. *Singing Cowboy Stars*. Salt Lake City: Gibbs-Smith, 1994. Print.

Regester, Charlene. "Lynched, Assaulted, and Intimidated: Oscar Micheaux's Most Controversial Films." *Popular Culture Review* 5.1 (1994): 47-55. Print.

Reid, Mark. *Redefining Black Film*. Berkeley: U of California P, 1993. Print.

Reyes, Luis, and Peter Rubie. *Hispanics in Hollywood: An Encyclopedia of Film and Television*. New York: Garland, 1994. Print.

Sampson, Henry T. *Blacks in Black and White: A Source Book on Black Films*. 2nd edn. Metuchen, NJ: Scarecrow, 1995. Print.

Shohat, Ella, and Robert Stam. *Unthinking Eurocentrism: Multiculturalism and the Media*. New York: Routledge, 1994. Print.

Slotkin, Richard. *Gunfighter Nation: The Myth of the Frontier in Twentieth-Century America*. 1992. Norman: U of Oklahoma P, 1998. Print.

Smith, Valerie, ed. *Representing Blackness: Issues in Film and Video*. New Brunswick: Rutgers UP, 1997. Print.

Spivak, Gayatri Chakravorty. "Can the Subaltern Speak?" *Marxism and the Interpretation of Culture*. Ed. Douglas Kellner. Urbana: U of Illinois P, 1988. 271-313. Print.

Stanfield, Peter. "Dixie Cowboys and Blue Yodels: The Strange History of the Singing Cowboy." Buscombe and Pearson 96-118. Print.

Streible, Dan. "The Harlem Theater: Black Film Exhibition in Austin, Texas: 1920-1973." Diawara *Black* 221-36.

Zwisohn, Lawrence. "The Western: Through the Years on Film and Television." *Songs of the West*. Rhino Records, 1993. Audio CD.

# 5 Space, Class, City

## Imagined Geographies of *Maud Martha*

*Maud Martha* is the only work of fiction by Gwendolyn Brooks (1917-2000), the first African American poet to win a Pulitzer Prize. It is a short novel or novella made up of a series of vignettes centering around the title character, a young black woman, covering the period from her childhood to early adulthood in Chicago. The frontispiece tells us that "Maud Martha was born in 1917 and she is still alive," creating a kind of immortality for the main character. The book was published in 1953 to positive reviews, although literary historians such as Mary Helen Washington argue convincingly that it was overshadowed at the time by Ralph Ellison's *Invisible Man*, published in the previous year and winner of the 1953 National Book Award (Washington 271-72). As Lattin and Lattin explain,

In 1940, Richard Wright told the story of Bigger Thomas growing up in black Chicago not far from where Maud Martha was to grow up. In 1953, the year Maud Martha was published, Ralph Ellison added the story of his protagonist harassed from the south to New York City. Judged by the standards of these two complex, powerful urban novels, *Maud Martha* could be easily dismissed. (181)

Washington's comparison of the reviews of *Invisible Man* and *Maud Martha* demonstrates the widespread neglect Brooks's book met with: while "Ellison's work was placed in a tradition" and "compared to Wright, Dostoevsky, and Faulkner," none of the reviews at the time mentioned Brooks's artistic lineage (272). None of the reviewers recognized, as Washington did thirty years later, that "[w]ith no college degrees, no social standing, lacking the militant or articulate voice, denied the supports black men could claim from black institutions, Maud Martha is the invisible woman of the 1950s" (272).[1]

The book itself is also markedly different from Ellison's and Wright's novels in its subject matter and its style: Maud does not experience the same intense search for identity that Bigger and Ellison's protagonist experience. Nor does the novel have comparable violent struggles between the black and white worlds, broad discussions of black nationalism, or tragic conflicts between characters. (Lattin and Lattin 181). In fact, Malin Walther suggests that in a chapter centering on Maud Martha's interactions with a mouse, Brooks's novel "re-Wrights" the disturbing scene in which Bigger Thomas kills a rat, resituating it in a more humorous and contemplative domestic setting with the result that Maud Martha sets the mouse free, rather than killing it as Bigger does the rat (143).

I want to demonstrate that, although it appears smaller and less dramatic than Wright's and Ellison's novels both in its length and in its reception, *Maud Martha* is also a "complex, powerful urban novel," not in the sense of gritty depictions of street life but in its quieter, more ethereal images of the inner life and reveries of its main character. Barbara Christian, in her essay "Nuance and the Novella: A Study of Gwendolyn Brooks's *Maud Martha*," identifies the historical importance of the text: it is one of the first novels by a black woman to focus on an ordinary person who is not only a victim of an unjust society, "not just a creation of her external world," but also an active individual who "helps create her own world by transforming externals through her thoughts and imaginings" (244). The text's portrayals of Maud Martha's inner life of the mind, as well as her day-to-day life at home, and in the beauty parlor, hat shop and department stores, produce an intimate portrait of a woman who is constantly made aware of her lack of status—because of her gender, racial identity, skin color, class—yet also constantly finds ways to reaffirm her worth. As Christian puts it, *Maud Martha* is "the embodiment of the idea that a slice of anybody's life has elements of wonder and farce, wry irony and joy" (247). The book's third-

---

1   I would like to express my gratitude to the American Studies Foundation of Japan for an overseas travel grant to attend the Modern Language Association 2007 Convention in Chicago, where I delivered an earlier, shorter version of this chapter.

person omniscient narrator puts into words thoughts and feelings that the characters seldom do; the reader has access to this narrator's humor and judgment as it tells the story, highlighting both the "wonder and farce" inherent in ordinary life.

This chapter considers two of the thirty-four vignettes in *Maud Martha*: chapter 11 "second beau" and chapter 12 "Maud Martha and New York." These chapters are set around 1935, when Maud Martha is eighteen years old. Her boyfriend David is the central character in chapter 11; the subsequent chapter focuses on Maud Martha herself. Through free indirect discourse, both chapters narrate the overlapping but quite different ways David and Maud Martha fantasize about worlds outside their own. While David longs to be a member of the collegiate bourgeoisie that he observes while taking classes at the University of Chicago, Maud Martha imagines herself in the luxury of high-society New York, a city she has never visited. Neither chapter directly refers to race, but it is a central issue in the novel, even when unspoken. Moreover, the fact that both characters' fantasies hinge on class mobility illustrates the attraction of the comfortable life that, then as now, often required the privilege that accompanied whiteness, as well as wealth and education.

To better understand the representations of class and space as co-constructions in *Maud Martha*, I would like to introduce a key concept from geographical theory: the "imaginative geography." According to Felix Driver, imaginative geographies are "representations of place, space and landscape that structure people's understandings of the world, and in turn help to shape their actions" (152). Driver cites Edward Said's coinage of the term in Orientalism to describe the ways in which Europe's "shared collective imaginations" of non-western cultures contribute to crucial binary oppositions by which westerners identify themselves against the Other (149). What geographers emphasize is the material, embodied nature of imaginative geographies: they are not just images. Rather they are products of, and influences on, physical lived experience as raced, gendered, classed, and otherwise marked and unmarked bodies in society. In the case of oppressive imaginative geographies, such as Orientalism, the importance of these representations cannot be disputed; on the other hand, not all imaginative geographies enable imperialism.

I suggest that reading provides access to another kind of imaginative geography, which can have more liberatory potential. Sheila Hones argues for an understanding of reading is a "spatial event" that involves the reader and the writer, along with the "traces of other readers and writers: novelists, geographers, colleagues, students, reviewers, editors" as well as the conditions under which the practices of reading and writing take place ("Text" n.p.). In this way the spatial event of reading "happens at the intersection of agents and situations scattered across time and space, both human and non-human, absent and present" ("Text" n.p.). I argue that, in the spatial event of reading, the text's imaginative geographies play a role in the development of literary meaning, in that a reader's impression is informed by the text's representations of the narrator's or the characters' thoughts, dreams, and actions as portrayed in the text. But they can also can be a product of reading literature, in that the act of reading fosters an imaginary experience of other places, other lives, and other bodies. As reader-response criticism teaches us, "readers actualize the text into a meaningful work that in turn stimulates response," so that the meaning of the text is the product of the "dynamic transaction" between the text and the reader (Schweickart and Flynn 4).

This transaction can be powerful, and even transformative; Janice Radway argues that reading is sometimes a physical experience:

> There are moments for me now when books become something other than mere objects, when they transport me elsewhere, to a trancelike state I find difficult to describe. [...] When this occurs, the book, the text, and even my reading self dissolve in a peculiar act of transubstantiation whereby "I" become something other than what I have been and inhabit thoughts other than those I have been able to conceive before. This tactile, sensuous, profoundly emotional experience of being captured by a book is [...] an experience that for all its ethereality clearly is extraordinarily physical as well. (209)

The physicality of this kind of reading resonates with the materiality inherent in the concept of imaginative geography. Rather than emphasize a divide between mind and body, Radway wants to investigate the blurring of that divide that occurs when she is in such a "trancelike state." Troubling the divide between mind and body, the spatial event of reading can transport us to new and unknown places, teach us about things we cannot learn in our "real" lives.

I argue that, in *Maud Martha*, representations of the characters' imaginative geographies express their spatial and classed identities in relation to the body in two ways: through fantasies of clothing and consumer goods, and through the imagination of the body in other places. Finally, I'd like to conclude by considering the imaginative geographies that can be produced by the readers' engagements with the text.

## CLOTHING, ACCESSORIES, AND PHYSICAL EMBODIMENTS OF CLASS

David wants to join the educated elite, "those guys" he sees on the University of Chicago campus. David's desire to become a part of the college-educated middle class brings with it a desire for the "tasteful" trappings he deems appropriate to that class. Although his plan to acquire these various things appears shallow and superficial, David's highly specific wants reflect his sensitivity to the role of taste in the social construction of class. Pierre Bourdieu argues that taste is a "systematic expression of a particular class of conditions of existence, i.e., as a distinctive life-style," which is the "product of the internalization of the structure of social space" (175). David's wish for class mobility is not expressed through any overt desire for wealth, but through a set of symbolic objects he wants to possess. He believes that owning these objects will enable him to build a more educated, middle-class identity. From the first line of this chapter, David's yearning for class mobility is gently derided by the narrator, whose descriptions of him make him appear arrogant and self-absorbed: the chapter opens with the joking admonition, "And—don't laugh!—he wanted a dog" (42).

David's catalog of desirable consumer goods becomes repetitive in the chapter's final paragraph, using the word "good" six times in his cliché-filled fantasy of the objects—the goods—he feels he needs to own in order to achieve the lifestyle and class identity he wants.

He wanted a dog. A *good* dog. No mongrel. An apartment—well-furnished, containing a *good* bookcase, filled with *good* books in *good* bindings. He wanted a phonograph, and records. The symphonies. And Yehudi Menuhin. He wanted some *good* art. These things were not extras. They went to make up a *good* background. The kind of background those guys had. (46, emphasis added)

This background, which he thinks "those guys" have, can be read to mean their upbringing, in which they were exposed to cultured conversations from an early age. David laments that he has not, as the college boys have, grown up surrounded by educated adults; in their homes, he imagines, their parents had had casual discussions "across four-year-old heads" about a book he has just begun to study, the American studies classic,

Parrington's Main Currents in American Thought. He had not mastered it. Only recently, he announced, had he learned of its existence. "Three volumes of the most reasonable approaches!—Yet there are chaps on that campus—young!—younger than I am—who read it years ago, who know it, who have had it for themselves for years, who have been seeing it on their fathers' shelves since infancy [...]." (43)

These students have the advantage, in David's imagination anyway, of being raised to be comfortable and at ease in the intellectual milieu that he so badly wants to inhabit. His yearning for a middle-class identity centers around the university, not only as a place of learning and ideas, but also as a community of people among whom David seems to feel uncomfortable (it goes without saying, too, although he doesn't indicate it directly, that most of them are white). If only he had "a good background" with a bourgeois upbringing like those students appear to have had, he seems to say.

But David's word "background" also implies a backdrop, the tableau in which their lives are played out. The performance of the academic is a physical act, supported by appropriate clothing and props. As mentioned above, the chapter opens with his desire for a dog; the narrator continues to describe David's newly contrived image as the "picture of the English country gentleman. Roaming the rustic hill. He had not yet bought a pipe. He would immediately" (42). In this scene, David is dressed in a tweedy professorial costume, wearing the right tie, purchased with much anxiety and planning, as well as socks, haircut, and shoes:

There already was the herringbone tweed. [...] There was the tie a man might think about for an hour before entering that better shop, in order to be able to deliberate only a sharp two minutes at the counter, under the icy estimate of the salesman. Here were the socks, here was the haircut, here were the shoes. (42-43)

He has also adopted the physical mannerisms he thinks appropriate: "The educated smile, the slight bow, the faint imperious nod" (43). In his fantasy, the herringbone-clad David is trying to act the part, ensconced in a stage set peppered with all the important "goods" to signify his desired status. His body and physical appearance are in the process of being made over to conform to an image of the class identity he aspires to, in addition to his intellectual pursuit of a university education.

In some ways similar to David's, Maud Martha's imaginative geography of a higher class involves costuming and adorning the body, but she expresses only a passing interest in intellectual pursuits and instead directs her imagination toward scenarios heavily indulging the senses. While David's physical makeover is part of his overall goal to become more like the middle-class university "chaps" and less like the working-class man he starts out as, Maud Martha is quite emphatically still herself in her fantasies. Like David, she is fascinated by the habits of a more privileged class, but her fantasies place her directly in their realm, skipping over the "icy estimate of the salesman" and other uncomfortable obstacles that David knows first-hand. The faraway location of Maud Martha's imaginative geography, New York City, and her own lack of experience there allow her to appropriate only the positive elements of that world, eliding the potential roadblocks. The opening of the chapter expresses her image of the city:

The name "New York" glittered in front of her like the *silver* in the shops on Michigan Boulevard. It was *silver*, and it was solid, and it was remote: it was behind *glass*, it was behind bright *glass* like the *silver* in the shops. It was not for her. Yet. (47; emphasis added)

The repetition of the words "silver" and "glass," along with the image of the glittering name, reinforces the metaphor in this passage that describes what New York means for Maud Martha—something as shining and expensive, "solid" as a precious metal. This passage also describes part of the allure of New York in its remoteness, "behind glass," something beautiful she can see "in front of her" but cannot touch. Perhaps because of her distance from its reality, perhaps because she hasn't (yet?) encountered the difficulties that David has in achieving his dream, Maud Martha's New York is almost entirely hopeful and doesn't entail a reworking of her body so much as a swirling daydream. The youthful sense of the future in the final word, "yet," strikes a contrast with David's anxiety and frustration, for Maud Martha is not at this point certain that she won't someday achieve the elegance and poise she admires in the idea of New York.

Gleaned from her cultural knowledge of New York as depicted in magazines and newspapers, her daydreams envision upper-class life there:

Maud Martha loved it when her magazines said "New York," described "good" objects there, wonderful people there, recalled fine talk, the bristling or the creamy or the tactfully shimmering ways of life. (48)

The adjective "good" here is emphasized with quotation marks, creating an echo of the previous chapter and David's humorous overuse of the word and his fetishization of tasteful "goods" for purchase, as discussed above. Also like David, Maud Martha envisions "fine talk" but here is none of David's envy or wistful regret. Rather, this chapter's imagery is overwhelmingly sensual, describing Maud Martha's excitement over the "tactfully shimmering ways of life" so different from her own and often focusing on the senses, as seen in the tactile metaphors such as "bristling" and "creamy."

Indeed, Maud Martha's New York dream is a sybaritic delirium of delicacies. Her epicurean litany of foods shows Maud Martha's fascination with the habits of New York polite society:

they ate things called anchovies, and capers; they ate little diamond-shaped cheeses that paprika had but breathed on; they ate bitter-almond macaroons; they ate papaya packed in rum and syrup; they ate peculiar sauces, were free with honey, were lavish with butter, wine and cream. (49)

The context, in the middle of the Depression, can explain some of Maud Martha's gourmet lusts, of course. But I also suspect she is a sensualist, chanting in repetitive anaphora (they ate; they ate; they ate). Food here is not merely a source of physical nourishment, but a sign of "lavish" living, which she physically craves. This is not a catalog of things she feels she needs in order to gain a particular status, as David's are; it is a list of exotic indulgences that she wants to sample for herself, for her own pleasure, even if she does not know what they are, as the expression "things called anchovies, and capers" suggests.

Maud Martha can hardly bear the opulence of her New York fantasies and her lust for these expensive objects extends beyond food, although hunger remains an apt metaphor. The physical craving overcomes her completely when she peruses magazine advertisements for an expensive pair of figurines: "Her whole body become a hunger, she would pore over these pages" (47). This physical desire is not only for the commodities being sold, nor is it for membership in a particular university community; it is for "what she felt life ought to be. Jeweled. Polished. Smiling. Poised" (50). Her yearning for effortless elegance shows an eye for both the product and the lifestyle: "especially did she care for the pictures of women wearing carelessly, as if they were rags, dresses that were plain but whose prices were not" (48-49). But for Maud Martha, the attainment of this elegance is not fraught with disappointment and self-denigration, as are David's ambitions; perhaps due to their remoteness, both geographical and experiential, the things she fantasizes about are at least theoretically within her reach if she only had the money to purchase them. Although she too imagines her own body swathed in expensive fabrics before a high-class backdrop, she screens out the negative implications that David cannot.

Crucial too is the fact that her imaginative geography of New York is formulated from the images and information she gleans from her own experience as a reader of texts:

She bought the New York papers downtown, read of the concerts and plays, studied the book reviews, was intent over the announcements of auctions. She liked the sound of "Fifth Avenue," "Town Hall," "B. Altman," "Hammacher Schlemmer." (49)

The New York in her imaginative geography captures her interest as a center of high culture, and again appeals to the senses, where even the sound of the names of streets, halls, and shops are attractive. Maud Martha has "studied" these texts and developed an idealized world that embodies everything she thinks life should be. For David, studying texts seems to mean reading volumes such as Parrington's, which signify for him the disadvantages he labors under in comparison to the other students. David's aspiration to enter the educated bourgeoisie is closer, more within reach: it is predicated on attending a university in Chicago where he already lives, and where he is already taking classes. Yet perhaps because he has come so close, he is all the more aware of the hindrances that still threaten to hold him back.

Like a child dreaming of fairy tales, Maud Martha places herself at the center of her fantasies of New York, and her wide-eyed optimism is only gently teased by the narrator: saying that she "was intent over the announcements of auctions" shows the utter seriousness of the inexperienced young woman and at the same time the absurdity of her reading about auctions that are inaccessible to her, both because of her location in Chicago and because of her status, as a young, working-class black woman. The grammatical inversions in this chapter are unique in that they don't occur in David's: formal, archaic-sounding constructions like "especially did she care," quoted above, also underscore the fairy-tale quality of the chapter, where the narrator seems to want to convey the naïve magic of her hopeful imagination. But these grammatical inversions also hint at the spatial act of transposition that is inherent in her imaginative geography, which is the other intriguing element of her and David's imaginative geographies.

## CO-PRODUCTION OF SPACE AND CLASS

David's ambitious shopping list of clothing and accessories—the pipe, the good bindings—are made to look silly and snobbish by the narrator, but his character's pathos comes from the contrast between those attempts to mimic the performance of middle-class academia and his stark imaginative geography of race and class in South Side Chicago, where he draws a firm boundary line between east and west. Of course, this imaginative geography is not merely an individual construction: it is informed by his own embodied experience of racial segregation in early twentieth-century Chicago. Accordingly, he separates his own neighborhood (and Maud Martha's) "[w]est of the Midway" from that of the university and its denizens "[e]ast of Cottage Grove" (44). He explains that he becomes "instantly depressed" and "want[s] to throw up" when he comes home from the university to the "mess" that is his own neighborhood (44). Here in Bronzeville, people "leaned against buildings and their mouths were opening and closing very fast but nothing important was coming out. What did they know about Aristotle?" (45). The brashness of the street life in this passage, where conversations are lively but not intellectual enough to suit him, contrasts with the polite restraint and intelligence David attributes to people in the university neighborhood, where "people were clean, going somewhere that mattered, not talking unless they had something to say" (44-45). The clownish image of "mouths [...] opening and closing very fast" makes his neighbors appear foolish, and although he stops short of calling the residents of his own neighborhood dirty, he implies it in this passage by asserting the cleanliness of the others "East of Cottage Grove" (44). Similarly, he condemns the poor condition of the buildings by blaming the inhabitants: "up in those kitchenette windows, where the lights were dirty through dirty glass—they could wash the windows" (45). His imaginative geography consists of a divided city, in which the clean, intelligent people are east of the line and the dirty, foolish, ignorant people are west of it. David often finds himself on what he considers to be the wrong side of the line, in more ways than one: as these passages demonstrate, he lives in an area he considers poor and dirty. But several times in this chapter he also seems to misapprehend his own location in relation to that line.

Through a kind of imaginative displacement, David's strict sense of boundaries sometimes gives way to a possibility for transgression. Although he is in Maud Martha's parents' house, he comports himself with such pomp that the narrator chides him again: "His scent was withdrawn, expensive, as he strode down the worn carpet of her living room, as though it were the educated green of the Midway" (43). The dramatic situation again resembles a performance through the narrator's choice of words, such as striding the carpet and "the educated green," that elevate him to the status of an actor or orator, but the "worn carpet of her living room" reminds us that he is just ranting in his girlfriend's house. But this passage also shows the slippage between the two parts of David's divided imaginative geography, as he is behaving here in a manner more appropriate there. The carpet in this passage almost becomes the green of the Midway, almost but not quite, thanks to the narrator's precise use of the simile "as though it were" highlighting the distinction. However, this kind of imaginary spatial displacement continues later in David's description of his own neighborhood as if it were elsewhere: "The unhappiness he felt over there was physical" (45). Though we know he is in the living room at Maud Martha's house, the sentence implies that he is speaking from elsewhere about "there," meaning their neighborhood, a place that makes him feel sick with unhappiness.

Perhaps because in his mind he is on the other side of the boundary, David even becomes forgetful about his neighborhood:

There was a fence on Forty-seventh and—Champlain? Langley? Forestville?—he forgot what; broken, rotten, trying to lie down; and passing it on a windy night or on a night when it was drizzling, he felt lost, lapsed, negative, untended, extinguished, broken and lying down too—unappeasable. (45)

Although he cannot remember the exact intersection, he identifies with that fence on 47th Street. It makes him feel "lost" and "untended" as well as "broken and lying down too"—the ragged fence can be read as a synecdoche for the African American community in the midst of the Depression. It also more specifically bears a symbolic burden for David, standing for all the things he associates with his own neighborhood, his own "background" that hasn't prepared him enough for a life at the university.

Like the fence, too, David is in his own estimate "untended," in that his working-class parents weren't able to provide for him the kind of privileged "background" that the students at the university appear to have. As the chapter explains, not everyone in his neighborhood is dirty like the windows mentioned above:

His mother had taken in washing. She had had three boys, whom she sent to school clean but patched-up. Just so they were clean, she had said. That was all that mattered, she had said. She had said "ain't." (44)

His mother did her best to tend her sons while washing other people's laundry to support her family, keeping them clean even if she couldn't replace their worn clothes, only patch them. "His father," we are told, "hadn't said anything at all," implying he was distant or even absent from the family (44). But David wishes he had been tended in other ways, raised in a more genteel, middle-class environment, by parents who didn't say "ain't" and who could afford to buy him new clothes (herringbone?).

Certainly the frustration David feels in his own neighborhood and thinking about his own upbringing could make him feel broken. But the fact that the fence is ineffective in its primary function as a boundary or barrier, broken and "trying to lie down," also suggests the impossibility of maintaining the rigid spatial boundaries he tries to invoke (45). His very presence taking courses on the University of Chicago campus—"the Midway"—is evidence of the permeability of those boundaries. That is not to say crossing is easy or taken-for-granted, but it is possible.

Maud Martha's imaginative geography also enables her to cross boundaries. However, she doesn't visit New York only to return to her own neighborhood depressed; she has never visited there at all. Instead, she completely projects herself into an assortment of scenes there. Unlike David, whose language betrays his insecurity and uncertainty about his location even though he attends the university, Maud Martha relocates herself at will. Whenever a train passes she imagines it's heading for New York and she is on board: "She sat inside with them. She leaned back in the plush" (47). The physical sensation of sitting in the train seat, feeling the plush fabric against her skin, is not mediated by a metaphor; rather, Maud Martha transports herself onto the train that she knows is going to New York. The imagined mobility in this passage is two-fold: she imagines that she is in another place (on a train) and on her way to another city.

She is on the train, looking out the window at all the "unfortunate folk who were not New York-bound and never would be" (48). Harry B. Shaw points out that Maud Martha's fantasy of New York "is more to escape a stultifying mental and aesthetic environment," while David wanted to "change his style to escape his own heritage" (262-63). Her escape, in this imaginative act of geographic transposition, performs a kind of switch, where she is no longer the unfortunate person who isn't going to New York, but rather she is going there, looking out at the unlucky ones. Similarly, she transposes herself to the famous Fifth Avenue:

She was on Fifth Avenue whenever she wanted to be, and it was she who rolled up, silky or furry, in the taxi, was assisted out, and stood, her next step nebulous, before the theaters of the thousand lights, before velvet-lined impossible shops; she it was. (49)

Maud Martha is there, decked out in silks or furs (again the focus on clothing). In her embodied imaginative geography she physically travels to and occupies the city in her imagination and she feels the textures of the plush, silk, fur, and velvet against her skin.

Maud Martha's fantasy, inspired by the magazines and newspapers she reads, also focuses on the distant and unknown, not only the cosmopolitan city of New York, but also the imported luxuries to be found there. The chapter is peppered with references to exotic imported goods. She revels in the idea of consuming expensive products from other countries: "Chinese boxes," "Italian plates" (48), "Russian caviar" (49), "a Persian rug," "tea, as in England" (echoes of the "English country gentleman") (50).

Maud Martha reserves her best metaphors for a decorative screen she envisions in a beautifully furnished home. The narration doesn't attribute it to a particular source, but fits in with the kinds of interiors that Maud Martha delights in. She describes the screen, thinking that it might be "Japanese. . . with rich and mellow, bread-textured colors" (50-51). The colors of the screen are, like the people she imagines inhabit the New York of her daydreams, rich and mellow. But here a visual attribute, color, has a tactile description that evokes the feel of bread, its rough crust and cushiony inside. The reference to food underscores the hunger metaphor that runs through the chapter, too: her appetite for the imagined New York permeates even her figures of speech. The fantasies in which she indulges are like her daily bread, feeding her spirit as well as her body with the sustenance she needs to thrive in the midst of the challenges in her life.

She acknowledges that her daydreams, in which she "dwell[s] upon color and soft bready textures and light, on a complex beauty, on gemlike surfaces," might not come true (51). But she defends the pleasure she derives from them:

What was the matter with that? Besides, who could safely swear that she would never be able to make her dream come true for herself? Not altogether, then!—but slightly?—in some part?

She was eighteen years old, and the world waited. To caress her. (51)

Maud Martha's pragmatism has struck a bargain with her daydreams, allowing her to enjoy the imagined New York even as she realizes that she probably won't ever attain that level of luxury. She optimistically elects to incorporate her sense of aesthetics into her life "slightly," as we can see in later chapters from her appreciation of "her finest wedding gift, a really good white luncheon cloth" (167). Although her fantasies are not "real," they have a real effect in her life.

## LITERARY GEOGRAPHIES OF *MAUD MARTHA*

Later in the book, in chapter 18, entitled "we're the only colored people here," Maud Martha and her husband go to the movies in a fancy, mostly white downtown cinema. After depicting their delicate dance of anxiety and forced nonchalance, the narrator explains the value of the movie for Maud Martha:

you felt good sitting there, yes, good, and as if, when you left it, you would be going home to a sweet-smelling apartment with flowers on little gleaming tables; and wonderful silver on night-blue velvet, in chests; and crackly sheets; and lace spreads on such beds as you saw at Marshall Fields. (77)

This description, inspired by the brief experience of the movie (along with trips to a downtown department store) and its ability to transport her to another kind of life, shows that Maud Martha still has the power to create imaginative geographies replete with sensual and luxurious details of color, texture, and fragrance.

In this later chapter, too, the narration provides a strong contrast with her reality, living in a kitchenette apartment in a run-down building:

Instead of back to your kit'n't apt., with the garbage of your floor's families in a big can just outside your door, and the gray sound of little gray feet scratching away from it as you drag up those flights of narrow complaining stairs. (77)

Unlike the New York chapter, Maud Martha is older now and has experienced more of the restrictions and disappointments that her past boyfriend David had also encountered. But her habit of creating pleasurable fantasies—"learning to love moments"—helps to sustain her even in the "gray" circumstances of her daily life (78). Like the imagined geographies of New York that thrilled her at eighteen, Maud Martha's imagined geographies of upper-class creature comforts continue to feed her craving. She might not any longer feel she is on the train or on Fifth Avenue, but she feels as if she "would be going home to a sweet-smelling apartment," which pleases her. By projecting themselves into imagined places and imagined embodied experiences, David and Maud Martha try to open themselves to possibility. As readers following these two fictional characters as they undergo this projection, we also project ourselves into other times, other places, other lives. Representations of class and space in the novel allow us as readers to temporarily access imaginative geographies that are not "real," but that can have real effects on our lives.

## WORKS CITED

Christian, Barbara. "Nuance and Novella: A Study of Gwendolyn Brooks's *Maud Martha*." Mootry and Smith 239-53. Print.

Driver, Felix. "Imaginative Geographies." *Introducing Human Geographies*. 2nd Edn. Eds. Paul Cloke, Philip Crang, and Mark Goodwin. London: Hodder, 2005. 144-55. Print.

Hones, Sheila. "Text As It Happens: Literary Geography." *Geography Compass* 4.1 (2010): 61-66. Print.

Lattin, Patricia and Vernon Lattin. "Dual Vision in Gwendolyn Brooks's *Maud Martha*." *Critique* 25.4 (1984): 180-88. Print.

Longhurst, Robyn. "The Body." *Cultural Geography: A Critical Dictionary of Key Concepts*. Eds. David Atkinson, Peter Jackson, David Sibley, and Neil Washbourne. London: I.B. Tauris, 2005. 91-96. Print.

Mootry, Maria, and Gary Smith, eds. *A Life Distilled: Gwendolyn Brooks, Her Life and Fiction*. Urbana: U of Illinois P, 1987. 254-70. Print.

Radway, Janice. Introduction. *A Feeling for Books: The Book-of-the-Month Club, Literary Taste, and Middle-Class Desire*. Chapel Hill: U of North Carolina P, 1997. Rpt. in *Falling into Theory: Conflicting Views on Reading Literature*. Ed. David Richter. Boston: Bedford-St. Martin's, 2000. 198-210. Print.

Schweickart, Patrocinio, and Elizabeth Flynn. Introduction. *Reading Sites: Social Difference and Reader Response*. Eds. Schweickart and Flynn. New York: MLA, 2004. 1-38. Print.

Shaw, Harry B. "*Maud Martha*: The War with Beauty." Mootry and Smith 254-70. Print.

Walther, Malin. "Re-Wrighting Native: Gwendolyn Brooks's Domestic Aesthetic in *Maud Martha*." *Tulsa Studies in Women's Literature* 13.1 (1994): 143-45. Print.

Washington, Mary Helen. "Plain, Black, and Decently Wild: The Heroic Possibilities of *Maud Martha*." *The Voyage In: Fictions of Female De-*

*velopment.* Eds. Elizabeth Abel, Marianne Hirsch, and Elizabeth Langland. Hanover, NH: UP of New England, 1983. 270-86. Print.

# 6 Home on the Range

## Space, Nation, and Mobility in *The Searchers*

> Through the process of domestication, the
> home contains within itself those wild or
> foreign elements that must be tamed; do-
> mesticity not only monitors the borders be-
> tween the civilized and the savage but also
> regulates traces of the savage within itself.
>
> AMY KAPLAN/"MANIFEST DOMESTICITY"

Focusing on representations of mobility, space, and national identity, this essay reads John Ford's movie *The Searchers* (1956) in terms of its deployment of American "domestic" space, meaning both "home-centered" and in opposition to "foreign." I argue that *The Searchers* represents American national identity using tropes of space and mobility, in both thematic content and cinematic form. Tracing the ways in which this movie represents race and gender within private domestic spaces as well as against sweeping desert landscapes foregrounds the primacy of space in the American national imagination in the 1950s. Ford's movies are often cited among the quintessential Westerns of cinema history and, as Ella Shohat and Robert Stam have written, the Western "played a crucial pedagogical role in forming the historical sensibilities of generations of Americans" (115). Space and mobility in Ford's work bear the burden of representing the nation, not only within the movie's narrative, but also within the wider context of American public culture. In the following essay, I interpret *The Searchers* in terms of how representations of public and private space and geographic mobility operate within the dramatic narrative and the visual economy of the movie, as well as within its contemporaneous cultural contexts of the Civil Rights Movement and the Cold War.

This chapter presents an interpretation of *The Searchers* centered around the movie's representation of different kinds of space: national and familial, public and private, foreign and domestic, indoor and outdoor. Because the term "space" is frequently employed in wildly divergent interpretive and theoretical strategies, I would like to clarify my use of the term here. As Michael Keith and Steve Pile point out in their groundbreaking essay collection, *Place and the Politics of Identity*:

In order to articulate an understanding of the multiplicity and flexibility of relations of domination, a whole range of spatial metaphors are being used [in contemporary theory]: position, location, situation, mapping; geometrics of domination, center-margin, open-closed, inside-outside, global-local; liminal space, third space, not-space, impossible space. (1)

Many theorists use such spatial metaphors to describe power relations, such as cognitive mapping, for example, but in the process of importing the terminology from the discipline of geography, they often fail to fully define those terms, using them as if space were "absolute," a kind of "container, a co-ordinate system of discrete and mutually exclusive locations" thus eliding the relationality of social identities within particular spaces (75). According to Neil Smith and Cindi Katz, "spatial metaphors are problematic in so far as they presume that space is not" (75).

In this chapter, I begin with the axiom that space is indeed problematic: within the spaces of the home as well as on the open range, "the social, the political, and the economic do not just take place in 'time' and 'space,' they are in part constituted by temporality and spatiality" (Keith and Pile "Introduction Part 1" 27). Throughout this chapter I will discuss space in terms of material, social, and metaphorical meanings; for example, the domestic space of the family homestead is comprised of the material, the physical house and the land it sits on; the social, the racial and gendered power relations that operate within and around that house; and the metaphorical function that the home takes on as a symbol for the nation. As Keith and Pile forcefully argue, "we may now use the term 'spatiality' to capture the ways in which the social and the spatial are inextricably realized one in the other" ("Introduction Part 1" 6). Drawing on theories from the disciplines of Social and Cultural Geography as well as American Studies and Cinema Studies, this chapter attempts to unravel the meanings and metaphors implicit in the spaces of *The Searchers*.

## WESTERNS, SPACE, AND MOBILITY

John Ford was fond of telling the story about how, during his early Hollywood career as an extra, he played a Klansman in D.W. Griffith's *The Birth of a Nation* and fell off his horse. His fondness for this anecdote provides a useful counter-point to those more familiar with Ford's celebrated status as a director: it links him, on horseback, with the Western genre for which he is famous, but humorously and humbly, while at the same time it places him firmly in the history of cinematic representations of race. Perhaps Ford's anecdote will take on additional resonance for readers of this chapter, which considers Ford's *The Searchers* within its specific cultural contexts and its representations of mobility, public and private space, and national and racial identity.

The trope of mobility suffuses his movies of all genres, and Ford, dubbed "America's cinematic poet laureate" by Andrew Sarris (90), is best remembered for his Westerns, movies in an inherently American genre that often represent conflicts around gender, race, and space. Mobility in Ford's work takes the physical form of horse, stagecoach, buckboard, locomotive, and Model T; figuratively, the movements are between town and country, civilization and wilderness. But the characters do not simply move from one discrete space to another, they also traverse spaces, usually depicted in wide angle landscape shots of deserts, mountains, gorges, and valleys. As Geoffrey O'Brien praises *The Searchers*, he emphasizes the primacy of movement across landscapes:

Ethan and Martin crossing an icy plain at night, or riding downhill through deep snow, or silhouetted against a red sky as they travel along a ridge; the 7th Cavalry […] crossing a newly thawed stream, the camera moving down a narrow crevasse, the whole VistaVision image given over to a singular moment of rocky abstraction. Not one shot felt like an interpolation or interlude; the visual life of the film was a continuous balancing of immensity and intimacy. Movement through space, whether of a hand in close-up or of an army in long shot, was always in the center of the drama. (O'Brien 19)

The crossing from one space to another, such as a man on horseback bisecting the frame, dwarfed against a Technicolor blue sky and blazing red mesas, has been called by Ford scholar Tag Gallagher a "Fordian symbol of the parade [...] a formalized progression, a *passage*" (384). Gallagher rightly notes the importance of movement across landscapes, but Ford's use of doorways is equally important, signifying not only movement, but liminal spaces, the site of a shift from one kind of space to another. The oppressiveness of Ford's interiors, particularly his shots of ceilings and doorways, conveys the constricted feeling that drives many of his characters out into the desert's open spaces. Ford's classic Western draws a boundary around American domestic space, signifying the permeable borders of both the family home and the nation itself.

*The Searchers* is a 1950s Western that, through its use of space and mobility, speaks to American concerns about domestic and national boundaries. These concerns are not always at the surface of the narrative, but I want to situate the movie within the context of the national mood in which it was produced. At the particular historical moment when this movie was made, the national imagination had two important preoccupations: the Civil Rights Movement and the Cold War. Both these issues relied on one primary trope in articulating a national agenda: mobility. In the Civil Rights Movement, social, economic, and geographic mobility became a question of survival for many African Americans, while during the Cold War mobility was the primary enemy as government policy centered around the containment of Communism. The "domestic" is the center of conflicts located simultaneously in the private sphere, where racial issues take the form of fear of miscegenation and the debate around segregation, and in the public sphere, where mounting international tensions foster the threats of nuclear war and Communist spies. This chapter argues that spatial concerns such as these necessitate a reading of *The Searchers* in terms of mobility and space, whereby we can discern the tenacious discourses of domesticity in twentieth-century American culture as they represent concerns about citizenship and national security.

Reading Westerns in terms of landscape and identity, many critics in American Studies and Cinema Studies have theorized the parameters of race, gender, and nation. Jane Tompkins's book *West of Everything: The Inner Life of Westerns*, while provocative in its analysis of landscape and gender, brackets the discussion of race in Westerns; this omission implies that race has no significant bearing on her definition of the feminine, private, domestic sphere, which she convincingly argues is central rather than peripheral to the genre. I concur with her argument that gender is pivotal to the ideological foundation of the Western, but not to the point of excluding other crucial factors of identity such as race and nation.[1] Rather, I suggest that the operation of these terms of identity within the power relations in Westerns are just as crucial as, and in many cases difficult to separate from, considerations of gender. Richard Maltby's essay "A Better Sense of History: John Ford and the Indians," on the other hand, focuses on Ford's Native American characters and traces a brief but thorough history of movie Indians and the debate around their authenticity (35). Maltby's primary concern is with the racial dynamics of representation, but rather than completely sidestep gender, he refers to several different women's roles. Linking gender and race, Maltby correctly points out that the "division of heroines into light and dark [and into] schoolmarm and saloon-girl" signifies not only at the level of gender roles within white society, but also that, through association with Indian men, however involuntary, white women can be "degraded out of their skin color into a self-perpetuating Otherness" (43). Gender, then, interacts with race in the cinematic landscape and mythic national home of the Western, which functions as "the primary site in which Hollywood could maintain a racist discourse, in which racism was offered and enacted as a theory of history" (Maltby 37).

---

1  For example, Tompkins describes the moment, while watching The Searchers, when she realized that representations of Native American women in Westerns complicate her reading of women as icons of domesticity: the character Look "is treated so abominably by the characters—ridiculed, humiliated, and then killed off casually by the plot—that I couldn't believe my eyes." Tompkins realizes that Look and many other stereotyped Indian characters have offended her to the point that her "unbelief at the travesty of native peoples that Western films afford kept me from scrutinizing what was there." Unfortunately, Tompkins maintains the book's focus exclusively on gender because she "couldn't bear to take [Look] seriously; it would have been too painful" (8-10).

In agreement with Maltby, I find the Western a rich text for interrogating representations of the intersecting factors of race and gender in American culture; absent from his article, however, is a prolonged accounting for the spatial dimensions of these crucial social issues in the Western. I suggest that the grids of power implicit in the Western, whether that power is rooted in gender, race, nationality, or most likely a combination, can best be discerned by attending to the representation of space and mobility. Ford's wide angle shots of the desert landscape contrast powerfully with his claustrophobic low angle interior cinematography, separating the spheres of men and women, outdoor and indoor, and quite clearly privileging the former. Ford's vistas draw audiences into such struggles, impelling us to identify with the land, with the heroes who also identify with it, and with the nation itself. Ultimately, *The Searchers* requires a spatial reading that considers the competing interests of the American "domestic" in both senses of the word: civic, national, and military spaces and the private, feminine site of the home.

In cinema, images exert a spatial control over the ideological location of competing interests as well: geographers Stuart Aitken and Leo Zonn argue for the importance of "representations of, and the meanings attached to, places and the environment in terms of their relationship to power and contestation" (6). Audiences of Westerns expect a certain iconography, bearing familiar ideological echoes of heroism and triumph over adversity. As Keith and Pile remind us, "simultaneously present in any landscape are multiple enunciations of distinct forms of space—and these may be reconnected to the process of re-visioning and remembering the spatialities of counter-hegemonic cultural practices" ("Introduction Part 1" 6). The photography of the Western landscape represents the American nation still in its expansion westward, but also as a dangerous, still unconquered space, justifying the need for national defense. In *The Searchers*, a settler homestead is attacked and family decimated: mother Martha and daughter Lucy are raped, murdered, and mutilated, father Aaron is killed, and the youngest daughter Debbie is kidnapped by Scar, a Comanche warrior. Debbie's uncle, Ethan Edwards (John Wayne), and her adopted brother, Martin, were away from the home during the attack; when they discover the ruin in its wake, they set off on a seven-year search to find Debbie. Ethan's role is both conqueror of the enemy and defender of the American family, located at the frontier where the contestation over land ownership and national sovereignty takes place.

According to David Harvey, the "conquest of space [...] first requires that it be conceived of as something usable, malleable, and therefore capable of domination through human action" (254). Harvey points to the American system of homesteading and land settlement, which figures prominently in *The Searchers*, as an example of the "pulverization and fragmentation of the space of the United States along [...] rationalistic lines" meant to allow "maximum liberty to move and settle in a reasonably egalitarian way" (255; 257). This kind of spatial organization of land ownership replaces earlier modes of communal land use; conversion from Indian territory to open range to privately owned land is a feature of most Westerns. White characters in *The Searchers* view this conversion as inevitable and just, in accordance with Manifest Destiny, while the Comanche and other Native Americans share neither their conception of the ownership of space nor their belief in divinely sanctioned white progress. As Harvey points out, conquest necessitates the instrumentalization of space as settlement requires the mapping and fragmenting of space; the ideology of American expansion is predicated upon a spatial model which conflicts with that of the Native Americans but which allows the white settlers to justify their cause. The question of power relations in frontier spaces is more complicated, as the settlement process blurs some class distinctions among whites but neglects the racial and gender inequalities upon which the community, and the nation, is founded. In this movie, the landscape is both the site and the subject of these conflicts and inequalities.

## LANDSCAPE AS SYNECDOCHE FOR THE NATION

Ford's movies all employ a marked opposition between interior and exterior space, usually privileging the exterior, often in the vast landscapes of the American West. From the audience's point of view, the overwhelming visual images of sublime outdoor spaces represent power relations in a double dilemma: on the one hand, they "arouse the viewer's desire for, wish to identify with, an object that is overpowering and majestic" (Tompkins 76) The majesty of the West invites the audience to identify with the American desert landscape and all it represents: ruggedness, natural beauty, strength, eternity, austerity. Tompkins reads the Western's "rejection of language and its emphasis on landscape" as signs of the genre's inherent, assertive masculinity, arguing that the "openness of the space means that domination can take place" (57; 74). On the other hand, the landscapes in Westerns can also be read as contested spaces where Native Americans battle European Americans, with Mexicans and Mexican Americans on either side, over the rights to the land, to the resources, and ultimately for control over the geographic, economic, and political spaces of the nation.

In *The Searchers*, the land signifies not only the nation, but the site of national and international conflict dependent on perspective and point of view: geographer Derek Gregory argues that "the very idea of landscape is shot through with ambivalences, tensions, and grids of power" (99). Certainly the fictional settings of *The Searchers* bear the traces of these ambivalences, as it is set in "Texas 1868." We know that white Americans live in Texas only because they appropriated the land from Native Americans and Mexicans, and in the 1860s much blood is still being shed as the Comanche resist.[2] But the characters in the movie perceive themselves as pioneers in a divinely sanctioned nation-building enterprise. The power relations within the contact zone of "Texas 1868" are by no means stable, as the isolated homesteaders are vulnerable to raids by the embattled Indian tribes; the movie emphasizes this in the constant pans across the apparently empty desert, corresponding to characters in the movie vainly attempting to spot possible Comanche aggressors hiding in the desert. The wide open spaces can hide violent attackers hoping to thwart white progress into the West, as the beauty of the wilderness also suggests danger.

The land itself occupies a prominent role in Ford's work as setting, motivation, and subject, even when realism must be sacrificed for iconicity. *The Searchers* is set in Texas, where the land is flat and grassy prairies alternate with dry sandy plains, but filmed in Monument Valley, Utah, with dramatic, unearthly towering formations of bright red rock: as Gallagher points out, "Perhaps *The Searchers*' 'Texas 1868' looks nothing like the

---

2 The movie couches the violence in more individualistic and emotional terms, as the Comanche warrior Scar seeks revenge against the whites who murdered his family; Ethan's murderous revenge mission also places him on equal footing with the Native American, while at the same time any legitimate grievance is elided.

*real* Texas; but it does look the way 'Texas' *ought* to look" (329). But for a thinking audience, the idea of starting small homestead ranches among the mesas and buttes of the southwestern desert seems foolhardy: there is little water, no arable land, and sparse vegetation for grazing herds. Ignoring the material reality of the landscape in order to represent the visual majesty of "the West," the cinematography of *The Searchers* sacrifices geographic accuracy and even credibility for sublime myth-making images. Within the ideological geography of the Western, America is a majestic, exceptional nation, whose appropriate landscape should also be majestic and exceptional; the sublime Monument Valley vistas are the idealized representation of all of America, the best of America.

But as Richard Maltby points out, in the critics' canonization of Ford's Westerns, "Monument Valley came to represent the landscape of the West and to encourage by the extremes of its appearance a view of Westerns as abstracted and allegorical," enabling the further abstractions of interpretation that read Westerns as parables of inevitable white progress" (39). Ford's wide angle shots of the desert signify its emptiness which waits to be filled, occluding the presence of Native Americans except as a threat to American manifest destiny who must be driven out or destroyed. Furthermore, the audience is conflicted by the identification of Ethan Edwards with the geography of Monument Valley, the quintessential American hero moving across the quintessential American landscape. At the same time the landscapes inspire audiences' admiration for the natural beauty of the land itself, the character of Ethan complicates that admiration. This ambivalence resides at the core of my reading of *The Searchers*: we are simultaneously awed and repulsed by the spectacle of the land as we are by the main character Ethan. The empty deserts of the cinematic West always echo with the absence of their previous inhabitants who are being driven out or exterminated by white "pioneers," and we are similarly drawn to reject Ethan at first but later cajoled to accept him again.

The opening scene shows Ethan riding up to his brother's family homestead, where his former beloved Martha now lives as his brother's wife. Ethan's figure is framed by the dark outlines of the doorway opening onto the sunny desert landscape; similarly, the concluding shot of the movie returns to a doorway framing the desert, again framing Ethan as he hesitates and turns his back on home. Ford's doorway framing device shows the audience that the domestic environs of the home are the dark antithesis of the bright, sunny desert landscapes; the indoor spaces of *The Searchers* are constricting and tight in complete contrast to the wide open outdoors. Ford shoots the indoor spaces as physically cramped and claustrophobic, the dimly lit rooms shot at a low angle, with heavy, timbered ceilings that seem to be closing in on people. Most obvious is Ethan's discomfort in the house, which critics ascribe to his love for his brother's wife Martha (Slotkin 464-65; Gallagher 324). This personal motivation is clear from the subtle actions of Ethan and Martha: for example, when she thinks she is unobserved, Martha gingerly caresses Ethan's coat and embraces it as if it were Ethan. But Ethan's awkwardness in the house also stems from his strong sense of belonging in the outdoors, in the masculine public sphere. Borne out not only in cinematography but in dramatic action, Ethan's discomfort in the home amplifies his belief that his life is out on the range and he likes it that way: when he enters the house he seems ill at-ease, jumping at the first opportunity to ride out into the desert. The opening theme song, too, expresses this preference: "What make a man to wander, what makes a man to roam/what makes a man to wander, and turn his back on home?" While Ethan's impossible love for his brother's wife provides one answer to the song's question, I suggest that Ethan's need to be outside rather than inside, to turn his back on home, also stems from his potential for violence, the gun in the hand, which is out of place in the private family home but which *The Searchers* depicts as necessary to the preservation of the national home.

This is the spatial contradiction between the public and private spheres that *The Searchers* presents but doesn't resolve: the necessity for a violent element residing outside the family home to keep the security that dwells within the home. Ethan's paradoxical motivation, the movie suggests, is love for that private home in which he is uncomfortable. But there is another home in *The Searchers* which also represents the national home, where Ethan is profoundly at ease: the desert landscape with a cold wind blowing. The cold wind does blow through several winters during Ethan's search to restore Debbie to the family, but it also suggests the Cold War that is waged to protect the national home from the hostile foreign threat. The simultaneous and contradictory emphases on private domesticity and public militarism in 1950s America are represented in the bunker-like family house that has no place for Ethan, even though its safety depends on his potential for violence.

*The Searchers* provides the audience with an urge to sympathize with Ethan, even as they must acknowledge his violence, because Americans in the 1950s wanted to see justification for their aggressive foreign policy of nuclear proliferation and massive retaliation. Richard Slotkin makes this point convincingly, although I differ with his strict separation of domestic and international:

Although the concern with racism suggests that we see the film as addressing the domestic or "civil rights" side of contemporary ideological concern, *The Searchers* is also a "Cold War" Western which addresses issues of war and peace from the perspective of a microcosmic community forced literally to choose between being "Red" and being dead. (464-65; see also Gallagher 324)

The fact that Ethan the Indian-killer is the hero, however ambivalent, makes *The Searchers* indisputably political, and critics for decades have tried to decipher the movie as "racist" or "anti-racist." I suggest here that such a debate is moot: *The Searchers* paints a damning picture of essentialist racism while at the same time it reproduces many appalling stereotypes and privileges the white point of view. Rather than dissect the film in such absolutist terms as "racist" or "anti-racist," this chapter attempts to unpack what the movie says about the contradictions and controversies of the 1950s. I read the spatial politics of *The Searchers* in context of not only civil rights in the domestic, national American home, but also in terms of the bigger picture of American Cold War foreign policy.

## CIVIL RIGHTS, WHITENESS, AND *THE SEARCHERS*

Ethan Edwards is a former Confederate soldier who also fought against Juarez in Mexico; he is a virulent Indian-hater, which to an audience in the 1950s bears heavy implications in the national upheavals around Civil Rights. The Supreme Court decision in *Brown* v. *Board of Education* (1954) was a major milestone on paper, but President Eisenhower, like many politicians at the time, didn't personally support the decision and failed to enforce desegregation in the South until forced to do so by the 1957 crisis at Central High School in Little Rock, Arkansas (Slotkin 154–55). In March of 1956, *The Searchers* opened in theaters across the country, in the middle of the 381-day Montgomery bus boycott begun by the civil disobedience of Rosa Parks in 1955. This assertion of the right to a seat, the right to public space, resonates strongly with the issues of race and contested spaces in *The Searchers*, particularly in the scene when Ethan and Martin first meet.

When Ethan meets Martin, the adopted son of Martha and Aaron, the family is seated around the dinner table and Martin walks in and sits down. They are introduced, and Ethan looks suspiciously at him, asking Martin if he is a "half-breed," to which Martin replies that his ancestors are all English and Welsh except for "one eighth Cherokee." Ethan is troubled by this answer but jokes that at least he isn't Comanche, a tribe he perceives (and the movie represents) as more inherently hostile than the Cherokees. Ethan's shock at a suspected half-breed sitting at the family dinner table acts out a racist white's reaction to the Civil Rights Movement's demands for equal rights to public spaces, particularly public sit-ins. Martin's defensive claim that he is seven-eighths white seems to satisfy his adoptive family, while Ethan, who represents unreconstructed American racism, is still suspicious of him. In this respect, the character of Martin in the movie is markedly changed from the character in the 1954 novel, also entitled *The Searchers*, by Alan Le May: the book's Martin is orphaned in childhood by a murder raid, as is the movie's Martin, but never described as having any Indian ancestry. By changing this character to be part Native American, the movie consciously brings the racial other into the security of the family home, a non-white presence within the nation who must be incorporated into the home so that outside enemies can be defeated.

In 1956, when *The Searchers* was released, the "private" problem of racial difference had already entered the public arena of the courts and the public spaces of city buses. Thus Martin's place at the family table in the movie signifies not only an orphan who is embraced by a white American family, but a racially mixed orphan. His partial whiteness appears to be his justification for his position in the family but their acceptance of him also suggests that their fear of the outside enemy, the hostile Comanche, enables them to be more flexible than the previous generation of white Americans, represented by Ethan the Indian-killer. Even Martin's name suggests that he is part of the white family, closely resembling Martha's, but this resemblance may also trouble Ethan since he loves Martha but sees Martin as a racial other, not quite white. Ethan's obsession with whiteness and racial purity mark his character from the beginning; his definition of family and nation are very clearly defined as exclusively white.[3]

Throughout the first two-thirds of *The Searchers*, Ethan's character reveals his ruthless hatred of Indians. Ethan's hatred becomes unbearable even for the most sympathetic viewers in the scene where he attempts to slaughter as many buffalo as possible so that Scar's clan will have fewer food sources. The scene is rightly noted by critics as a major turning point in audience identification with Ethan, when it becomes impossible to sympathize with him because of his sadistic racism, and here our identification shifts to Martin, the younger, more rational man (Gallagher 327). The buffalo scene is immediately followed by the searchers' discovery of an Indian camp strewn with the corpses of women and children recently massacred by Custer's 7th Cavalry; in both scenes, our sympathies, and Martin's, lie with the victims, innocent buffalo and innocent Indians, rather than with Ethan and the Cavalry. But the parallel construction of sympathies places the Indians at the same level as buffalo, their deaths clearly presented to the audience to foster sympathy, not identification, suggesting that wholesale slaughter is wrong while at the same time the Indians are animals.

Slotkin's reading of the parallels between the buffalo and the cavalry massacre scenes is instructive:

Martin is appalled by the mentality the massacre reveals in his own people—they are no better than Comanches. This perception chimes with his growing realization (in the buffalo-killing passage) that Ethan is motivated by the same "spirit of massacre" that drives both Scar and the cavalrymen. (468)

This moment in *The Searchers* marks the audience's simultaneous distancing from Ethan and growing understanding of Scar, whose violence has the same motive as Ethan's: personal revenge. At the same time, Martin is portrayed as the real voice of reason: his rejection of violence and vengeance throughout the movie represents the peace-loving American ideal which

---

3    For a revealing reading of the character of Ethan in the novel, the script, and the finished movie, see Eckstein. His research shows that not only is the character of Ethan made much more negative (violent, racist) in the transition from novel to script, but also that Ford introduced significant changes during filming to further demonize Ethan's character.

nonetheless needs to be comfortable with violence, embodied by Ethan. Martin recognizes in Ethan's and Scar's personally motivated behaviors, as well the U.S. government's participation in retaliatory murder via the Cavalry massacre, the "cycle of victimization and revenge from which it is possible that no one will escape alive and untainted" (Slotkin 469). Douglas Pye also points out that the juxtaposition of the two massacres "marks eloquently the way in which Ethan's racial hatred is repeated at the institutional level in the genocidal actions of the U.S. cavalry" (229).

Reading the buffalo slaughter and Cavalry massacre scenes, and in particular Ethan's unrepentant white warrior persona (he never surrendered his Confederate saber after the Civil War), in terms of the American Cold War strategy, the simultaneous sympathy for and dehumanization of the Indians makes more sense. The U.S. announced its policy of "massive retaliation" in 1954, which held that any attack, however limited and whether conventional or nuclear, would be answered with a nuclear attack (Hobsbawm 235). If provoked, wholesale slaughter would thus be unavoidable, and the Soviets, like the Indian women and children, would remain at the level of buffalo, whose deaths the U.S. cannot prevent.

Together with the overt comparison between the slaughter of Indians and buffalo, Ethan's blunt questioning of Martin about racial ancestry signifies his obsession with race. His seeming adherence to the "one drop rule"[4] definition of whiteness marks his contemporary significance for the audiences of the 1950s, who can read him as a staunch segregationist. Maltby cites critics' habit of reading Ethan as a scapegoat racist character: "'Our racial prejudice and our guilt for it,' says Brian Henderson, 'are placed on [Ethan's] shoulders, then he is criticized, excluded, or lampooned, mythically purging us of them [...] Ethan is excluded for our sins; that is why we find it so moving.'" (qtd. in Maltby 41). But Ethan's gradual acceptance of Martin, and his indifference to Martin's engagement with Laurie, a white woman, prevent us from believing that Ethan sees Martin as "pure Indian" and therefore not white. Ethan's character development, from

---

4   The legal convention of "hypodescent" in U.S. racial categorization in which a person with "one drop" of African American blood cannot be considered white, even if a majority of the person's ancestors are white. For a thorough examination of the one drop rule including its history and in current debates, see Hickman 1161.

staunch racist into a more flexible variety, prevents him from being merely a scapegoat. Ethan is, after all, played by John Wayne at the peak of his popularity. I suggest that Ethan's role shifts from racist scapegoat to sympathetic loner. That shift itself demonstrates the function of Ethan's character: first, to show that white racists can be rehabilitated to accept non-whites into the domestic spaces of the family home, and second, that even rehabilitated racists have an important role in the nation's defense against foreign enemies.

Allowing the "mostly white" Martin into the private sphere of the home allows Ethan to concentrate on the real enemy outside the home, in the public sphere: he can still hate Comanche and be a good American. The audience's split sympathy, with Ethan and with Martin, is never fully resolved, but the complicated ending of the film gives some clear signals about who really holds the authority over the home: the man who declines to cross its threshold at the end. As a Cold War Western, *The Searchers* must demonstrate the need for Ethan's violent presence on the scene just outside the home: the Red menace, which is more important than "domestic" matters.

## COLD WAR CONTEXT IN *THE SEARCHERS*

Richard Slotkin points out that the number of feature-length Westerns produced during the years immediately following World War II increased dramatically, "from 14 in 1947 to [...] 46 in 1956" (347). Even after the movie Western's peak in the mid-1950s, Westerns became enormously popular with growing American television audiences (Slotkin 348). The continued national interest in the myths of the West demonstrates an enduring sense of pride in that segment of American history. This interest is especially noteworthy when we consider that most Westerns only concern themselves with a relatively narrow window of time in the history of the United States: "Westerns privilege a period of roughly fifty years, and return time and again to particular sites and events" in the latter half of the nineteenth century (Shohat and Stam 115). At this point in history, the nation is busily developing the vast spaces of the west, from the early pioneer towns to the Gold Rush to the consolidation of the country with the railroad.

The historical time and place of the isolated Texas frontier homestead surrounded by murderous Comanche engages a familiar narrative in the Western genre: the terror of a lone outpost encircled by enemies about to attack. This "imagery of encirclement" common in Westerns rests on the notion that the frontier whites are surrounded by hostile savages, and, because the Western's "point-of-view conventions consistently favor the Euro-American protagonists," the sense of encirclement creates an atmosphere of tension as the family nervously awaits attack (Shohat and Stam 120). Portrayed as vulnerable and outnumbered, the family is forced into self-defense and struggles to stay together against the onslaughts of savage attackers. In the tense, silent scene as the family wordlessly prepares for the Comanche attack, the teenage daughter Lucy finally deciphers the unspoken fear of her parents and screams in horror.

Most American audiences in 1956 were familiar with the feeling of being surrounded by hostile enemies waiting to attack: the demonization of the Soviet Union had only escalated since the 1948 Gallup poll in which "76 percent of Americans believed that Russia was out to rule the world, and [...] 63 percent expected a full-scale war within the next twenty-five years" (Chafe 109). The certainty of coming nuclear war lasted through the 1950s, and the fear of outside attack pervaded the private domestic sphere that was so much a part of American national identity during that decade. This combination of exalted domesticity and escalating national defense manifested itself in strange ways: Elaine Tyler May begins her book *Homeward Bound: American Families in the Cold War* with a story, originally published in *Life* magazine, of a newlywed couple embarking on their two-week honeymoon in their bomb shelter, which she rightly calls "a powerful image of the nuclear family in the nuclear age" (3-5). *The Searchers* participates in the convergence of these two popular Cold War discourses by evoking the feeling of encirclement and the sense that the family is digging in to protect itself from a coming attack: the Edwards' homestead ranch house resembles a bunker designed for self-defense: it has small shuttered windows, thick adobe walls, low ceilings, and a heavily timbered overhanging roof. The ending of the movie, with the nuclear family reconstructed as the reunited couple Martin and Laurie (his fiancée) walk back into the house with the rescued Debbie while Ethan remains aloof and outside the house, reinforces *The Searchers*'s message about the convergence of domesticity and national defense.

Richard Slotkin interprets *The Searchers* as a Cold War Western, meaning that it can be read as an allegory of U.S. foreign affairs during the postwar period, and my reading shares this premise. However, Slotkin's assessment of the movie's participation in Cold War discourses differs from mine in its specifics, in that his focuses only on American foreign policy, which vacillates between "search and rescue" and "search and destroy" in the escalating conflicts in Vietnam:

> Through Ethan Edwards, Ford metaphorically explores the logic of the "savage war"/Cold War analogy . . . and finds that it produces an overwhelming, and finally malign, pressure to choose "destruction" over "rescue." American policy-makers would explore that same logic in articulating and putting into practice a new doctrine for counterinsurgency in the Third World. (472)

The carving up of the Third World by the Cold War superpowers was certainly worrisome for many Americans in the 1950s, but hardly as much cause for wide public concern as other fears that posed threats closer to home, such as the possibility of Soviet attack or nuclear war.

Slotkin's Vietnam interpretation is convincing insofar as it identifies a similar logic in the movie and in U.S. foreign policy, but I have two problems with it. First, my interest lies more in how *The Searchers* participates in familiar public discourses about foreign policy with which audiences could identify in 1956: not whether to rescue or destroy Indochina, but how to fortify America against the enemies outside and within the national home. Second, and more important, I propose that rather than adopting an exclusively "foreign policy" framework for reading the movie as Slotkin does, we should attend to both foreign and domestic. Only then can we discern how the movie articulates the ways in which foreign policies are inseparable from "domestic" policies, both in the sense of the American national home and private family home.

## THE CONVERGENCE OF COLD WAR AND CIVIL RIGHTS DISCOURSES IN *THE SEARCHERS*

Along with the fear of nuclear war with the U.S.S.R., internal problems also worried Americans in the 1950s, as Billy Graham warned of "barbarians beating at our gates from without and moral termites from within" (Chafe 109). *The Searchers* constructs a complicated picture of the American home: the Indians ("Reds") are indeed poised for attack, but there are also "domestic" threats to unity, including racial others demanding to be seated at the family dinner table. Moreover, the intimate connections between these concerns appear frequently in the reactionary political discourse of the time: Georgia Governor Eugene Talmadge claimed that African American Civil Rights protests were motivated by "Communist doctrines from outside the state" (Chafe 107). I argue that the movie's representations of mobility and domesticity communicate the national concerns about an international threat—Communists attacking America and infiltrating the nation with spies—as well as a "domestic" threat— increasing tensions about civil rights. In this reading, I depart from Slotkin's interpretation of the film because his focus brackets the domestic in order to elaborate American anxieties over international enemies, re-enacting the separation of spheres that I suggest limits our understanding of the text. As Amy Kaplan and Elaine Tyler May argue in the contexts of the American nineteenth century and the 1950s respectively, private and public spheres—domestic and international—are two sides of the same coin. National concerns about international military threats become implicated in "domestic" concerns about allegedly private issues: segregation and racism in American society and institutions. Domestic unity, including racial desegregation, makes a stronger nation that can stand up to the outside threat and better combat the "moral termites from within." I read *The Searchers* as a 1950s Western that expresses American fears of the threat from outside the "home" or nation, as well as the growing anxieties about black demands for the full rights of citizenship, for equal membership in the national "family." The fact that both internal and external threats are portrayed as Native Americans, albeit of different tribes, only underscores the racial and ethnic undertones and the inseparability of these two seemingly "separate" spheres.

Anti-communism, according to historian Eric Hobsbawm, "was genuinely and viscerally popular in a country built on individualism and private enterprise where the nation itself was defined in exclusively ideological terms ('Americanism') which could be virtually defined as the polar opposite of communism" (235). In my reading of *The Searchers* as a Cold War narrative, nationalistic and xenophobic anti-communism takes the form of nationalistic and racist Indian-hating, which motivates Ethan's character.

Ethan's definition of American is white, defined as the polar opposite of Indian (or black, recall his loyalty to the defeated Southern Confederacy), but
we discover that his definition of white is not purely biological in the scene
where he and Martin look for Debbie among a group of former captives of
the Comanche.

These white women are visibly traumatized and when a soldier remarks, "It's difficult to believe they're white," Ethan replies, "They ain't
white anymore—they're Comanche." The scene suggests that the women's
insanity derives from their captivity: this representation of their madness
creates a problem of perspective that Pye argues is, when read alongside
Debbie's seemingly assimilated life with the Comanche witnessed later, a
contradiction within the film's racial-ideological narrative:

> At the heart of this troubled and troubling process of negotiation is miscegenation it-
> self, the sexual act which is the focus of Ethan's and Laurie's fear and hatred. [...]
> In the material we have looked at here, two attitudes are present: in one, inter-racial
> marriage can produce the well-balanced Martin and apparently well-integrated Deb-
> bie; in the other, miscegenation can be imagined only as rape and its results as mad-
> ness, violence and death. (234)

The white captives scene does indeed trouble any reading of the film as
"anti-racist," as Pye points out, because the point-of-view shots structurally
equate Ethan's reactions to the captives with Martin's and the soldier's
even as, portraying the horror of the women's situation, the objective shots
of the captives evoke the same reaction from the audience (233). Ethan
leaves the scene with his hatred of Comanches and miscegenation justified,
even intensified, while Martin is silent and upset. Both men appear to be
wondering whether Debbie will be insane when they find her, and if so,
whether her insanity will signify a sexual relationship with a Comanche.
This fear is verbalized by Martin's fiancée, Laurie, in words that horrify
Martin: when he explains to her that he wants to bring Debbie back to live
as part of their white community, Laurie replies viciously, "Fetch what
home? The leavin's of a Comanche buck sold time and again to the highest
bidder with savage brats of her own?" To Martin's dismay, Laurie argues
that they should kill Debbie because that is what Martha, Debbie's mother,
would have wanted (recall that Martha was raped and murdered by Comanche at the beginning).

Like Laurie's appalling tirade, Ethan's response to the fear of miscege-nation is to declare his intention to kill Debbie when they find her, because whether she is insane or happily partnered with a Comanche man, she will no longer be white, as the captives "ain't white anymore— they're Coman-che." When the searchers do finally see Debbie, she wears Indian clothing with her hair in braids and doesn't show any signs that she recognizes them; afterwards, Ethan echoes his reaction to the captives when he shouts at Martin, "She ain't Debbie—she's Comanch'!" Reading this response in terms of the Cold War, Slotkin argues that this is Ethan's turn from "search and rescue" to "search and destroy," mirroring American foreign policy in Vietnam and other Third World spheres of influence (471). But here is where a combined reading of foreign policy with domestic civil rights dis-course makes the text more coherent than Slotkin's approach: Debbie as the object of the search signifies the problem of the other, both as an ally of the "Reds" and as a racialized other within the "white" nation. The two men's views of her represent the two attitudes available to Americans in the 1950s: Martin's acceptance of racial difference and love for Debbie as a family member even though she is not his blood relation, and his abhor-rence of the revenge massacres mark him as a liberal integrationist. Ethan, on the other hand, is a violent Indian-hater who would kill his niece rather than let her live as a "Red," thus combining anti-integrationist with anti-communist sentiment. Given this split into opposite corners, Ethan's subse-quent change of heart and Debbie's return to the fold become the keys to the cultural meanings of *The Searchers*'s ending.

Ethan's change of heart—he doesn't kill Debbie when he has the oppor-tunity, but instead swings her in the air like a girl—is tempered by his ab-rupt and solitary departure at the end of the film. We can read him as less monstrous than he was at the beginning, but he still isn't "domesticated" enough to join the happy family. Instead Ethan walks away, having saved Debbie and returned Martin to his future wife, and the door closes. Ethan is "partially redeemed," in Stowell's words, because he doesn't follow through with killing Debbie (131). But he also still remains outside the family home. Ethan isn't a family man, a ladies' man, or a company man: we are made to believe that he belongs "out there," riding the range, alone with his gun and his horse, ready to fight Indians and rescue white women. His role as security force protecting the home gives him the authority to control membership in the family, and his decision to allow certain racial others into the fold suggests that they do live up to his standards of whiteness after all.

The younger generation in the character of Laurie is just as racist as Ethan though in the end she too is willing to allow Debbie back into the family, as Ethan eventually relented in his vow to kill her. But the "white" family at the end of the movie depends on Ethan's power to protect their home. As the nation in the 1950s began to make concessions to Civil Rights, accepting African Americans into the white national family, American militarism continued to escalate the arms race using the Red threat as justification. In this light, domestic stability depends on the military muscle that keeps outside threats at bay, embodied in the public imagination as John Wayne[5] and in the movie as his character Ethan Edwards, whose dogged pursuit of Debbie he sees as his nature. He describes himself to Martin as "a critter who just keeps coming on" regardless of hardship or passing time. Ethan's perseverance and determination has sinister overtones, because his determination to persist in his search, his revenge, and ultimately his defense of the white family, is represented as a justification for genocide.

Critics have debated the ending of *The Searchers* for decades, and I find Pye's argument, along with Slotkin's, most compelling.[6] I concur with Pye's premise that *"The Searchers* allows no comfortable identification with or disengagement from its hero (who is both monstrous *and* John Wayne)" (229). Slotkin's interpretation is also convincing in his recognition of the unresolved audience identification. Rather than argue for an absolutist ideological reading of "racist" or "anti-racist," making Ethan fully sympathetic or unsympathetic, he points out the ambivalence of the ending:

---

5   For an excellent analysis of the cinematic meanings associated with Wayne, see Thomas.

6   Gallagher reads Ethan's change of heart as evidence that Ethan's character is a symbol of the racist society, citing other characters including Laurie who endorse his plan to kill Debbie (333). Thus he can interpret Ethan's reversal of that decision as evidence that white racist society can also change. This doesn't account for Ethan's departure at the end; in fact, according to this logic, Ethan would be welcomed into the home by the family that he has restored.

The moral confusion of the ending is responsible for two recurrent misreadings of the film. A "left" misreading sees it as an exemplar of the very racism it decries. A "right" misreading sees Ethan Edwards as an entirely heroic figure whose harsh manner and personal isolation are the consequences of his devotion to his mission and his unique understanding of the red menace. (472)

Slotkin aptly points out that a left misreading would focus on race and the film's relevance in the debates over civil rights, whereas a right misreading would take Ethan as a valiant defender of America against the Soviet threat. I suggest that each of these two (mis)interpretations on its own is indeed a misreading, but that if we allow for both readings at once, we may find what shred of resolution the film will allow. Because of the movie's insistent contrasts between indoor and outdoor, private and public, family and nation, we are drawn to interpret these spaces in terms of one another. The play on the meaning of domestic throughout this essay is an attempt to weave together these seemingly discrete spaces by emphasizing the social relations that connect them.

Ethan's violent presence outside the home makes possible the domestic scene at the end of the film, just as the renewed fervor for domesticity in the 1950s also depended on the military-industrial complex, including nuclear arms. In other words, audiences in 1956 could read the movie as a parable showing how the restoration of the private sphere and its continued security is only feasible if the public sphere is secured by force. As Amy Kaplan points out, "The idea of foreign policy depends on the sense of the nation as a domestic space imbued with a sense of athomeness, in contrast to an external world perceived as alien and threatening" (582). The emphasis on the external threat gives even racist whites a reason to accept racial difference: knowing that the home must be strong and secure allows the racist Laurie to accept Debbie and Martin although she knows Debbie has been living with an Indian husband for years and may have mixed-race children and Martin is one-eighth Cherokee. This domestic scene has obvious integrationist and assimilationist overtones, but the presence of the warrior patrolling the periphery makes the happy reunion seem somehow ominous, like the honeymooners in the bomb shelter. Ethan turns away and disappears into the landscape as the door closes and the final frame fades to black.[7] Ethan's location outside the home doesn't prevent him from exercising authority over the family: he identifies its limits, deciding who lives, who dies, and who remains in the family.

## CONCLUSION

In *The Searchers*, Ethan is always in motion: riding up to the house, across the western states, into the desert. The landscapes that frame his obsessive search for Debbie and his self-identification as a "critter who just keeps coming on" suggest that he is a natural stalker and conqueror, even though we know he has been on the losing side of at least two wars. Ethan's nature is to kill, and the movie suggests that he is as "savage" as he claims the Indians are: he is a classic Indian-hater "whose knowledge of Indians engenders profound and undying hatred rather than sympathetic understanding" (Slotkin 462). The movie portrays Ethan as a nomadic killing machine, set against the backdrop of Monument Valley landscapes that Ford made into visual icons of the American West, signifying the open spaces of the growing nation and the western territories waiting to be conquered. *The Searchers* portrays a Western landscape within whose time and space we can read signs of an ongoing struggle for a renegotiation of national identity along racial lines, taking place in a context of an ongoing, albeit cold, war.

Beginning with his part as extra in *The Birth of a Nation*, John Ford has played a role in American cinematic representations of race and nation. This chapter has argued that Ford's representations of American national identity during the 1950s are intimately bound up in questions of space, mobility, and domesticity. In its movements between foreign and home, public and private, *The Searchers* articulates the ideological complexities of the 1950s. His attention to the mobility trope in American history offers a geographic and social narrative of the power relations that reside in the landscapes of the movie as well as the "domestic" and foreign policy issues

---

7    Gallagher reads the doorway shot that begins *The Searchers* as a sign of sex: the darkness of the womb, Ethan's ambivalent feelings for Martha, who opens the door, but that doesn't explain the final doorway shot as Ethan turns away (334–45).

plaguing the country at the time of its production. As John Wayne makes his way through the landscapes of Monument Valley, audiences have access to the contested spaces that have always made up the United States, both within its borders and in its relations with other countries. The desert setting in Monument Valley memorializes the American landscape, and Ethan in the middle distance completes the vision: the lone ranch house, occupied by the family and protected by the abrasive but loyal warrior.

## WORKS CITED

Aitken, Stuart C., and Leo E. Zonn. "*Re*-Presenting the Place Pastiche." *Place, Power, Situation, and Spectacle: A Geography of Film*. Eds. Stuart C. Aitken and Leo E. Zonn. Lanham, MD.: Rowman and Littlefield, 1994. 3-26. Print.

Cameron, Ian, and Douglas Pye, eds. *The Book of Westerns*. New York: Continuum, 1996. Print.

Chafe, William H. *The Unfinished Journey: America Since World War II*. 3rd edn. New York: Oxford UP, 1995. Print.

Eckstein, Arthur M. "Darkening Ethan: John Ford's *The Searchers* (1956) from Novel to Screenplay to Screen." *Cinema Journal* 38.1 (1998): 3–24. Print.

Gallagher, Tag. *John Ford: The Man and His Films*. Berkeley: U of California P, 1986. Print.

Gregory, Derek. *Geographical Imaginations*. Oxford: Blackwell, 1994. Print.

Harvey, David. *The Condition of Postmodernity: An Enquiry into the Origins of Cultural Change*. Oxford: Blackwell, 1990. Print.

Hickman, Christine B. "The Devil and the One Drop Rule: Racial Categories, African Americans, and the U.S. Census." *Michigan Law Review* 95.5 (1997): 1161-265. Print.

Hobsbawm, Eric. *The Age of Extremes: A History of the World, 1914–1991*. New York: Vintage, 1996. Print.

Kaplan, Amy. "Manifest Domesticity." *American Literature* 70 (1998): 581-606. Print.

Keith, Michael, and Steve Pile, eds. *Place and the Politics of Identity*. New York: Routledge, 1993. Print.

Keith, Michael, and Steve Pile. "Introduction Part 1: The Politics of Place."
    Keith and Pile 1-21.

---. "Introduction Part 2: The Place of Politics." Keith and Pile 22-40.

Le May, Alan. *The Searchers*. New York: Harper, 1954. Print.

Maltby, Richard. "A Better Sense of History: John Ford and the Indians."
    Cameron and Pye 34-49.

May, Elaine Tyler. *Homeward Bound: American Families in the Cold War
    Era*. New York: Basic, 1988. Print.

O'Brien, Geoffrey. "The Movie of the Century." *American Heritage* 49.7
    (1998): 16+. Print.

Pye, Douglas. "Double Vision: Miscegenation and Point of View in *The
    Searchers*." Cameron and Pye 229-35.

Sarris, Andrew. *The John Ford Movie Mystery*. London: Secker and War-
    burg-BFI, 1976. Print.

Shohat, Ella, and Robert Stam. *Unthinking Eurocentrism: Multiculturalism
    and the Media*. New York: Routledge, 1994. Print.

Slotkin, Richard. *Gunfighter Nation: The Myth of the Frontier in Twentieth
    Century America*. Norman: U of Oklahoma P, 1998. Print.

Smith, Neil, and Cindi Katz. "Grounding Metaphor: Towards a Spatialized
    Politics." Keith and Pile 66-81. Print.

Stowell, Peter. *John Ford*. Boston: Twayne, 1986. Print.

Thomas, Deborah. "John Wayne's Body." Cameron and Pye 75–87.

Tompkins, Jane. *West of Everything: The Inner Life of Westerns*. New
    York: Oxford UP, 1992. Print.